Race,
Economics,
and
Corporate America

Race,
Economics,
and
Corporate America

by
John W. Work

SR Scholarly Resources Inc.
Wilmington, Delaware

©1984 by John W. Work
All rights reserved
First published 1984
Printed and bound in the United States of America

Scholarly Resources Inc.
104 Greenhill Avenue
Wilmington, Delaware 19805

Library of Congress Cataloging in Publication Data

Work, John W., 1932-
    Race, economics, and corporate America.

    Bibliography: p.
    Includes index.
    1. Discrimination in employment—United States.
2. Afro-Americans—Employment. I. Title.
HD4903.5.U58W66   1984   331.6'3'96073   84-1233
ISBN 0-8420-2217-1

To
Edith Carr McFall Work
and
to the memory of
John Wesley Work III

Contents

Preface

IT HAS BEEN twenty years since the passage of the 1964 Civil Rights Act, and more than a decade since the issuance of the Kerner Commission Report on Civil Disorders. Yet a review of current economic and social factors would indicate that the 1964 Act and the Kerner Report recommendations have had a limited impact on the economic status of black Americans relative to the total society. Specifically, Title VII of the Act prohibits employment discrimination on the basis of race, color, religion, sex, and national origin. That such various kinds of discrimination exist has been substantially documented, their differences in origin and manifestation notwithstanding. Employment discrimination based on race was cited by an Urban League Report[1] as a major problem confronting blacks in the 1970s. This theme is also found in the earlier Kerner Commission Report[2] as a main cause of black unrest in the nation. Despite the ominousness of such reports, we remain, as a nation, unable—or unwilling—to significantly combat these racist forces which short-circuit and otherwise artificially interrupt black labor flows throughout the economy. This inability is especially foreboding for the future of the society when black populations in the major cities of America have grown and now constitute substantial proportions, proportions on which the burden of unemployment and underemployment rest

---

[1]Robert B. Hill, *The Widening Economic Gap* (Washington, D.C.: National Urban League, 1979).

[2]*Report of the National Advisory Commission on Civil Disorders* (New York: Bantam Books, Inc., 1968).

heaviest. By not addressing these employment problems forthrightly as priority issues, we are permitting our major cities to slowly but surely become monuments to ignorance and bigotry.

I have spent nearly the past twenty years as a member of corporate management and as a consultant to major corporations in the human resources area. Our firm has undertaken, and continues to undertake, studies on behalf of clients regarding the employment dynamics which characterize corporate white-collar workplaces. There remains a substantial interest in the question of how private-sector internal labor market dynamics affect and determine occupational assignments, promotion rates, and salary levels of black and other minority employees, in particular. This book, then, analyzes and elevates many of the findings and conclusions from earlier internal labor market surveys and studies. While there are clearly social class and other forces operating within corporate workplaces, it is my contention that the central force is economic in nature; thus, the analyses and findings are principally within that framework.

I was provided access to employee data for the year 1978 by a major corporate bureaucracy in New York City. In return, I was required to respect the firm's request for anonymity when presenting and analyzing the data in this volume. The data describe 2,721 graded employees in the offices of the corporate headquarters in terms of educational level, salary level, sex, length of service, and race. The data on race were actually divided into minority and nonminority categories. It is assumed, however, that a significant majority of the employees in the minority category are black and, therefore, consistent with the thrust of this work. are referred to throughout as black employees.

While this data base does not readily lend itself to an analysis of every hypothesis in this book, it does provide a basis for a systematic analysis of the internal labor market and the impact on black employees relative to white employees. Of course, using data from a single firm requires the assumption that the patterns of employment and their dynamics are similar in most white-collar corporations. In the real world, however, it is reasonable to suspect that different firms and industries in fact respond differently to a black employee presence even though the range of that response is likely to be relatively small, given the nature of racial discrimination.

This book, which is both an essay and a study, is about black white-collar employees in the corporate bureaucracies of America. It attempts to analyze and enhance our understanding of the upward mobility—to a lesser extent, occupational mobility—patterns of black corporate employees. While the book is written expressly for economists and other social scientists, corporate managers, and government officials, I hope it will appeal to a wider audience interested in the employment developments occurring in the corporate sector. With the exceptions of Chapters VIII and IX, the discussion throughout is not especially technical. Finally, the corporate data base will be of value to analysts interested in this subject. Such data are only occasionally, if not rarely, available for broad use.

A number of individuals were good enough to read the manuscript at various stages and make useful suggestions and criticisms. While they are more than I can name here, Judy Edelstein, despite her heavy academic and consulting schedule, read, criticized, and edited Part 1, correcting mistakes in content and reviewing sources. A great debt is owed to Lloyd Burgess who reconsidered the manuscript each time a revision was made and was invaluable in helping to bring consistency to the ideas developed. He cannot be thanked enough. Cleavan Daniel reviewed Chapters VIII and IX and the overall statistical presentations. While my interpretations might be called liberal, they are less so because of his valuable persistence. He has my gratitude. Significantly, my early professor, Lloyd L. Hogan, who unknowingly started all this more years ago than either of us probably cares to remember and who has remained a friend over the years, reviewed the entire manuscript with an emphasis on methodology and content. An original principal in the Black Economic Research Center and former editor of *The Review of Black Political Economy*, Hogan made suggestions which were so highly valued and incorporated. A very special expression of gratitude is reserved for Philip Johnson at Scholarly Resources. His rather detailed suggested revisions have further improved the work. The result is a more even thematic development which actually strengthens the case. Last, but not least, I could not have had better manuscript preparation than that provided by Aida Arroyo who typed and revised the manuscript, it seems, repeatedly. Her attention to detail, including my oversights, and the coordination of the "revisions file," contributed to a good final product. I thank all of these kind and interested people for their input and their moral and professional support. In the final analysis, the good things about this volume must be shared, but its shortcomings are mine alone.

PART 1

Qualitative Bases of Discrimination

I

Introduction

THIS WORK is an outgrowth of several years of study with respect to particular economic aspects of black employment in the corporate internal labor markets of America. As a result, there can be little doubt that racism, both individual and institutional, has shaped an employment discrimination pattern which tends to delimit the quest of black people for jobs in the private sector and promotes their relegation to certain types of jobs, if employed.

In their search for jobs, blacks are further disadvantaged by the generally inferior educational structures and living conditions found in the central cities of America and by the sheer debilitating effect of a pervasive and oppressive racism on the black psyche. Let us be clear about one fact: the fate of black Americans implied by these conditions is shared by no other ethnic or racial group in America. Philip Green states:

> The major difference is fundamental: conscripted slavery is hardly similar, psychologically or sociologically, to voluntary emigration motivated by hope. Over the generations black people, in contrast to other "immigrant" groups, have correctly perceived American society as unremittingly closed, tyrannical, and hostile.[1]

Of particular interest is the development and role of institutional racism in the reinforcement and perpetuation of a disparate black existence. Since conditions of employment, with particular

---

[1]Philip Green, *The Pursuit of Inequality* (New York: Pantheon, 1981), p. 52.

reference to income and occupation, are related axiomatically to social and economic status, it is a reasonable presumption that improvements in employment and income could significantly narrow the general economic differences that characterize black/white relations in America. But racism serves to stall such potential improvements and, as a result, supports the relegation of a majority of American blacks to low-income ghetto areas with relatively low-quality educational and health care facilities, substandard housing, and other living conditions that heap ignominy and demotivating experiences upon the many who reside there.

Obviously, there are blacks in America who earn "average," "above average," and even substantial wages and salaries and who do not live under these impoverished conditions. They tend to be college graduates and holders of advanced and professional degrees; they are engaged in white-collar and professional occupations; and often they reside in neighborhoods and communities with the better housing and educational opportunities and embrace general middle-class values. But racism is pervasive. While this group has succeeded in varying degrees in its struggle for a rewarding and fulfilling livelihood and may be largely exempt from the everyday enervating sting of racism to which those blacks in lower socioeconomic categories are subjected, racism is directed toward peoples of color, and black people in particular. Thus, while blacks of higher socioeconomic status are enabled by their incomes to enjoy many of the *personal* benefits and pleasures afforded by the society, they are denied, through the magic of institutional racism, full access to socioeconomic institutional benefits (e.g., higher levels of employment including occupational access, higher levels of political life, capital acquisition).

It is interesting to note that many view blacks of high socioeconomic status as evidence that racial discrimination has been reduced to a point where it is no longer the major factor in determining economic welfare.[2] Some economists have gone to great lengths to demonstrate that the gap between the earnings of black and white workers over approximately the past two decades has steadily narrowed, and that as younger and better–educated and better–qualified blacks replace older blacks in the work place, this narrowing will continue.[3] The implication, of course, is that racism is in the decline. Such a conclusion is suspect when one examines

---

[2]On this point, Wilson controversially argues that "class" is the more likely arbiter of socioeconomic success and not race. See William Julius Wilson, *The Declining Significance of Race*, 2nd ed. (Chicago: University of Chicago Press, 1980).

[3]While there are a number of writers who take a similar position, in particular, see James Smith and Finis Welch, "Black-White Male Wage Rates: 1960–70," *American Economic Review*, 67 (June 1977), 323–38; and *Race Differences in Earnings: New Evidence* (Santa Monica: The Rand Corporation, R–2295–NSF, March 1978).

internal labor market dynamics. For there, where promotions, salary increases, occupational assignments, critical corporate experiences, and other factors promoting upward mobility are determined, significant gaps between whites and blacks remain. Edward Lazear has argued that the apparent narrowing in the wage gap is the likely result of equal employment opportunity and affirmative action pressures but that while pecuniarily compensated, blacks are denied important on–the–job and other internal labor market experiences essential for upward mobility, thereby effecting differences in black/white lifetime earnings curves.[4] Specifically, our studies show this to be the case in corporate white–collar internal labor markets and that such black/white differential development is a principal function of racism. As Michael Reich contends, racism is as persistent as ever:

> The decline of a black agrarian class of small–holding and tenant farmers and the incorporation of blacks into the urban class structure has occurred in a manner that has not eliminated racial inequality, but has reproduced it in another setting.[5]

The central intent of this volume, then, is to examine the current impact of racism on one principal dimension of the overall employment process, viz., the upward mobility paths of blacks employed in corporate America. Even though equal employment opportunity laws have opened corporate doors to blacks—that is, black men and women are *hired* by corporations at generally established entry points—our studies reveal that the internal labor market mechanisms, which control career directions and rates of mobility, remain significantly influenced by an institutional racism that not only limits access to higher organizational levels but also to certain occupational groups.

Of considerable concern are the implications of neoclassical and orthodox economic thought, and the writings of economists and other social scientists who generally embrace that school of thought, on descriptions and analyses of corporate internal labor market operations. Essentially, the orthodox approach explains the generation of income, and black/white income differences, in terms of the quality and level of worker productivity, which, in turn, is some function of education and training. With fortification from other social sciences, one learns that *quality* of education, IQ and other inheritances(?), family background, father's occupation, and behavior traits

---

[4]Edward Lazear, "The Narrowing of Black–White Wage Differentials is Illusory," *American Economic Review*, 69 (Sept. 1979), 553–64.

[5]Michael Reich, "The Persistence of Racial Inequality in Urban Areas and Industries, 1950–70," *American Economic Review*, 70 (May 1980), 128.

related to social class are additional factors in employment earnings determination. Thus, if one desires to explain the disparity in black and white earnings (or occupational exclusion), one need search no further than these factors.[6] Racism is never accorded its rightful place in orthodox writings—writings, which when popularized, help to shape the thinking of whites about blacks.

Limited to an economic discussion and analysis of the qualitative dynamics of internal labor markets in the corporate offices of America, and to a lesser extent external markets, there are at least five reasons for this volume.

First, a review of the published writing about the racism underlying the economic and employment status of corporate blacks reveals that much of this work—irrespective of a writer's posture—has been done by individuals in universities and research institutes, those connected with various government and nonprofit social agencies, journalists, and writers at large. Less frequently has this subject been addressed by individuals residing in corporate and other private-sector institutions. Having spent the largest part of a professional career in the corporate sector, this writer hopes to further explicate the subject of black employment dynamics, and the problems of upward mobility.

Second, the general field of theoretical economics, and most of those who wear the mantle of orthodoxy within that field, have shied away from analyses and explanations of employment discrimination based on a concept of racism. As a result, there exists a relative paucity of published work in this area.

Third, racial discrimination in external and internal labor markets can have a profoundly negative impact on the viability of America's key cities, and, thus, on the future of America. Countless newspaper and other popular press articles cite as authoritative explanations of inflation, stagflation, unemployment, underemployment, and the plight of cities and urban areas such diverse concepts as underinvestment, inadequate consumption and aggregate demand, tight monetary policies, high taxes, structural unemployment, low corporate profits, the welfare crisis, eroding tax bases, too rapid technological growth, poor and unresponsive educational systems, problems of income distribution, flaws in statistical measures of employment, inappropriate economic priorities, large government budget deficits, teenagers and women flooding the job market, wage

---

[6]On the other hand, if these factors do not strike one as being sufficiently exhaustive or explanatory, then one might try including an individual's "luck" as a catch-all explanatory factor. Jencks did! See Christopher Jencks, *Who Gets Ahead?: The Determinants of Economic Success in America* (New York: Basic Books, 1979), pp. 306–11.

increases induced by union pressures, and international trade problems. Black unemployment and underemployment, however, are generally viewed as *results*—never causes. Given the fact that by 1978 approximately 55 percent of the black population lived in America's central cities,[7] it is reasonable to suspect that a significant underutilization and misallocation of such a sizable labor resource would likely have an exacerbating impact on the declining economies of those major cities. If such a thesis is at least partly valid, then its import for urban economic analysis is unmistakably clear.

By way of digression, this notion begs the question: in view of the history of racial discrimination in this country, why have the economic problems of the sixties and seventies not been in evidence in past decades? In fact, they have been; but at least four factors have pushed problems of ghetto and urban poverty and black unemployment and underemployment into bold relief during the post–World War II period. First, until recently, economists have paid little attention to the problems of urban poverty and black employment patterns. Second, the continuing black population shifts from rural to urban areas, in addition to relative increases in that population, have heightened the opportunity and perceived need for employment discrimination in business and private institutions by white employers. Third, advancing technological production methods, to some degree, increasingly delimit employment opportunities for blacks with relatively few skills and, in the long run, reduce the number of employment opportunities usually available in the *secondary labor markets*.[8] And fourth, more of an hypothesis than an empirical explanation, I am persuaded that inherent in the matured capitalist economy of the United States are forces producing conditions which preclude a ready accommodation of employment discrimination such as that experienced by blacks in the pre–World War II years. While advancing technology and increasing productivity can explain relative increases in real income, it is apparently this same technology and productivity that gives rise to a mode of production which will no longer tolerate the inefficient utilization and underemployment of blacks (or anyone else) where that group is significantly represented in major labor markets around the country.[9] In this sense, employment discrimination and the resulting underemployment are contributing *causes* of the general malaise of the economy rather than a result of it. Thus,

---

[7]Bureau of the Census, *The Social and Economic Status of the Black Population in the United States, 1790–1978*, Current Population Reports, p. 23, No. 80.

[8]This terminology is central to the dual labor market theory and will be described in a later chapter.

[9]This point is also made by William K. Tabb, *The Political Economy of the Black Ghetto* (New York: Norton, 1970), pp. 61–62.

in part, the rationale for equal opportunity laws and affirmative action programs. And while these have been limited in their overall effectiveness given the intensive and extensive character of racism, such programs probably do tend to blunt the full impact of discrimination, to some degree.[10]

Fourth, affirmative action has been unfairly and pejoratively saddled with terms such as government compliance, quota system, and reverse discrimination, among others. Based on such terms, three arguments are most frequently put forth by corporate employers in opposition to affirmative action. First, there are the "constitutionalists" who are offended by affirmative action programs which violate constitutional guarantees of equal treatment for all citizens, and, according to them, discriminate against whites in employment and upward mobility. Second, there are the "business administrators" who argue that affirmative action programs require that unqualified people be employed and upgraded so that productivity and profits are likely to be negatively affected. Third, the "laissez-faire" types see evil in big government encroaching on decisions to hire and promote in a manner violative of traditional corporate prerogatives. In addition, the voluminous paper work required by affirmative action legislation—and the cost—detracts from an institution's *raison d'être*, so the argument goes. Needless to say, these arguments are specious, but they serve to further undermine the progress of black employees.

The fifth, and final, reason for this essay is found in a haunting passage from W. E. B. DuBois's *Dusk of Dawn*:

> It is difficult to let others see the full psychological meaning of caste segregation. It is as though one, looking out from a dark cave in a side of an impending mountain, sees the world passing and speaks to it, speaks courteously and persuasively, showing them how these entombed souls are hindered in their natural movement, expression, and development; and how their loosening from prison would be a matter not simply of courtesy, sympathy, and help to them, but aid to all the world. One talks on evenly and logically in this way, but notices that the passing throng does not even turn its head, or if it does, glances curiously and walks on. It gradually penetrates the minds of the prisoners that the people passing do not hear; that some thick sheet of invisible but horribly tangible plate glass is between them and the world. They get excited; they talk louder; they gesticulate. Some of the passing world stop in curiosity; these gesticulations seem so pointless; they laugh and pass on. They still either do not hear at all, or hear but dimly, and even what they hear, they do not understand. Then the people within may become

---

[10]See Chapter III.

hysterical. They may scream and hurl themselves against the barriers, hardly realizing in their bewilderment that they are screaming in a vacuum unheard and that their antics may actually seem funny to those outside looking in. They may even, here and there, break through in blood and disfigurement, and find themselves faced by a horrified, implacable, and quite overwhelming mob of people frightened for their own very existence.[11]

This book, then, is yet another attempt to seize the attention of those who would pass us by.

The central theme of this essay is that racism governs the corporate internal labor market as regards black employees and constitutes the major explanation for income, occupational, and upward mobility discrimination. Comprised of six chapters, Part 1 attempts to provide a qualitative basis on which to examine the issues surrounding employment discrimination. Following Chapter I, the introduction, Chapter II summarizes some of the early racial attitudes of Europeans toward Africans and, later, attitudes of Americans toward black slaves. The chapter ends with a definition of *racism*. Chapter III presents a brief history of black workers in America since 1865 for the purpose of tracing black employment patterns and gaining a better understanding of the development of contemporary racism in the corporate workplace. Chapter IV presents three major theoretical approaches which attempt to explain employment discrimination and the resulting differences in income, occupational mobility, and upward mobility accruing to black and white corporate employees. Chapters V and VI reflect our studies with respect to corporate internal labor market dynamics and the ways in which they affect black employees in the overall employment process, i.e., hiring, promotions, training, career paths, compensation, and the like. The two major categories of black corporate employees are defined, and the demand—and to a lesser extent, supply—factors impacting these groups are identified and discussed. Part 2 is an empirical investigation and contains the final four chapters. Chapter VII presents work force data for 1978 from a single corporation, describing employees by race, sex, salary, level of educational attainment, and length of service. Chapters VIII and IX construct measures and models designed to explore the broad issues of employment discrimination and test important hypotheses on the basis of the corporate data made available for this study. The final chapter is a summary of this work with recommendations. It concludes that the *quality* of employee length of service is a major determinant of upward

---

[11]W. E. B. DuBois, *Dusk of Dawn* (New York: Schocken Books, 1968), pp. 130–31.

mobility in the corporate internal labor market; moreover, it concludes that black corporate employees tend to be precluded from those corporate experiences necessary to support significant upward mobility. Finally, the Appendix contains individual data for the 2,721 employees in the data base.

II

Race, Class, and Racism

INTRODUCTION

THIS BOOK ARGUES that *racism* is the engine for the employment dynamics that control the positioning and mobility of blacks in corporate internal labor markets. Though it may be possible to define and describe racism in a very few sentences, such an initial approach probably would not lend maximum substance to the thesis. What is needed, at least, is a brief discussion of the historical character of race relations and its persistence over time. Moreover, the development of contemporary race relations into an apparently viable doctrine of white superiority–black inferiority requires some examination, especially the support of this "doctrine" by economic (and other) thought and writings. It is this doctrine which, when defined, we will call racism; and, throughout the remainder of this book, our purpose will be to assess its impact on the corporate internal labor market patterns of black white-collar employees.

Neoclassical economics, in particular, avoids use of the word *racism* in its analyses of black/white employment relations. It prefers the relatively less offensive term *discrimination* and imputes to it the simplicity of "employer tastes" in preferring white workers over black workers. No serious recognition is granted to that set of pervasive, societally institutionalized values shaped by the notions of white superiority–black inferiority. Such an omission is significant for, among others, the following reason: while the sometimes arcane writings of economists are not generally read by the public at large, the sense and thrust of their works are frequently distilled in general trade publications for consumption by large segments of the society including corporate executives and elected officials, only to be further spread to even larger segments of the society, including the average law-abiding citizen. Thus, such writings often form the basis for conventional wisdom. A major example of this sort of conventional wisdom is the set of rationalizations for individual and institutional racism in labor markets, which feeds on itself so as to continue the relegation of blacks, in the main, to the least-paying positions and to a relatively few occupations, from which upward mobility is often precluded. In the meantime, a social consciousness is shaped, and one need not venture far—employment centers, educational institutions, et al.—to observe or experience a lack of interest in the overall economic conditions of blacks in America, and their relationships to major social and economic institutions.

Why is this the situation? What is the *raison d'être* for the continuation of racist employment patterns, and through what mechanisms are such patterns justified, maintained, and encouraged? It is the contention of this work that a systemic racism—not simple prejudice or discrimination—is at the center of black/white employment relations.[1] This chapter, then, is devoted to a general discussion of early European racist thought, its subsequent use in the justification for American slavery, the subtle embrace of racist thought by some contemporary observers of the economic and social scenes, and, finally, a definition of *racism*.

NEOCLASSICAL DISCRIMINATION—AN OVERVIEW

Neoclassical economics does not admit of racism in its analyses of employment discrimination based on race. At best, racism is recognized as an exogenous variable—i.e., noneconomic in character, existing outside the economic system or where black and white employees are assumed to be homogeneous in the production process; at worst, it is either ignored or euphemistically replaced by the more acceptable word "discrimination." Few, if any, economists of the orthodox persuasion explicitly give racism its due in explanations or descriptions of racial discrimination. For example, Milton Friedman, a leading exponent of the neoclassical view, states, in

[1]Some economists make the strong argument that racism is an integral part of capitalism; to answer these questions requires an analysis of capitalistic dynamics. In particular, see Michael Reich, *Racial Inequality: A Political-Economic Analysis* (Princeton: Princeton University Press, 1981).

what amounts to a meretriciously intellectual appeal probably to large numbers of white readers:

> It is hard to see that discrimination can have any meaning other than a "taste" of others that one does not share. We do not regard it as "discrimination" . . . if an individual is willing to pay a higher price to listen to one singer than to another, although we do if he is willing to pay a higher price to have services rendered to him by a person of one color than by a person of another. . . . Is there any difference in principle between the taste that leads a householder to prefer an attractive servant to an ugly one and the taste that leads another to prefer a Negro to a white or a white to a Negro?[2]

Gary Becker, in his seminal discrimination study,[3] utilizes exclusively the notion of employer "taste" for discrimination. The analysis is an excellent example of why a severely bounded, perhaps dispassionate, and scientifically staid approach to a study of black/white labor and employment relations in America yields very little of value toward meaningful policy developments, or even to a furthered understanding of employment discrimination based on race. Not only does Becker never use the word *racism* in his book, and the word *race* but infrequently, his predominant use of *discrimination* is sterile with respect to relevant reality and subject to the narrow constraints of marginal productivity analysis. This socioeconomic naiveté—feigned or otherwise—is revealed in the following statement:

> An employer may refuse to hire Negroes solely because he erroneously underestimates their economic efficiency. His behavior is discriminatory not because he is prejudiced against them but because he is ignorant of their true efficiency.[4]

Likewise, Christopher Jencks has stated:

> while we cannot blame discrimination by *current employers* for the portion of the earnings gap attributable to white/nonwhite differences in personal characteristics, neither can we simply dismiss the possibility that this portion of the gap is due to discrimination. To the extent that discrimination in education causes white/nonwhite differences in educational attainment, or

---

[2]Milton Friedman, *Capitalism and Freedom*, 2nd ed. (Chicago: University of Chicago Press, 1982), p. 110.

[3]Gary S. Becker, *The Economics of Discrimination*, 2nd ed. (Chicago: University of Chicago Press, 1971).

[4]Ibid., p. 16.

past discrimination by employers causes white/nonwhite differences in social background, discrimination is an indirect cause
of the entire earnings differential.[5]

Failure to recognize the existence and role of racism as an
explicit—or endogenous—variable in one's model of racial discrimination in employment markets is to rationalize the decisions of
white employers regarding black employees, violate the sensibilities
of racism's victims, and construct what amounts to an apologia for
continued denial of a full range of employment opportunities to black
Americans.

Being "ignorant of their true efficiency," as Becker puts it, has
led to the development of an added dimension to the marginalist
approach—namely, the statistical theory of racial discrimination in
labor markets. An initial proponent, Edmund S. Phelps, comments:

> the employer who seeks to maximize expected profit will dis-
> criminate against blacks . . . if he believes them to be less qual-
> ified, reliable, long-term, etc. on the average than whites . . . and
> if the cost of gaining information about the individual applicants
> is excessive. Skin color . . . is taken as a proxy for relevant data
> not sampled. The a priori belief in the probable preferability of
> a white . . . over a black . . . candidate who is not known to differ
> in other respects might stem from the employer's previous sta-
> tistical experience with the two groups . . . or it might stem from
> prevailing sociological beliefs that blacks . . . grow up disadvan-
> taged due to racial hostility or at least prejudices toward them
> in the society.[6]

Even here, it is assumed "that treating two groups of workers differently may be the *rational* response of firms to uncertainty about
an individual's productivity."[7] (My italics)

In the internal labor market, measures of employee productivity
are some function of investments in human capital—i.e., education,
training, and experience—and performance, in addition to innate
abilities. Models that begin with assumptions that black and white
employee groups have equal *means* with respect to innate abilities
but different *standard deviations* in innate and acquired abilities[8]
provide more information about institutional behavior and values

[5]Christopher Jencks, *Who Gets Ahead?: The Determinants of Economic Success
in America* (New York: Basic Books, 1979), p. 208.

[6]Edmund S. Phelps, "The Statistical Theory of Racism and Sexism," *American
Economic Review*, 62 (Sept. 1972), 659.

[7]Shelly J. Lundberg and Richard Startz, "Private Discrimination and Social
Intervention in Competitive Labor Markets," *American Economic Review*, 73 (June
1983), 340.

[8]Ibid., p. 344.

than either black or white employee productivity. Such models fail to explain how differences based on race arise, and they ignore the institutional impact on corporate managers charged with assessing employee performance.

Moreover, the strict neoclassical theories tend to focus on wage differences generated by discrimination to the exclusion of other internal manifestations of racial discrimination in employment.[9] To put it differently, the various approaches assume that employer assessments of employee productivity—relatively high for whites and relatively low for blacks—are registered principally in wage adjustments rather than in upward mobility opportunities (promotions, occupational access, training, etc.). Such a singular approach reduces the need to identify racism in the overall process by emphasizing "taste for discrimination" decisions of an individual employer, as if those decisions were made in isolation from institutional customs and societal values, inter- and intra-group dynamics, and the clear inexactitude of performance evaluations.

EARLY AFRICAN-EUROPEAN RELATIONS

It would appear that contemporary racist thought has an extremely long history; and if we are to gain a better understanding, it may be useful to begin with early African-European relations. The objective is not to be exhaustive in this regard, but rather to capture some sense of how contemporary race relations came to be. An interesting question, then, is: to what extent were the perceptions of Europeans in the sixteenth and seventeenth centuries regarding Africans accurate and unbiased, or ill-motivated and, perhaps, fraught with conspiratorial undertone? Moreover, to what extent do historical accounts of whites become the accepted "history," the final word, as it were, regarding black people?

What is curious is that the historical record, from the viewpoint of Africans' oral histories, does not square in all respects with the picture painted by European sources. To be sure, there are different emphases and interpretations; however, one can observe major differences in the selection and character of events chronicled, and further note that these may well be shaped by a society's needs to justify current policies.

---

[9]A partial exception to this is Bergmann's "crowding" thesis. While effects of discrimination on black and white wages are examined, Bergmann recognizes occupational discrimination based on race and argues that blacks are "crowded" in low-level and few occupations relative to whites. See Barbara R. Bergmann, "The Effect on White Incomes of Discrimination in Employment," *Journal of Political Economy*, (Jan.–Feb. 1971), pp. 294–313.

The social evidence on this subject is currently in abundance. We begin by reviewing, principally, Winthrop Jordan's findings regarding initial English attitudes toward Africans, and some relevant portions of Chancellor Williams's history of the African peoples. In addition, Lerone Bennett's history of the American Negro provides an important citation.

Jordan's interesting work begins with a description of the initial reactions of Englishmen to Africans in the sixteenth century before England's involvement in the slave trade.[10] Having gone there and having observed *physical* differences for the first time—principal among these the Africans' blackness—many Englishmen, nonetheless, viewed the West Africans that they encountered as merely a different kind of people. Needless to say, such perceived differences were not exactly neutral in character, but rather strange and a source of fascination. Their view of Africans as "un-Christian," "ugly," "libidinous," living unlike Englishmen, and reflecting, at best, a lower-level civilization, however, tended to support feelings and thoughts of significant English superiority. Simply on the basis of their blackness alone, with which Englishmen seemed preoccupied, Africans seemed to be thought of in a negative context, since, as Jordan notes, the English connotation of *black* before the 16th century was, indeed, emotionally negative, in contrast to the connotations of nobility, purity, and beauty associated with the color white. Black was "evil," "deadly," "horrible," "dirty," "wicked."

In addition to this matter of African blackness, which was a source of considerable consternation and speculation in the seventeenth century, and which gave rise to theories of causation ranging from the natural (the sun) to the theological (descendants of Ham), the characteristics of Christianity and heathenism, and being "civilized" versus being "savage" dominated the thinking of Englishmen.[11] It is clear that such thinking principally served to distinguish Africans from white people and establish the latter as superior in every important respect. If blacks were perceived as deviant, or beastly, or otherwise akin to the lower animals, and they were so perceived, then, indeed, it was a

> tragic happenstance of nature that the Negro's homeland was the habitat of the animal which in appearance most resembles man. ... A few commentators went so far as to suggest that Negroes had sprung from the generation of ape-kind or that apes were themselves the offspring of Negroes and some unknown African beast.[12]

---

[10]Winthrop D. Jordan, *White Over Black: American Attitudes Toward the Negro, 1550–1812* (Chapel Hill: University of North Carolina Press, 1968), chap. 1.

[11]Ibid., pp. 20–27.

[12]Ibid., pp. 29–31.

Jordan states that while this particular suspicion did not enjoy wide currency, tales of sexual relations between Negroes and apes and of attacks on Negro women by apes were more common and persistent. Of course, this was not a big step to take when West Africans were already considered libidinous, bestial, lecherous, and lustful. After all, "sexuality was what one expected of savages."[13]

As the slave trade and the system of slavery grew in America, these and other white views of Africans, and their implications for broad aspects of African life, were surely communicated—views that established Negroes as a lower type of human and formed the basis for much of the thinking about them that was to come.

In an impressive and fascinating account of African peoples and their civilization from 4500 B.C. to more recent times, Chancellor Williams[14] presents a provocative analysis of the genesis of black slavery. It began with the enslavement of the Mamelukes, the whites of North Africa, by the Arabs in the thirteenth century. The revolt of this group, located in Egypt, and the resulting overthrow of their Arab rulers "so shocked the white world that the general enslavement of whites ended forever . . . [and] Black Africa became the exclusive hunting ground for slaves."[15] This historical development, over time, "led to the general degradation of a whole people. The way was now both open and easy for all the relevant branches of science and scholarship to proclaim theories on the inherent inferiority of Blacks."[16]

According to Williams, when the Portuguese arrived in West Africa in the fifteenth century, they found a level of political structure and administrative machinery equal to any in Europe.[17] Moreover, Lerone Bennett has written:

> European penetration and the slave trade debased much that was vital in African culture. The popular myth depicts the conquering white man carrying the blessings of civilization to naked savages who sat under trees, filed their teeth and waited for fruit to drop into their hands. The truth is less flattering to the European ego. On the West Coast of Africa . . . there were complex socio-economic institutions. Political institutions ranged from

---

[13]Ibid., p. 33.

[14]Chancellor Williams, The Destruction of Black Civilization: Great Issues of a Race from 4500 B.C. to 2000 A.D. (Chicago: Third World Press, 1976). Williams's long and intensive research establishes the existence of advanced black civilizations in Egypt, circa 4500 B.C., an area which was actually Northern Ethiopia. Attributing this foremost of civilizations to black people has tended to be dismissed by white scholars. On this matter, see Thomas F. Gossett, Race: The History of an Idea in America (New York: Schocken Books, 1963), p. 66.

[15]Ibid., p. 162.

[16]Ibid., p. 163.

[17]Ibid., p. 261.

extended family groupings to village states and territorial empires. Most of these units had all the appurtenances of the modern state—armies, courts, and internal revenue departments. Indeed, more than one scholar has paid tribute to "the legal genius of the African."[18]

How can these accounts of civilized African life appear so inconsistent with the British accounts cited in Jordan's work? Undoubtedly, an answer to this question is of far greater complexity than this study is prepared to develop; however, it is not unreasonable to assert that significant cultural and physical differences between the Europeans and the Africans would have readily translated into a superiority/inferiority framework, and thereby served usefully for the conquest and exploitation of the African continent and for the later justification of the slave trade and the system of American slavery. Why would the Europeans have made seemingly attractive offers of Christianity, trade, and material benefits if feelings of a superior culture were not present? In fact, according to Williams, such offers were rarely made good on, since it appears that the aims of the Europeans were ultimately directed toward conquest of African nations. It is clear that these aims were eventually realized and have been maintained to a significant extent even to this day. The major conclusion, in any event, is that such efforts succeeded in debasing the African cultures, "reducing blacks to non-persons" and establishing a basis for the slave trade.[19] What is also clear is that the slave trade did indeed flourish, and Europeans viewed their captives as barbaric and generally inferior peoples.[20] These notions were to persist in the American colonies.

RACE THEORIES AND AMERICAN SLAVERY

The first half of the seventeenth century in the American colonies was a period of indentured servitude, and while black servants were certainly different from white servants in terms of length of servitude and color, theories of race were not as prevalent as they

---

[18]Lerone Bennett, Jr., *Before the Mayflower: A History of the Negro in America, 1619–1964*, rev. ed. (Baltimore: Penguin Books, 1966), p. 23.

[19]Williams, *Destruction of Black Civilization*, pp. 261–65.

[20]According to Williams, it is true that initially many African kings and chiefs supplied captives of war and other prisoners to the slave trade in the belief that they were "supplying workers needed abroad—and at great profit to themselves." However, even after the real intent of this trade activity became clear, some African leaders, eager for guns, wealth, and power, "became as brutal as the whites in dealing with their own kind." Ibid., p. 268.

would become later in the century.[21] But as Jordan has pointed out, "in all societies men tend to extrapolate from social status to actual inherent character, to impute to individuals characteristics suited to their social roles."[22] Thus, as the role of the white indentured servant declined and the labor requirements of the colonies increased, blacks were legally recognized as different from other servants and, by the latter part of the century, categorized as "slaves for life."[23] At this stage in the development of the institution of slavery, its justification rested on notions of heathenism (non-Christian) rather than race; slavery was seen as a means through which to convert heathens.[24] But heathenism, in this case associated with blacks who had already been described as savage and lacking in traits derived from civilization, implies an inferiority based on color and race. By the eighteenth century, in turn, arguments for enslavement based on Christian concepts of heathenism vanished. The system of slavery went largely unchallenged, and black slaves were seen as an inferior people.[25] As a matter of fact, many Christians were now beginning to question the wisdom and worth of conversion and to wonder whether the effect on slaves would be beneficial or harmful (relative to the highly valued institution of slavery).[26]

Into the eighteenth century, whether based on physical differences, spiritual deficiencies, lack of civilization, or comparative mental capacities, theories—not necessarily scientific—abounded, and the most influential argued that blacks were simply a lower human species with inferior traits and attributes. Even so notable an American as Thomas Jefferson wrote a literally vile piece on blacks that described them as typically ugly, smelly, incapable of high-level affection and emotionalism, dull of imagination and inferior in reasoning abilities.[27] Clearly, the notion that blacks were a separate human species was taking hold. Adding supposedly scientific rigor to this argument in the late eighteenth century was White's new application of the "great chain of being." This English physician arranged the skulls of man and beast from lowest to highest in terms of "intelligence and active powers suited to their stations in the general system." The Negro was thought to be somewhere between white men and apes, but closer to apes than white men.[28]

---

[21]Gossett, *Race: The History of an Idea*, pp. 29–30.
[22]Jordan, *White Over Black*, p. 179.
[23]Gossett, *Race: The History of an Idea*, p. 30.
[24]Ibid., p. 31.
[25]Ibid., chap. 3.
[26]Jordan, *White Over Black*, pp. 180–86.
[27]Gossett, *Race: The History of an Idea*, pp. 42–43. Also, see Jordan, *White Over Black*, p. 458.
[28]Ibid., pp. 47–48.

The concept of the "great chain of being" was beginning to lose some of its popularity in the nineteenth century when Darwin's theory of evolution came onto the scene. While the Darwinian thesis "left no doubt that all human races belong to a single species . . . , [it] . . . did not change the argument that some races are superior to others."[29] On the contrary, Darwin's theory did promote a concept of differences which was applied to racial groups; and, into the twentieth century, much effort was expended in attempts to effect scientific measurements of such racial differences.[30] Interestingly, Darwin's biological approach "provided a new rationale within which nearly all the old convictions about race superiority and inferiority could find a place."[31]

As was stated earlier, the thoughts and writings of contemporary scholars often contribute to the shaping of conventional wisdom regarding, among others, race and racial practices. Such wisdom tends to not only rationalize such thoughts and practices but reinforces them. This was no less true in the late years of the nineteenth century or the early years of the twentieth century.

The proponents of Social Darwinism, the application of the principles of evolution and natural selection in organisms to social phenomena including the condition and position of blacks in society, had a field day with the issues of race. The sociologist Herbert Spencer, for example, argued that in view of the evolutionary process, which by its nature is excruciatingly slow, virtually nothing could be done about primitive civilizations since the primitive state "merely reflected the state of . . . biological evolution."[32] More specifically, Spencer compared the mental development of primitive peoples with that of a child. Spencer's position, according to Gossett, was that "the minds of primitive races had all the limitations of the minds of children, except that their childhood of intellect was permanent."[33] Of course, this type of thinking provided a foundation for many writers of the late nineteenth and early twentieth centuries.

The eugenics movement, also from the late nineteenth century, emphasized genetics and hereditary influences in determining the ablest of men, and the inferiority of blacks. Thus, it was easy to explain the social and economic conditions of the impoverished masses, which included blacks, in terms of their stock of inherited traits.[34]

---

[29]Ibid., p. 67. Also, see Jordan, White Over Black, pp. 509–10.
[30]Ibid., pp. 68–69.
[31]Ibid., p. 145.
[32]Ibid., p. 148.
[33]Ibid., p. 149.
[34]Ibid., pp. 156–59.

CONTEMPORARY THOUGHT

What stands out boldly is that many of the finest American and European thinkers of their day considered the matter of race of substantial importance. Moreover, there can be no question but that theories of race continue to play a major role in contemporary American life through their impact on social values and on the relative economic positioning of blacks vis-à-vis whites.

In relative terms, not much has changed for blacks in America as regards their participation in the economic life of the society, their economic rewards, or the degree of racism to which they are subject.[35] In response to this assertion, there will be those who will observe that there has been a noticeable diminution in the practices of individual racism, as evidenced by the increased presence of blacks in better jobs in the corporate and government sectors. Such changes may merely reflect, however, practices growing out of changing social and economic variables—e.g., growth in technology, population growth and shifts, improved national and international communication systems, changing forms of work and workplaces. But it does not then follow that racist thought and practices have subsided; on the contrary, they are accommodated by a changing economic and social framework induced, in large measure, by the needs for economic growth and social survival.

The important consideration to be borne in mind is that all of the anti-black rantings and race theories—antiquated or current, and irrespective of basis—attempt to structure concepts of white superiority, black inferiority, or both, based on perceived black/white physical and behavioral differences. This appears to be true whether the basis is the Christian notion of oneness in mankind or polygenics; cranial measurements or color; cultures of civilization or traits of savagery; innate superiority or innate inferiority. And it remains true whether the racist discourse is coarse or sophisticated; clothed in dispassionate scientific jargon or otherwise; or written or spoken by lettered or virtually illiterate proponents.

For example, the work of contemporary scholars such as Arthur Jensen and Christopher Jencks is geared to measuring not only differences in intelligence, but imputing such differences to group factors of heredity. Thus, according to Philip Green, "Jensen argues that whatever else compensatory education can do, it cannot *equalize* IQs, or intelligence."[36] The basic difference between this approach to innate inferiority and the approaches developed in the past is that

---

[35]On this point, see Robert B. Hill, *The Widening Economic Gap* (Washington, D.C.: National Urban League, 1979).

[36]Philip Green, *The Pursuit of Inequality* (New York: Pantheon, 1981), p. 39.

current methods of measurement and evaluation—despite the possibility of perverse use—are technically superior and more refined.

Another example of a link with the past can be found in the "culture of poverty" thesis which has enjoyed ready acceptance by many observers of the social and economic scene. Charles Sackrey provides an excellent statement of the thesis:

> A poor ghetto—whether black, Puerto Rican, Irish, or WASP—has its own particular ethos, a considerable range of behavioral characteristics displayed by its members which makes their plight insensitive to most antipoverty measures, including income flows. John Kenneth Galbraith's "insular and case poverty" . . . and Banfield's "lower-class behavior" are both attempts to symbolize those kinds of personal characteristics which make the poor "different" from other Americans. Such traits as helplessness, despair, a relatively strong propensity to break laws written by others, large numbers of illegitimate children, family size considerably beyond the capacity of family income, a tendency to be impulsive and present-oriented, fatherless families, and, especially important, a harsh and defeating self-contempt—all are said to lead to a life style outside the mainstream of American economic and social life.[37]

It is this "lower-class behavior," according to those who embrace this thesis, that entraps, especially, poor blacks in a constant state of poverty.

A major criticism of this theory is that it does not answer the basic question of how people get trapped in the "culture of poverty," or how it is maintained. Green contends that without accounting for a "structure of white oppression, then black inferiority is the only available alternative."[38] With respect to the educational process, Kenneth B. Clark has raised specific questions as to the substitutability of this theory for theories of inferiority, the role that the theory plays in obscuring basic reasons for slow educational growth, and the development of rationalizations for "educational default."[39]

Criticisms notwithstanding, the advancement of variations on this theme are numerous. Of overall importance here, however, is the emphasis on class rather than race as the explanation of discrimination and its justification. Bradley R. Schiller, in an attempt to give credence to the "culture of poverty" thesis, analyzed the educational and career progress of the black and white sons of families receiving

---

[37]Charles Sackrey, *The Political Economy of Urban Poverty* (New York: Norton, 1973), p. 54.

[38]Green, *Pursuit of Inequality*, p. 51.

[39]Kenneth B. Clark, *Dark Ghetto: Dilemmas of Social Power* (New York: Harper & Row, 1965), p. 131.

public assistance. He concluded that since poor whites made as little educational progress as did poor blacks, then class and not race is the primary operator. Schiller also noted that occupational barriers are similar in their restraint of poor black and white youngsters. Thus, "poverty, not race, is the greater obstacle to early socio-economic achievement for black AFDC children."[40]

William Julius Wilson argues that the progress of blacks is, today, more a function of economic class than a function of race. In particular, Wilson believes this to be true in labor markets:

> Basic changes in the system of production have produced a segmented labor structure in which blacks are either isolated in the relatively nonunionized, low-paying, basically undesirable jobs of the non-corporate sector, or occupy the higher-paying corporate and government industry positions in which job competition is either controlled by powerful unions or is restricted to the highly trained and educated, regardless of race.[41]

Such are the current attempts to substitute class discrimination for race discrimination. Of course, notions of inferiority associated with behavioral traits remain derivable from the "culture of poverty" arguments.

As was stated above, the "culture of poverty" thesis is not entirely new, but rather a variation on a theme. The American Economic Association,[42] of all the possible associations, in 1896 published "Race Traits and Tendencies of the American Negro" by Frederick L. Hoffman, whose position was that the Negro's poverty and plight could not be remedied by improving living conditions since his gross immorality was racially innate.[43] He did think, however, that the Negro could possibly make some progress if he were "willing to subject himself to the same stern disciplines which had developed and conditioned the race of white men."[44]

---

[40]Bradley R. Schiller, "Class Discrimination vs. Racial Discrimination," *Review of Economics and Statistics*, 53 (Aug. 1971), 263–69.

[41]William Julius Wilson, *The Declining Significance of Race*, 2nd ed. (Chicago: University of Chicago Press, 1980), pp. 15–16. That there is a segmented labor market is a well-established fact. But that highly trained and educated blacks occupy the higher-paying positions regardless of race is simply not true. In particular, see my Chapters VIII and IX.

[42]The imagined lineage from Hoffman to Friedman and other contemporary economists—while it would make a fascinating caricaturized display—reminds one of the relatively close proximity to the avowed racists of yesteryear.

[43]Gossett, *Race: The History of an Idea*, pp. 281–82.

[44]Gossett, *Race: The History of an Idea*, p. 282. This contention is bandied about with some frequency in a variety of forms in contemporary writings. For example, it relates to "a tendency to be impulsive and present-oriented" quoted earlier from Sackrey. Neoclassical proponents of human capital theory, discussed in later chapters,

Even Paul Samuelson, writing in the eleventh edition of his now-famous textbook, borrows from the "culture of poverty" theme:

> Finally, if a black child comes from a broken home where no books line the shelves, and where one parent is hard-pressed to care for many children on a limited relief check, then, already at the age of six, the beginning student is under a handicap with respect to learning performance and educational achievement.[45]

Clearly, white America has a vested interest in the social and economic status quo and presumes the correctness of theories—adequate or otherwise—that ignore important factors in an effort to justify the continued degradation of black Americans. It is Clark's thought that:

> Speculation appears to reflect primarily the status of those who speculate. Just as those who proposed the earlier racial inferiority theories were invariably members of the dominant racial groups who presumed themselves and their groups to be superior, those who at present propose the cultural deprivation theory, are, in fact, members of the privileged group who inevitably associate their privileged status with their own innate intellect and its related educational success. . . . the implicit caste and class factors in this controversy cannot and should not be ignored.[46]

To be sure, racism has a basis in American life and affects its every aspect. In the next and final section of this chapter, a definition of racism is developed which underlines our meaning in this book.

RACISM DEFINED

To begin with, *racism* is a term that both defines and describes the current patterns of living and working relationships between black and white Americans. Based on attitudes and relationships formed several centuries ago, these current patterns are such that

---

often describe blacks as not willing to forego current income in favor of future returns. Arrow sums up the neoclassical position which imputes to blacks and whites differently chosen investment schedules when he states: "the investments are not the usual types of education or experience, which are observable, but more subtle types of personal deprivation and deferment of gratification which lead to the habits of action and thought that favor good performance in skilled jobs." See Kenneth J. Arrow, "The Theory of Discrimination," *Discrimination in Labor Markets*, ed. Orley Ashenfelter and Albert Rees (Princeton: Princeton University Press, 1973), p. 27.

[45]Paul A. Samuelson, *Economics*, 11th ed. (New York: McGraw-Hill, 1980), p. 734.

[46]Clark, *Dark Ghetto*, p. 131.

blacks tend to have relatively limited access to those socioeconomic and political institutions whose social products and services bear directly on the standard of living and the quality of life for society's members. Furthermore, blacks receive negatively disproportionate shares of such products and services.

What does not seem to be debatable is that first-rate developmental opportunities for full participation in labor markets are foreclosed to blacks. Generally, this means that blacks are discriminated against not only in terms of wages, but also in terms of access to varied and higher-paying occupational categories and to critical training and job-related experiences. With relatively lower incomes, housing standards and residential options are lower and fewer. Low-income communities provide inferior public educational facilities and poor health-care systems. Thus, to complete the cycle, blacks are limited in their labor market mobility on the grounds that they lack sufficient "qualifications" including capabilities (largely developed according to educational opportunity) and acceptable worker traits and habits (the result of lower-status community life).

Those writers who would emphasize that this is an example of discrimination based on "class" rather than "race" and who further argue that educated and well-trained blacks are not discriminated against in their bids for the better jobs are simply not knowledgeable regarding internal labor market dynamics. Even those well-educated and well-trained blacks who embrace middle-class values are victimized in the employment process relative to similarly prepared whites—and, in some instances, to less well-prepared whites. Admittedly, the discrimination faced by the better-educated and trained black is often not as pointed or as egregious as in the case of less well-prepared blacks; but, that the result is discriminatory nonetheless, and based on racial implications of black inferiority, cannot be easily denied.

Suffice it to state that white individuals who act, in their particular capacities or on behalf of an institution, against blacks in a racially motivated manner are in fact reflecting society's institutional values. Thus, in the internal labor market, in particular, unrewarding employment decisions made by individual white managers regarding black employees are a likely reflection of that corporate organization's racist values which, in turn, mirror the values of the larger society. To that extent, then, racism is institutional but is practiced by white individuals who perceive a vested interest in not only the maintenance of the corporate organization's racist values but in having successfully acted on behalf of the organization.

A second major form of institutional racism is that less clear variety rooted in seemingly passive institutional policies. For example, consider a corporate policy, written or unwritten, that states that in order to become a sales manager in the headquarters operation, the successful candidate must be educationally credentialed, must have no fewer than five years of successful sales experience in a field operation, must have served as an assistant manager in a field operation for at least two years, and must be a member in good standing of the hypothetical American National Good Salesperson Association. Certainly, these seemingly fair requirements have no racist overtones until it is realized that field operations typically will not hire blacks as salespersons in the first place because "whites won't buy from them"; and those few who have been hired and who have performed well for five years as salespersons are found not to be members of the Association because that organization has a practice of not admitting non-whites to membership. Therefore, no blacks are eligible for manager positions. This form of institutional racism is *quiet* in the sense that the existing policy, which "we have had for fifty years" and which is nonracist and applies to everybody equally, is self-operating within institutional norms. That is, it is not necessary for a white manager to exercise judgement.

Racism may be defined in a number of meaningful ways.[47] For the purposes of this work, however, we define *racism* as a set of institutionalized and negative social values, and whether expressed within or outside of institutions by individual whites or groups, or through silent functions of the institution itself, is reflective of systemic patterns of racial discrimination rooted in an historically generated and societally approved system of beliefs in white superiority—black inferiority which serves to foreclose full and equal access *to* socioeconomic and political institutions, delimit paths of mobility *within* such institutions, and to justify a deficient distribution of social goods and services *from* institutions to black people and other peoples of color with an intent to dominate and control. This impact on internal corporate labor markets is the central theme of this work.

SUMMARY

Neoclassical economics has tended to diminish, at best, if not ignore, the role of racism in its analyses of employment discrimination. It views racism as outside the economic system, and, by so

---

[47]For other exemplary definitions of racism, see Stokely Carmichael and Charles V. Hamilton, *Black Power: The Politics of Liberation in America* (New York: Vintage Books, 1967); Robert W. Terry, *For Whites Only* (Detroit: Detroit Industrial Mission, 1970); Louis L. Knowles and Kenneth Prewitt, eds., *Institutional Racism in America* (Englewood Cliffs: Prentice-Hall, 1969); and Calvin C. Hernton, *Sex and Racism in America* (New York: Grove, 1965).

doing, creates a model of discrimination based on marginal productivity analysis which rationalizes the behavior of employers in terms of profit-maximizing motives. Such an approach is consistent, in fact, with socioeconomic explanations which tend to maintain and protect the white superiority–black inferiority basis for race relations in America.

Racism would appear to have its foundations in the historical developments of race relations dating back to before the sixteenth century. In particular, the early European experiences on the West Coast of Africa were shaped by initial impressions of heathenism and of the uncivilized and even savage nature of the blacks. Though there is historical evidence to the contrary, the European slave trade capitalized on concepts of African inferiority and exploited the Christian commitment to convert heathen.

The need to develop justifications for the early institution of American slavery produced theological, social, and presumably scientific tracts, as well as personal tirades purporting to establish the inferiority of blacks relative to whites. This development of a system of rationales for slavery and its brutalities, while a source of some debate, nonetheless continued unabated beyond the period of legalized slavery and into the twentieth century.

Though less violent in tone and armed with more sophisticated analytical techniques, current efforts on behalf of racism continue in America through the use of IQ and achievement tests to "prove" the innate mental inferiority of blacks relative to whites. Racism is also perpetuated through the development of "culture of poverty" explanations which generally claim that low-status behavior and lifestyle—in some theories portrayed as inherited traits—preclude escaping the poverty trap and participation in the mainstream of American life.

This chapter ends with a definition of racism which emphasizes the role of institutionalized values and practices in race relations, generally, and in the life of black Americans, in particular.

III

Black Employees in Corporate America:
An Historical Perspective

INTRODUCTION

THE USE OF the word "historical" in this chapter's title is something of a misnomer since the significant history of white-collar blacks in the corporate bureaucracies of America is descriptive of so recent a past. Nonetheless, the purpose of this chapter is to establish a basis for the chapters that follow. Specifically, the employment discrimination faced by black Americans today doubtless has its roots in the system of slavery. While that system may have legally met its demise by the end of the Civil War, the racism, which was its underpinning, has remained a major thread in the fabric of our society and continues to impact blacks in matters of education, housing, health care, and income and employment. Thus, it would be useful to briefly examine the general patterns of black employment following the Civil War as an introduction to the internal labor market dynamics which currently influence the career paths and occupational status of white-collar blacks in the corporate sector.

BLACK WORKERS, 1865–1910

Freed black workers, following the Civil War, continued to experience the manifestations of the earlier slave system as well as other forms of subjugation. C. Vann Woodward writes:

Slavery was only one of several ways by which the white man
has sought to define the Negro's status, his "place," and assure
his subordination. Exploitation of the Negro by the white man
goes back to the beginning of relations between the races in
modern times, and so do the injustices and brutalities that
accompany exploitation. Along with these practices and in justification and defense of them, were developed the old assumptions of Anglo-Saxon superiority and innate African inferiority,
white supremacy and Negro subordination. In so far as segregation is based on these assumptions, therefore, it is based on
the old pro-slavery argument and has its remote ideological roots
in the slavery period.[1]

In addition, Eugene D. Genovese has suggested that by the time
of the Civil War, the system of slavery and its social and cultural
values had become indispensable to southern whites and their tra-
ditions.[2] Thus, not only were notions of black inferiority well
entrenched in the South's *modi operandi*, they also shaped the
employment contract between black workers and white employers
and continued to foster an occupational segregation.

It is clear, then, that the slave system and its ideology had—
and continues to have—a profound influence on the development
and character of the black work force in America. The system's
requirement that blacks be perceived as inferior to whites in order
to support the latter's needs to dominate and control lived on and
created a black work force, after 1865, which was allowed to hold
only the most menial of jobs—the dirtiest, the lowest level, the least
rewarding psychologically, the lowest paying, and, finally, those jobs
with virtually no career opportunities. Thus, while the Emancipation
Proclamation and the Thirteenth Amendment freed the slave population and made it legal for that group to seek and choose employment opportunities for wages, the transition from slave labor to wage
labor did not come easily for white employers. Those who did hire
blacks signed contracts enforceable by the Freedman's Bureau—a
creation of the Congress in 1865—which defined the conditions of
employment. Though such contracts often were not adhered to, they
gave freed men an opportunity to earn money under the wage system
and facilitated the transition from slave to wage labor.[3] Nonetheless,
unemployment among freed black workers was high due to white
employer hostility and was further intensified by the increased flow

---

[1]C. Vann Woodward, *The Strange Career of Jim Crow*, 2nd rev. ed. (New York:
Oxford University Press, 1966), p. 11.

[2]Eugene D. Genovese, *The Political Economy of Slavery* (New York: Vantage
Books, 1965), pp. 34–55.

[3]Charles H. Wesley, *Negro Labor in the United States, 1850–1925* (New York:
Russell and Russell, 1927), p. 131.

of European immigrant labor which drove many freed black workers from even common labor and personal service jobs.[4]

European Immigration and Black Employment

The role of European immigrant labor in fashioning the fate of black workers before 1860, and in the decades that followed, was pivotal and deserves some attention before returning to the main theme.[5] Three important developments associated with European immigration are boldly in evidence.

First, and the most major of the developments, even prior to the Emancipation Proclamation and the Civil War, European immigration, which had not been significant before 1820, began to increase dramatically as news of substantial economic opportunity in the United States reached that continent and as the forces of the Industrial Revolution were being felt. In addition, the end of the Napoleonic Wars, the Irish famine of 1846–47, and the French and German Revolutions of 1848, because of their impact on the general economic life of Europeans, were reasons for emigrating.[6] Thus, over five million Europeans came to America between 1821 and 1860.

Wesley writes that from about 1840, particularly in the major cities of the East (New York, Philadelphia, and Boston), feelings of antagonism were easily generated between free blacks and immigrants. Considering that many immigrants came with few skills and with considerable cultural and language differences, it is not surprising that even menial jobs became a point of competition and

Table 3.1 European Immigration to the United States,
1821– 60
(in thousands)

Period	Numbers of Immigrants
1821–30	152
1831–40	599
1841–50	1,713
1851–60	2,598

Source: Wesley, Negro Labor, p. 75.

[4]For further discussion of the employment plight of freed blacks after the Civil War, see E. Franklin Frazier, The Negro in the United States (New York: Macmillan, 1949), chap. 23; and Charles H. Wesley, Negro Labor, pp. 82–85.
[5]This section relies heavily on Wesley's classic history of black labor.
[6]Wesley, Negro Labor, p. 74.

conflict. Given the presumed sympathies of white employers with white immigrants, the result was that many blacks who had followed such occupations as waiter, porter, barber, cook, and maid found themselves being replaced by white immigrants. Since relatively few immigrants made their way to the South—as a result of the South's general attitude toward labor—such occupations tended to remain the province of southern black workers.[7]

Without doubt, immigrants adopted the same attitudes of race prejudice as other American whites, including refusals to work alongside blacks in similar occupations. Hence blacks were not hired on the same employment terms as whites. While this had always been true in the South, Wesley states that

> Even in Massachusetts, this situation existed. . . . At Philadel-
> phia, the prejudice was so unrelenting in the trades that many
> were compelled to abandon their pursuit of them. In New York
> City, they were deprived of the opportunities for advancement
> and culture because of the prejudice of color.[8]

The second important development occurred in the years following the Civil War. Though immigrant labor continued to compete with black labor especially in the North, the South did not view the prospects of free black labor with great favor. Southerners' racist views of blacks as unreliable—except, perhaps, when under the whip—along with the heavy movement of blacks from rural agrarian life to urban settings and some migration from the South to the North, led them to encourage the migration of European labor with the intent of replacing black workers and meeting increasing labor needs. Wesley contends that this move was also in the interest of preserving the southern way of life.[9] Despite newspaper advertisements, and even the formation of state immigration associations,[10] the numbers of European immigrants attracted to the South were less than had been hoped for.[11] Thus, black labor retained a semblance of its role in a depressed agricultural South.

The third development, one of great significance, occurred in the early part of the twentieth century, specifically during the years

---

[7]Ibid., p. 76. Also, see W.E.B. DuBois, *Black Reconstruction in America* (New York: Harcourt, Brace, 1935), pp. 17–20.

[8]Ibid., p. 78.

[9]Ibid., p. 194.

[10]A number of southern state legislatures established associations for the purpose of inducing immigrants to come south. For example, South Carolina legislated such a commission in 1866; the Alabama political machinery during this time created a similar act on behalf of German immigrants; and the state of Virginia chartered several such associations. See Wesley, *Negro Labor*, p. 195.

[11]Ibid., p. 197.

of World War I. As background for this development, it should be recalled that the Industrial Revolution had brought with it extremely heavy demands for labor to be utilized in, for example, factories and railroading. While this industrial development took place principally in the North, and the South remained largely agricultural, European immigrants were essentially looked to for the satisfaction of these labor requirements. Indeed, they continued to come in increasing numbers:

> In the 1880s, 5,300,000 immigrants came to the United States; in the depression decade of the 1890s there were 3,700,000; and in the first decade of the twentieth century these figures rose to 8,200,000. . . . The population flow from the South to the rest of the country was relatively small, averaging only little more than 50,000 a year, of whom only about 20,000 a year were black.[12]

Table 3.2 European Immigration to the United States
Selected Years, 1910–1922
(in thousands)

Year	Numbers of Immigrants
1910	1,042
1912	838
1914	1,219
1916	299
1918	111
1920	430
1922	310

Source: Wesley, *Negro Labor*, p. 290.

From Table 3.2, it can be observed that the European migration continued virtually unabated until World War I, at which point the number of immigrants was reduced sharply. The fact remains, however, that the development and growth of manufacturing and other industrial activities, at this point largely related to the required war effort, was being deprived of its major source of abundant and cheap labor. And herein is contained the seeds for an interesting socioeconomic development—namely, the attraction and employment of large numbers of blacks. Wesley makes an observation that is all the more interesting when viewed in the context of the general black employment picture up to this point:

---

[12]Dan Lacy, *The White Use of Blacks in America* (New York: McGraw-Hill, 1972), p. 99. His figures include Asian immigrants to the West Coast.

This change in the number of immigrants into America was at the basis of the Negro migration during the war. It is difficult to conceive of successful results for so extreme a movement of the Negro population without the condition of decreasing immigration.[13]

In sum, a concatenation of events from the middle of the nineteenth century to the early decades of the twentieth century—not the least of which was the massive European immigration beginning in 1840, and including the growth of the Industrial Revolution in the North, the Emancipation and the Civil War, the decline of agriculture in the South, and World War I—finally resulted in a mass movement of blacks from the South to the North.

Black Employment Conditions

Interestingly enough, though the great majority of blacks prior to the Civil War were agricultural and domestic workers, substantial numbers of black skilled craftsmen were heavily relied upon in the South.[14] Following the war and during Reconstruction, however, white hostility, the competition for jobs, and the emergence of white labor unions all served to force black artisans out of craft activities and into menial jobs. In the North, where there were also black artisans, white artisans were opposed to their employment; and, as we have seen, the flow of European immigrants lent support to the exclusion of blacks from skilled occupations.[15]

In 1877, the Reconstruction period was effectively ended when federal troops were withdrawn from the South. According to Woodward, this act signalled "the abandonment of the Negro as a ward of the nation, the giving up of the attempt to guarantee the freedman his civil and political equality, and the acquiescence of the rest of the country in the South's demand that the whole problem be left to the disposition of the dominant Southern white people."[16] The door to the disfranchisement of freed blacks was now open, and the way made clear for the enactment of Jim Crow laws:

---

[13]Wesley, Negro Labor, p. 291.

[14]Lucian B. Gatewood, "The Black Artisan in the U.S., 1890–1930," The Review of Black Political Economy, 5 (Fall 1974), 19–33.

[15]Needless to say, this history is replete with instances of violence and racist legislation in the manner of the Ku Klux Klan and the Black Codes, respectively. See Gatewood, "The Black Artisan," pp. 24–25.

[16]Woodward, Jim Crow, p. 6.

The South universally hailed the disfranchisement of the Negro as a constructive act of statesmanship. . . . Their view was summed up by J. K. Vardaman, of Mississippi: "I am just as opposed to Booker Washington as a voter, with all his Anglo-Saxon reenforcements, as I am to the coconut-headed, chocolate-colored, typical little coon, Andy Dotson, who blacks my shoes every morning. Neither is fit to perform the supreme function of citizenship." . . . Once the Negro was disfranchised, everything else necessary for White Supremacy could be done. . . . Whites solemnly resolved to keep the races completely separate. . . . Beginning in Tennessee in 1870, Southerners enacted laws against intermarriage of the races in every Southern state. Five years later, Tennessee adopted the first "Jim Crow" law and the rest of the South rapidly fell in line. Negroes and whites were separated on trains, in depots, and on wharves. Toward the end of the century the Negro was banned from white hotels, barber shops, restaurants, and theatres after the Supreme Court, in 1883, outlawed the Civil Rights Act of 1875. By 1885, most Southern states had laws requiring separate schools. With the adoption of new constitutions, the states firmly established the color line by the most stringent segregation of the races.[17]

In addition to a broad-based white hostility, black workers were further thwarted in their employment efforts by the increased utilization of white women in factories and other industrial organizations. The Jim Crow laws clearly precluded white women and blacks from working together.[18]

Such a prohibition was not only rooted in a general despising of blacks, but in an ideology that imputed inferior human status, savage bestiality, and insatiable sex drives to black males, in particular. Although white protestations were directed toward concerns about miscegenation and the "stock-polluting" consequences of "blood mixing,"[19] more broadly "the white man's self-esteem is in a constant state of sexual anxiety in all matters dealing with race relations,"[20] an anxiety likely related to the white ideology. Of especial importance for this volume, however, Hernton goes on to conclude that:

The racism of sex in the United States is but another aspect of

---

[17]John Hope Franklin, *From Slavery to Freedom* (New York: Alfred A. Knopf, 1947), pp. 337–38.

[18]Arnold M. Rose, *The Negro in America* (Boston: Beacon Press, 1956), p. 102.

[19]Hernton is very clear about the fact that such concerns have not deterred white men from relationships with black women. See Calvin C. Hernton, *Sex and Racism in America* (New York: Grove, 1965), pp. 176–77.

[20]Ibid., p. 7.

the unequal political and economic relations that exist between the races.[21] (His italics)

Unlike the Jim Crow laws which legislated behavior, this aspect of racism was—and, in large measure, continues to be—codified in an extralegal fashion dictating that black men in the South, in particular, were to have virtually no contact with white women. According to Lacy,

> The utmost caution was required of black men to avoid any conceivable affront to a white woman or any remotest suggestion that they existed as members of opposite sexes of the same species. Any act, however innocent, of a black man that offended or frightened a white woman, however irrational or hysterical, might quite literally cost him his life. In a hundred other ways the code separated and subordinated blacks, but in none so ruthlessly as this.[22]

Thus, as white women increasingly became a part of the labor force, their mere presence was a probable obstacle to black employment.

Labor Unions and Black Employment

Labor and trade unions and groups have a long history in the United States, but the first national federation of such unions was the National Trades Union founded in 1834, and it remained active for just a short time. It was not until 1866, following the Civil War, that the National Labor Union was founded. It attempted to embrace as many affiliate unions as it could, and its pronounced intentions to include all workers and to prohibit exclusion from membership on the basis of race are commonly cited in the literature. Doubtless, this was, in principle, true, but Gatewood has pointed out that black delegates were not invited to the national convention until 1869, and, at that point, "urged . . . to form their own labor organizations."[23] During this time, it should be noted, white workers' resistance and hostility toward black workers were so intense, in both the North and South, that the likely implementation of a nonracial policy was viewed by the leadership as virtually impossible if the organization was to remain viable. In addition, the National Labor Union was politically supportive of the Democratic party when most blacks

---

[21]Ibid., p. 176.
[22]Lacy, *White Use of Blacks*, p. 130.
[23]Gatewood, "The Black Artisan," p. 26.

supported Republicans.[24] In fact, black delegates at the 1869 National Labor Union convention, as well as at other labor meetings and conventions, were so shamefully treated and discriminated against that black workers determined the need to form their own national organization; thus, the short-lived Colored National Labor Union was formed in December 1869.[25]

In that same year, the Knights of Labor launched its federation with the avowed purpose of representing all workers irrespective of color. With more than a modicum of success in forming "Local Assemblies," in 1886 there were an estimated 60 thousand black members in a total membership of 700 thousand.[26] Some of these units contained black and white members, and others only black members. While there were such examples of integrated union efforts, white hostility remained in evidence, and in the South craft unions generally created segregated locals for black members.

The American Federation of Labor came onto the scene in the 1880s as the Knights of Labor began its decline. An important difference between the older federations and the newer AFL was that the latter, while also promoting the ideals of nonracist policies, organized along craft lines a policy which, by definition, was exclusionary. This development "had the detrimental effect upon black workers of serving to exclude from the ranks of organized labor almost the entire black work force, largely consisting of agricultural workers, laborers, and other unskilled persons."[27] By the end of the century, AFL leadership had substantially capitulated to social custom and was admitting local unions that either barred black membership or established Jim Crow auxiliaries. Moreover, white hostility and fear of black competition, especially in the skilled trades, supported these and other restrictive actions. To be sure, there were significant numbers of black artisans in the South who were ultimately driven from the unions and out of their occupations. An interesting example of this development is cited by Meier and Rudwick:

> In Nashville, where blacks outnumbered whites as artisans in 1880, whites joined the unions, often learned the skills from the black members, and then, having achieved a commanding majority, voted to eliminate the Negroes from membership as rapidly

[24]On this point, see Ray Marshall, *The Negro Worker* (New York: Random House, 1967), p. 16.

[25]Gatewood, "The Black Artisan," p. 26.

[26]These statistics are frequently found in the literature. For example, see Gatewood, "The Black Artisan"; Marshall, *The Negro Worker;* and August Meier and Elliott Rudwick, *From Plantation to Ghetto,* 3rd ed. (New York: Hill and Wang, 1976).

[27]Gatewood, "The Black Artisan," p. 27.

as possible. By 1910 control of the crafts in the city had passed
to the whites.[28]

Clearly, the labor movement was turning its back on black workers in both the North and the South. Thus, by 1902, black membership in the AFL approximated only 3 percent of that federation's one
million members.[29]
This, then, was the lot of the black worker during and for
approximately three decades after the Reconstruction era. Despised,
denied entry, and in many instances brutalized, the black workers
of this period were segregated socially, politically, and in employment. Access to employment opportunities in both the North and
the South, other than to unskilled and semiskilled occupations, was
effectively blocked by labor unions, which were controlled by whites
and supported by Jim Crow laws, and in the North by immigrant
European workers.

BLACK WORKERS AFTER THE TURN OF THE CENTURY

At the turn of the century, blacks remained concentrated largely
in the South, and the employment status of blacks in the South and
North was not significantly different from earlier decades: "statistics
on occupations by race for the period 1890–1930 would . . . seem to
indicate that black workers were reported principally to be in agricultural, menial, and unskilled occupations. Few black workers . . .
were engaged in skilled occupations during this period."[30] Around
1910, however, blacks began moving from farms and agricultural
occupations in small numbers to northern cities where, initially, they
were found largely in private household occupations. "By 1920, the
proportion of blacks in the North had increased to 14.1%; most of
these were concentrated in large cities, where they found jobs in
rapidly growing industries."[31] However, employment continued to
be limited, for the most part, to those jobs requiring the least skill
and paying the lowest wages.[32] For example, in either northern or
southern factories, blacks would most likely be employed as laborers
or janitors. Those blacks who did hold skilled and supervisory positions were found generally in shops where only blacks worked. Of

---

[28]Meier and Rudwick, *From Plantation to Ghetto*, p. 209.
[29]Victor Perlo, *Economics of Racism U.S.A.*, 2nd ed. (New York: International
Publishers, 1976), p. 199.
[30]Gatewood, "The Black Artisan," p. 19.
[31]Eboh C. Ezeani, "Economic Conditions of Freed Black Slaves in the United
States, 1870–1920," *The Review of Black Political Economy*, 8 (Fall 1977), 112.
[32]Ibid., p. 113.

considerable interest is the fact that, as the impact of industrial expansion and technological development was felt, jobs which became mechanized "were defined as white jobs" and ceased to be held by blacks.[33]

A consequence of these predictable occupational patterns of black workers through the first three or four decades of the 1900s has been described by Ray Marshall:

> These job patterns obviously tended both to reflect and to perpetuate the racial caste system. Restricting Negroes to inferior jobs strengthened the image of them as "inferior" people, and the low incomes associated with these jobs made it difficult for them to acquire the education, housing, and physical means necessary for participation in the mainstream of American life.[34]

WHITE-COLLAR BLACKS, 1910–60

An important economic development began to take shape between 1890 and 1910. This was the emergence of the large corporate bureaucracies which were to dominate the economic life of Americans and which gave rise to the class of white-collar workers. According to Rosabeth Kanter, this group doubled its numbers

Table 3.3 White-Collar Workers, by Race and Sex, 1910–60
(in thousands)

Year	Totals			White		Black	
	Workers	Whites	Blacks	Males	Females	Males	Females
1910	7,908	7,764	144	5,882	1,882	101	43
1920	10,556	10,375	181	7,096	3,279	121	60
1930	13,590	13,335	255	8,662	4,673	164	91
1940	14,657	14,377	280	9,429	4,948	177	103
1950	20,745	20,177	568	12,186	7,991	323	245
1960	28,584	27,522	1,062	15,890	11,632	564	498

Source: Dale L. Hiestand, *Economic Growth and Employment Opportunities for Minorities* (New York: Columbia University Press, 1964), Table II, pp. 7–9.

Note: "The data for 1930 and earlier include all who considered themselves workers; the data for 1940 and later only those who were employed." See *Economic Growth*, p. 10.

[33]Marshall, *The Negro Worker*, p. 93.
[34]Ibid., p. 93.

between 1900 and 1920;[35] however, blacks played an insignificant role in this growth or the growth which occurred in subsequent decades. Between 1910 and 1930, the black worker's share of white-collar jobs was less than 2 percent, and it remained less than 4 percent by 1960.[36]

Table 3.3 depicts the patterns of growth and compares black and white employment in white-collar occupations during the period 1910–60. A general review of that data clearly supports Kanter's observations.

Another view of the data is contained in Table 3.4. Here, the percentage change in employment is shown over the period 1910–40. Note that the changes for white employees were equivalent to the increases in total white-collar employment, and declined only very slightly thereafter. While their numbers are relatively small, the percent increases in total black representation exceeded the increases in total white-collar employment in every decade except 1910–20. In the period 1940 to 1960, the percent increases for black employees more than doubled similar increases for white employees. Broadly, from 1910 to 1920, females, and to a lesser extent, black females, showed relatively substantial increases in their representations. By 1950, while the total numbers of white-collar workers continued to grow, white females and black males and females grew at much higher percentage rates.

Table 3.4 Percent Change for Black and White Workers in White-Collar Occupations, 1910–60
(percent)

	Totals			White		Black	
Year	Workers	Whites	Blacks	Males	Females	Males	Females
1910–20	34	34	26	21	74	20	40
1920–30	29	29	41	22	43	36	52
1930–40	8	8	10	9	6	8	13
1940–50	42	40	103	29	62	83	138
1950–60	38	36	87	30	46	75	103

These rates of percent increase notwithstanding, black employees in the white-collar occupations remained at less than 4 percent

---

[35]For a discussion of this development, see Rosabeth Moss Kanter, *Men and Women of the Corporation* (New York: Basic Books, 1977), chap. 1. Also, C. Wright Mills, *White Collar: The American Middle Classes* (New York: Oxford University Press, 1951), chap. 9.

[36]Dale L. Hiestand, *Economic Growth and Employment Opportunities for Minorities* (New York: Columbia University Press, 1964), pp. 20–21.

Table 3.5 Black Workers as a Proportion of White Workers in White-Collar
Occupations, 1910–60
(percent)

Year	Total Blacks/Total	Black Males/ White Males	Black Females/ White Females
1910	1.8	1.7	2.3
1920	1.7	1.7	1.8
1930	1.9	1.9	2.0
1940	1.9	1.9	2.1
1950	2.7	2.7	3.1
1960	3.7	3.6	4.3

of the total number of white-collar employees by 1960. (See Table 3.5.) Clearly, the gains shown by black employees after 1940, while relatively small, reflect the implications for changing labor patterns associated with World War II and its aftermath.

A word about World War II and its effects on black employment then and in subsequent years is in order. When A. Philip Randolph, journalist, civil rights leader, and organizer of the Brotherhood of Sleeping Car Porters, realized that America's development of a war industry was absorbing many of the Great Depression's unemployed, he and countless others complained that blacks were not being employed in the factories and plants being retooled for the war effort. These complaints seemed to have fallen on deaf ears, including President Franklin Roosevelt's. Thus, to attract attention to the employment needs of black Americans, Randolph threatened to initiate a "March on Washington" in which he promised to lead, perhaps, as many as 100 thousand blacks through the streets of the capital. Deciding that such a march and such a distraction from the war effort should be avoided, President Roosevelt signed Executive Order 8802, which established the Fair Employment Practices Committee aimed at requiring federal contractors to hire without regard to race. The result of this action, combined with labor shortages as the war progressed, produced the second "Great Migration" of blacks from the South to the North and West. Certainly more than at any other time since the Emancipation, many black workers, possessed primarily of agricultural and personal service skills, found themselves in factory training programs leading to more useful and higher-level trades and skills. In some instances, blacks were employed in the aircraft and shipbuilding industries in clerical, administrative, and, to a lesser extent, professional occupations. These employment gains were to form a new pattern of employment for years to come.

A second important result of World War II was the rapid growth of urban ghetto areas due to wartime migration, areas which became power bases for civil rights activism and political activities. In particular, it is generally agreed that President Harry Truman's election in 1948 was owed, in large measure, to black voters. He, in turn, provided significant impetus for later civil rights legislation by signing an executive order barring racial segregation in the armed forces and by bringing issues of black employment and racial discrimination in America to the fore. Though Congress would not pass a civil rights bill, the Truman years were a turning point in American race relations.

The final point that ought to be made is that following the war, returning servicemen, black and white, benefited from the GI Bill which provided financial support for educational pursuits and home mortgages. Unquestionably, there were many black returnees who for a variety of reasons, including low levels of literacy, were not able to take full advantage of the government-sponsored opportunities. On the other hand, many did take advantage with the result that an increasing number of blacks were graduated from college and from graduate and professional schools.

Tables 3.6, 3.7, and 3.8 describe clerical and sales worker patterns of employment during the period 1910–60. As a sub-category of white-collar workers, the patterns of black employment in the clerical and sales worker category reveal relatively important gains. The percent increases for all blacks exceeded the percent increases for all workers in every decade except 1920–30. Again, the changes in black representation during the 1940–60 period were dramatic. On the other hand, the proportional representation of black clerical and sales workers did not rise above 2 percent until 1950, and by

Table 3.6 Clerical and Sales Workers, by Race and Sex, 1910–60
(in thousands)

	Totals			White		Black	
Year	Workers	Whites	Blacks	Males	Females	Males	Females
1910	3,828	3,789	39	2,713	1,076	32	7
1920	5,705	5,642	63	3,464	2,178	48	15
1930	7,950	7,867	83	4,815	3,052	62	21
1940	7,642	7,548	94	4,391	3,157	69	25
1950	11,164	10,895	269	5,334	5,561	158	111
1960	13,985	13,496	489	5,532	7,964	289	200

Source: Dale L. Hiestand, *Economic Growth and Employment Opportunities for Minorities* (New York: Columbia University Press, 1964), Table II, pp. 7–9.

Note: "The data for 1930 and earlier include all who considered themselves workers; the data for 1940 and later only those who were employed." See *Economic Growth*, p. 10.

Table 3.7 Percent Change for Black and White Clerical and Sales Workers, 1910–60
(percent)

	Totals			White		Black	
Year	Workers	Whites	Blacks	Males	Females	Males	Females
1910–20	49	49	62	28	102	50	115
1920–30	39	39	32	39	40	29	40
1930–40	−4	−4	13	−9	3	11	19
1940–50	46	44	186	22	76	129	344
1950–60	25	24	82	4	43	83	80

Table 3.8 Black Workers as a Proportion of White Workers in Clerical and Sales Workers Occupations, 1910–60
(percent)

Year	Total Blacks/Total	Black Males/ White Males	Black Females/ White Females
1910	1.0	1.2	0.7
1920	1.1	1.4	0.7
1930	1.0	1.3	0.7
1940	1.2	1.6	0.8
1950	2.4	3.0	2.0
1960	3.5	5.2	2.5

1960, those black workers had increased their representation to 3.5 percent of the category. The data indicate that black males were more numerous than black females thoughout the period; however, black females showed the stronger percent increases such that their 18 percent share of black employment in this category in 1910 had grown to 41 percent by 1960. With respect to white employees, white females clearly dominated the clerical and sales category by 1960. The trend would point to continued female dominance in the decades to follow, with black females gradually increasing their share.

WHITE-COLLAR BLACKS, 1959–77

The current patterns of black white-collar employment reflect the racism previously described. As one takes account of the many impacts of racism, it is easy to discern the institutional and cyclic effects on black people arising from current employment discrimination: the income and occupational differences between blacks and whites and the consequential poorer housing, lower levels of nutrition and health care, relative political powerlessness, and lower-quality education. So that while an observer may be inclined to cite black/white education and training differences, for example, as a major explanation for the current white-collar employment patterns of blacks, it is necessary to recognize that such differences are themselves the result of racist policies and practices.

Though we have not discussed the broad-based efforts of black men and women to combat employment discrimination over the decades, it would be a mistake to assume the passivity of that group since 1865. On the contrary, that the 1960s and 1970s witnessed an interesting turn of events regarding black employment in the United States is directly attributable to a black activism of long standing. Much of this activism, and the relief which it seeks, has been and continues to be aimed at the powers of government. Thus, presidential executive orders and congressional enactment deserve mentioning as we examine the data in this section.

Though President Roosevelt signed an Executive Order in 1941 which established the first Fair Employment Practices Committee (FEPC) directed at employers who held federal contracts, and President Eisenhower, in 1953, brought into being the President's Committee on Government Contracts (PCGC), which was designed to promote nondiscrimination in employment, it was President John Kennedy who in 1961 signed Executive Order 10925, which created the President's Committee on Equal Employment Opportunity. This order was especially significant because it aggressively promoted fair employment practices in the federal government, those corporations in the private sector holding federal contracts, and labor organizations. In 1964, a Civil Rights Act was adopted by the Congress with Title VII of that Act specifically prohibiting employment discrimination in the private and government sectors on the basis of race, color, religion, or sex. Further, in 1965, President Lyndon Johnson signed Executive Order 11246, which requires employers to actively seek out minority candidates for employment so as to redress past acts of employment discrimination. This latter Order is the basis for what has come to be known as affirmative action.

Examining the 1959–77 employment patterns for black white-collar workers, one would expect, on the basis of the legislation cited, to observe significant increases in black representation in the white-collar category. Thus, in addition to the primary goal of examining the data of the period for its trends, a secondary goal is to be mindful of the legislation of the 1960s, and of changes in black employment patterns which may be related.

The white-collar data in the section are comprised of clerical workers (not including typists and secretaries) and salaried managers and administrators. These data were selected because they are likely to represent well the current patterns of black employment in corporate organizations in at least these two important occupational categories.

Clerical Workers

As was noted earlier, white females began to occupy a majority of the clerical positions circa 1950, but among black workers, black males held more clerical positions than black females in that period. Considering now the compilation of clerical workers shown in Table 3.9, it is interesting to note that as white female employment continued upward through 1977, white male employment reached its peak in 1968 and declined slightly through 1977. The data reveal a somewhat different picture for black employees. While the number of black females continued to grow through 1977, their numbers began to exceed those for black males in 1965, and significantly so by 1968—despite a continued growth in black male employment.

Table 3.9 Clerical Workers (Not including Typists and Secretaries), by Race and Sex, 1959–77 (in thousands)

		Totals		White		Black	
Year	Workers	Whites	Blacks	Males	Females	Males	Females
1959	6,999	6,668	331	2,725	3,943	199	132
1962	7,583	7,171	412	2,841	4,330	225	187
1965	8,261	7,745	516	2,971	4,774	252	264
1968	9,476	8,686	790	3,039	5,647	329	461
1971	9,794	8,870	924	2,892	5,978	347	577
1974	10,708	9,611	1,097	2,935	6,676	373	724
1977	11,586	10,343	1,243	2,915	7,428	396	847

Source: U.S. Bureau of Labor Statistics, *Handbook of Labor Statistics, 1978,* Bulletin 2000, June 1979, Table 18, pp. 75–81.
Note: The data for blacks comprise "Blacks and Others."

Table 3.10 highlights this perspective in terms of the growth of clerical jobs over the period 1959–77. A comparison of the percent increases of total white and black employment with percent increases in total employment reveals that blacks made substantial progress

Table 3.10 Percent Change for Black and White Clerical Workers
(Not including Typists and Secretaries), 1959–77
(percent)

	Totals			White		Black	
Year	Workers	Whites	Blacks	Males	Females	Males	Females
1959–62	8	8	25	4	10	13	42
1962–65	9	8	25	5	10	12	41
1965–68	15	12	53	2	18	31	75
1968–71	3	2	17	–5	6	6	25
1971–74	9	8	19	2	12	8	26
1974–77	8	8	13	–1	11	6	17

during this period. A further comparison of males and females confirms that black females exhibited higher rates of percent increases than either white females or black males; that black males had higher rates of percent increases than white females except in the decade of the seventies; and that white males generated the lowest rates of increases, including two periods of decreasing rates. Broadly, the percent change for white employees over the eighteen-year span was 55 percent compared with a 276 percent increase for black employees.

The numbers of black clerical workers as percentages of the total and of white workers are shown in Table 3.11. By 1977, black clerical workers had increased their share of total clerical jobs to more than 10 percent. Though black males increased their share of jobs held by a declining white male clerical work force to a substantial 13.6 percent by 1977, black females registered an 11.4 percent of the jobs held by white females.

Broadly speaking, there are at least several possible explanations for these changes in clerical occupations and the relative

Table 3.11 Black Workers as a Proportion of White Workers in
Clerical Positions (Not including Typists and Secretaries), 1959–77
(percent)

Year	Total Blacks/Total	Black Males/ White Males	Black Females/ White Females
1959	4.7	7.3	3.4
1962	5.4	7.9	4.3
1965	6.3	8.5	5.5
1968	8.3	10.8	8.2
1971	9.4	12.0	9.7
1974	10.3	12.7	10.9
1977	10.7	13.6	11.4

increases in black representation. Furthermore, it should be borne in mind that this occupational category tends to comprise the lower-level corporate jobs—jobs typically held by Category I employees.[37]

First, as is discussed in the next section of this chapter, equal employment opportunity and affirmative action legislation clearly has had a positive impact on the employment of blacks, at the clerical level in particular. At this level, institutional customs and norms are least assaulted by a black presence. Corporations seemingly are therefore more willing to hire clerical blacks relative to higher-level blacks to satisfy the intent of EEO legislation.

A second contributory explanation is found in the geographical location of an available supply of clerical workers. As segments of the white population have moved farther away from corporate organizations located in central business districts, these organizations have been forced to turn to the available in-city black population for lower-level employees.

Third, since the late 1940s and 1950s, rapid technological growth has created higher-level jobs into which many whites, who would have been lower-level clerical workers several decades ago, have moved. Consequently, blacks are shifting into vacated clerical jobs.

Fourth, it is probably true that Category I blacks are more easily hired at lowest salaries than are Category I whites. The most obvious reason is that blacks tend to have fewer employment opportunities than comparably credentialed and qualified whites; and while turnover rates may exceed those for higher-level positions, the costs of turnover at this level to corporations is fairly minimal. Also, this low-salary impact may be greater on black females than on black males.

Finally, as more blacks move into clerical jobs, and specifically such jobs within particular corporate departments, the label "Negro job,"[38] though often unspoken, may be attached; and whites will either not work in these jobs, or do so for only a short time. Therefore, blacks will constitute the bulk of hiring in such departments.[39]

---

[37]Category I is our designation for corporate employees who generally have minimal educational achievements and skills, and who fill the lower-level jobs in corporate structures. See Chapter V.

[38]This term is used here in its historical context. In major cities of the United States, the term "minority" is currently vogue.

[39]Schelling would call this the "tipping phenomenon." While his primary interest was determining the point of irreversibility when residential neighborhoods become all black, the concept may be easily applied to employment: "If blacks come to dominate an occupation, whites may decline to enter or begin to evacuate. More effectively, personnel managers may act like real estate brokers, even inadvertently, in advertising and recruiting among blacks and in supposing that whites will no longer be interested." Thomas C. Schelling, "A Process of Residential Segregation: Neighborhood Tipping," in *Racial Discrimination in Economic Life*, ed. Anthony H. Pascal (Lexington: D.C. Heath, 1972), p. 182.

It is interesting to note that this creation of "Negro jobs" in corporations is a rather obvious extension of the concept as developed and utilized in the late nineteenth century, but with one important difference. Unlike the white-collar offices of the early twentieth century, today's corporate structure is gargantuan and multi-dimensional with literally thousands of white-collar employees including, in some corporations, large numbers of black clerical and technical personnel. This corporate structure is hierarchical to a fault, employing a greatly variegated corps of "specialists," thereby creating many more departments, divisions, and units than dreamed of decades ago. It is obliged by federal and many state laws to alter employment patterns with respect to minorities and women and is significantly more visible to the general public and to governmental regulatory bodies. It possesses a sphere of influence that is likely to be nationwide and possibly world-wide in return for which it, at least, must demonstrate occasionally a perceived social and economic responsibility, and in urban areas it is faced by a large black presence which is effectively vocal and organized and spends sizable consumer dollars. Posturing itself as meritocratic and non-discriminatory, today's corporation is induced, enabled, and required by these factors to create *higher-level* "Negro jobs."

Over and above first-line supervisory jobs which often go to blacks in units that are predominantly black, the corporation has successfully fashioned relatively high-level positions for blacks in EEO units, some personnel and public relations functions, and special marketing areas, principally where their efforts are directed toward the black public or black employees. One should not imagine that this circumstance is entirely new. On the contrary, Rose, writing in the post–World War II period, observed that:

> Neither in the South nor in the North are Negroes in professional, business, or administrative positions except in rare instances and except when serving exclusively the Negro public—and even in this they are far from having a monopoly.[40]

Since Rose wrote, the number of blacks in corporate positions above the clerical level—and even in high-level management positions—has increased tremendously. Moreover, a few blacks have successfully assumed important nontraditional corporate positions. But, the concept of the "Negro job" is alive and well and living in most of the major corporations of America.

Regarding apparent changes in male/female patterns, as better jobs above the clerical level developed, white males were shifted to them; and the likelihood is that blacks and white females filled many

---

[40]Rose, *The Negro in America*, p. 69.

of the vacancies. While labor force participation rates for black males, black females, and white females have increased, corporate jobs still tend to be largely identified as "female" and "male," and female jobs tend to be concentrated in the clerical category. Kanter observes:

> Managerial and clerical jobs, then, are the major sex-segregated, white-collar occupations, brought into being by the development of the large corporation and its administrative apparatus. A sex-linked ethos became identified with each of these occupational groupings. Ideologies surrounding the pursuit of these occupations and justifying their position in the organization came to define both the labor pool from which these occupations drew and ideal images of the attributes of the people in that pool.[41]

Doubtless, Kanter is correct in her assertion. However, as blacks (and other minorities) have increased their numbers in corporate work forces, and have been largely relegated to clerical and other lower-level positions, the forces of racism and sexism have some points of commonality, especially as concerns black females. The overlap tends to make even more complex this aspect of corporate life. Such is the subject for another study.

In this occupational category, then, black workers have made solid gains based on steady increases in representation over the eighteen-year span. While the largest gains were made by black females, the trend for black males continues upward.

Salaried Managers and Administrators

In the corporate occupational hierarchy, this category is a top one, and one which tends to exclude black workers. Table 3.12 shows the patterns of employment in the salaried managers and administrators category during the period 1959–77. Clearly, blacks were significantly underrepresented in this occupational category which more than doubled between 1959 and 1977. As regards the various groups of managers and administrators, Table 3.13 reveals that with the exception of the 1962–65 period, the numbers of black and white females grew at faster rates than the total category and white males. However, white females were far better represented in the category than either black males or black females. For example, by 1977, white females had increased their representation to 21 percent of the total category, and to 28 percent of white males. The story of black worker representation during this period is less encouraging and demonstrates

---

[41]Kanter, Men and Women, p. 19.

that this group was not a significant proportion of the managers and administrators category.

Table 3.12 Salaried Managers and Administrators, by Race and Sex, 1959–77
(in thousands)

		Totals			White		Black	
Year	Workers	Whites	Blacks	Males	Females	Males	Females
1959	3,432	3,383	49	2,883	500	36	13
1962	4,052	3,972	80	3,361	611	62	18
1965	4,437	4,351	86	3,724	627	67	19
1968	5,522	5,405	117	4,602	803	89	28
1971	6,502	6,273	229	5,251	1,022	171	58
1974	7,135	6,863	272	5,634	1,229	202	70
1977	7,832	7,469	363	5,829	1,640	259	104

Source: U.S. Bureau of Labor Statistics, *Handbook of Labor Statistics, 1978*, Bulletin 2000, June 1979, Table 18, pp. 75–81.
Note: The data for blacks comprise "Blacks and Others."

Table 3.13 Percent Change for Black and White Salaried Managers and Administrators, 1959–77
(percent)

		Totals			White		Black	
Year	Workers	Whites	Blacks	Males	Females	Males	Females
1959–62	18	17	63	17	22	72	39
1962–65	10	10	8	11	3	8	6
1965–68	25	24	36	24	28	33	47
1968–71	18	16	96	14	27	92	107
1971–74	10	9	19	7	20	18	21
1974–77	10	9	34	4	33	28	49

Table 3.14 Black Workers as a Proportion of White Workers in Salaried Manager and Administrator Positions, 1959–77
(percent)

Year	Total Blacks/Total	Black Males/ White Males	Black Females/ White Females
1959	1.4	1.3	2.6
1962	2.0	1.9	3.0
1965	1.9	1.8	3.0
1968	2.1	1.9	3.5
1971	3.5	3.3	5.7
1974	3.8	3.6	5.7
1977	4.6	4.4	6.3

From Table 3.14, one can see that black managers and administrators constituted less than 5 percent of the category as late as 1977. While their numbers increased over the period 1959–77, so did the category; thus, black representation in percentage terms tended to remain small.

THE EFFECTS OF EEO AND AFFIRMATIVE ACTION LEGISLATION

It is generally agreed that Title VII of the 1964 Civil Rights Act and the subsequent Executive Order defining affirmative action have had positive impacts on the general employment status of black Americans.[42] With respect to the white-collar data in Tables 3.9 and 3.12, a cursory and something less than a rigorous analysis would seem to cautiously support that broad agreement. While the percent-change estimates for the total numbers of clerical and management workers, and the total numbers of black and white workers in those categories, show substantial increases over the period 1959–1977, a straightforward view of legislative impact can be obtained by a direct comparison of relative changes in the employment status of black and white employees before and after 1965. Specifically, the major expectation would be that the representation of black employees in the period 1965–77 would significantly exceed that of the 1959–65 period, and that the rate of their growth in percentage terms would exceed similar rates for white employees.[43]

Clerical Workers

The calculations of percent change shown in Table 3.15 constitute a beginning point. Obviously, the small number of black employees throughout the period tends to exaggerate the size of the percent change relative to the larger number of white employees. Nonetheless, comparisons of percent changes before and after 1965 are useful.

---

[42]For example, see Richard B. Freeman, "Decline of Labor Market Discrimination and Economic Analysis," American Economic Review, 63 (May 1973), 280–86; G. H. Mashayekhi, "Economic Situation of Non-Whites after 1964: An Empirical Analysis," The Review of Black Political Economy, 8 (1978), 336–45; and Bernard E. Anderson and Phyllis A. Wallace, "Public Policy and Black Economic Progress: A Review of the Evidence," American Economic Review, 65 (May 1975), 47–52.

[43]In this crude and simplified approach, no consideration is given to the state of the economy, e.g., whether levels of total employment are high or low; or to the types of industries hiring blacks; or to the job levels within the occupational categories.

Table 3.15 Percent Change in Clerical Workers, 1959–65 and 1965–77
(percent)

	Totals			White		Black	
Period	Workers	Whites	Blacks	Males	Females	Males	Females
1959–65	18	16	56	9	21	27	100
1965–77	40	34	141	−2	56	57	221

The percent change in clerical workers from 1965 to 1977 was more than double the change from 1959 to 1965 for total workers, total whites, and total blacks. Though the number of white males actually declined in the 1965–77 period, Table 3.15 shows that the other three groups more than doubled their representation. Thus, it would appear that a significant transfer of jobs from white males to blacks and white females occurred in the later period. Ignoring other factors, one might infer that EEO and affirmative action policies effected positive increases in black male and female representation. However, a review of Table 3.9 emphasizes the vast differences in the black and white female clerical population.

Managers and Administrators

Table 3.16 summarizes the changes in employment patterns for those workers in the managers and administrators category. The large percent increase, especially for black employees in the 1965–77 period, points to the fact that blacks increased their numbers in this period and did so at a higher rate than in the 1959–65 span. Of course, a review of Table 3.12 highlights the relative insignificance of black representation in this occupational category. Again, a cursory view leads to the conclusion that jobs in the managers and administrators category were transferred in the 1965–77 period from white males to blacks and white females. What is evident, however,

Table 3.16 Percent Change in Managers and Administrators, 1959–65 and
1965–77
(percent)

	Totals			White		Black	
Period	Workers	Whites	Blacks	Males	Females	Males	Females
1959–65	29	29	76	29	25	86	46
1965–77	77	72	322	57	162	287	447

is that the bulk of such a transfer benefited white females, in the main. Such a result may reflect the intensely negative attitude of many white managers and institutions toward blacks generally and toward those who seek positions in this category, in particular. This is to say that under the duress of affirmative action requirements, which white managers (and white employees) tend to view with disdain in any event, it may be more palatable to satisfy such requirements with white females than with blacks. Overall, however, a comparison of the 1965–77 row with the 1959–65 row lends credence to the notion of an affirmative action impact which had some value for black male and female employees.

Black Share of New Jobs

Another way to gauge the impact of the EEO and affirmative action legislation and the progress of black white-collar employees is to estimate the percentage of new jobs which accrued to blacks. Table 3.17 presents the percentage of new jobs in the clerical category and the managers and administrators category gained by blacks over the period 1959–77.[44]

Here, blacks are getting significant shares of clerical jobs reaching a peak of 42 percent in 1968–71. Given that the black share of clerical jobs is significant over the period, it is noteworthy that the black female share is substantial throughout. Compared with the percentages in 1959–65, black workers generally increased their share of these jobs in the post–1965 years, but with decreasing shares in the years 1971–77.

In the managers and administrators category, blacks did not fare well up to 1968. From 1968 to 1971, and 1974 to 1977, in particular, substantial gains were registered by this group, but less so by black females than by black males.

It is likely that the EEO and affirmative action legislation played an important role in the changing black and white employment patterns described in this chapter's tables. While the percentages tend to be overstated, the relative and comparative differences before and after 1965 indicate favorable changes in the latter period for black males and females in the white-collar category.

Notwithstanding such changes, the numbers of black employees continued to be relatively small during the period—especially in the

---

[44]See "Note" in Table 3.17. In addition, for problems associated with combining black workers with nonwhite workers, see Robert B. Hill, *The Widening Economic Gap* (Washington, D.C.: National Urban League, 1979), pp. 13–15.

Table 3.17 The Black* Share of New Jobs in the Clerical and Salaried Managers and Administrators Categories, 1959–77

Year	Increases in New Jobs		Total Black Share		Black Male Share**		Black Female Share**	
	Clerical	Managers and Administrators	Clerical	Managers and Administrators	Clerical	Managers and Administrators	Clerical	Managers and Administrators
	(in thousands)		(percent)		(percent)		(percent)	
1959–62	584	620	14	5	5	4	9	1
1962–65	678	385	15	2	4	1	11	–
1965–68	1215	1085	23	3	6	2	16	1
1968–71	318	980	42	11	6	8	37	3
1971–74	914	633	19	7	3	5	16	2
1974–77	878	697	17	13	3	8	14	5

*Note: Since the data used are actually "Black and Other," the percent estimates for black employees are overstated. See "Note" in Tables 7 and 10.

**Total percent will not always equal due to rounding.

managers and administrators group. Moreover, the *character* of white-collar jobs held by blacks is hidden in these numbers, that is, blacks tend to be relegated to certain types of jobs in the clerical and managers and administrators categories and virtually barred from certain other job groups within these categories. Legislation has not been successful in this regard.

Income Distribution for Clerical Workers and Managers and Administrators

A reasonable assumption would be that as blacks move in greater numbers into higher occupational categories, salaries would be equivalent to those of white workers in similar occupational categories. On the other hand, since salaries are, among other things, a function of longevity, and since black workers have less longevity on the average than white workers in the selected white-collar categories, then salary differentials would not be unexpected. This is an argument often presented by employers guilty of job discrimination within occupational categories. In fact, salaries are importantly a function of job level, also. Thus, persistent salary differentials within occupational categories do tend to reveal job discrimination.

Table 3.18 compares percent of earnings by occupational category for black and white workers. Only 3 percent of the black clerical workers earned $15,000 in 1977 compared with 7 percent of the white clerical workers. A larger percentage of black clerical workers earned salaries in the $6,000–$14,000 range than did white clerical workers, and a larger percentage of white clerical workers earned under $6,000 in 1977 than did black clerical workers. A key observation is that over one half of the black clerical workers are in the middle salary range, and only 3 percent are in the top range, which probably includes first-line supervisors and others in authority as

Table 3.18 Occupations of Workers by Earnings and Race, 1977
(percent)

	Black Workers			White Workers		
	$15,000 & over	$6,000-$14,999	Under $6,000	$15,000 & over	$6,000-$14,999	Under $6,000
Clerical	3	55	42	7	47	46
Managers	30	48	22	52	35	13

Source: Excerpted from a larger table. See Robert B. Hill, *The Widening Economic Gap* (Washington, D.C.: National Urban League, 1979), Table 11, p. 30.

well as the more skilled positions. Of the total number of white clerical workers, fewer than one half are in the middle salary group, and 7 percent are in the top salary group. Considering the difference in the size of the two groups, it is clear that white workers dominate this category in every important way.

This result is even more dramatically displayed in the data for managers. Over one half of the white workers in the managers category are in the top salary group in contrast to less than one third of all black workers in that group.

EEO and affirmative action laws have contributed to an increased representation of black males and females in white-collar occupations. However, these laws seemingly have had the least impact on the *internal labor market* where promotions, the allocation of job and career opportunities, and salaries are determined. The dynamics that govern this market are simply too complex and elusive for legislation, which can neither account for nor anticipate, in a comprehensive manner, the internal labor market employment circumstances governing promotions and assignments. Thus, managerial judgment and corporate policies, significantly influenced by institutional values and customs, remain the arbiter. The nature and role of internal labor market dynamics will be examined in subsequent chapters.

SUMMARY

The history of black workers in America has been broadly traced in this chapter with an emphasis on black white-collar workers, since a goodly portion of them are likely to be found in the corporate sector of the economy. The single most important conclusion to be drawn from this chapter is that the relegation of black workers to the lowest-paying, lowest-level, and least-skilled and least-critical jobs has its roots in slavery and the decades which followed, and that the particular form of racism which characterized that early period is today institutionalized in the work places of America. Specifically, it would seem that the patterns of life for blacks fashioned under Jim Crow—including segregation of the races, labor union discrimination, and the exclusion of blacks from meaningful employment in the larger white society in the late nineteenth century and first half of the twentieth century—have given rise to a well-developed institutional racism in this second half of the twentieth century. This form of racism can be observed currently in the corporate bureaucracies, as it limits the opportunities of white-collar blacks not only in terms of occupational mobility but also in terms of upward mobility.

Within the white-collar category, blacks have made the greatest gains in clerical occupations. By 1977, blacks held approximately 10 percent of the clerical jobs in contrast to less than 5 percent of the jobs in the managers and administrators category. (Both of these figures are overstated since they contain other minorities.) Much of the change in the patterns of employment reflected in those percentages can likely be traced to the Equal Employment Opportunity laws enacted by the Congress in 1964. However, these laws do not appear to have had much of an impact on the internal labor markets which control career advancement, salaries, and upward mobility. It is therein that institutional racism is strongest.

IV

Theoretical Approaches to the Economics of Employment Discrimination

INTRODUCTION

THIS CHAPTER DISCUSSES the major theories that attempt to explain wage and income, and occupational differences between white and black workers, via the demand side of the labor market. Two of these theories embrace the neoclassical concept of marginal analysis, and the radical theory rests on the pervasiveness of racism and its role in the American capitalist society.

The first theory determines wage differentials based on perceived differences in black-white productivity generated by employers' *tastes for discrimination*; it implies the existence of statistical discrimination, a concept which argues that race provides a visual and inexpensive basis for hiring presumably productive workers and not hiring presumably unproductive workers. The second approach describes a segmented labor market based on the behavioral characteristics of workers and presumed levels of worker productivity. And the third, as stated above, views racism as an essential element in the American capitalist society for controlling wages and the total work force. Typically, these approaches aim to determine why the differing wage rates and relative numbers of black and white workers exist, and whether the economic gains and losses attributable to discrimination accrue to white workers, black workers, employers, or some combination thereof. Our major concern, however, is the usefulness of these theories for understanding the corporate internal labor market. Discussed in greater detail in Chapter V, the corporate internal labor market embraces the set of forces within the workplace that control, evaluate, and allocate labor in terms of upward mobility and career advancement opportunities—i.e., promotions, assignments, training, salaries, communications, terminations.

As we shall see, the "taste for discrimination" approach is probably the least useful for an understanding of internal labor market dynamics. The dual labor market theory and the radical theory, however, do offer realistic explanations of the forces that shape management employment decisions. Following a discussion of the sources of racist employment practices, the neoclassical model of wage discrimination is explained. The final two sections are brief descriptions of the dual labor market theory and the radical theory, especially their emphasis on the socioeconomic factors impacting wage differentials, job assignments, and rates of upward mobility.

MAJOR SOURCES OF RACIST BEHAVIOR

White corporate managers' utilization of black workers in either the external or internal labor markets is some function of perceived white superiority–black inferiority: white managers prefer members of their own race over members of the black race. As this racial preference manifests itself to varying degrees, depending on the individual, managers (employers) are said by Gary S. Becker to exhibit a "taste for discrimination."[1] In a similar vein, Richard Perlman states that "overt discrimination may be practiced by employers who indulge their racial prejudices by discrimination against qualified blacks in the various aspects of employment—hiring, promotion, layoff, and wages."[2] These are descriptions of directed and individual prejudices and discrimination and in the employment process are generally operative at the point of one-on-one decisions. That is to say, a white manager brings to bear an internalized taste for discrimination on a decision to hire, promote, train, or fire a black employee.

A second major source of racist behavior in the corporate sector is generated by occupational group value systems and customs. There are occupational groups which perceive the inclusion of blacks as a threat to the group's view of itself, and the larger society's view of the group, as a lofty and important bastion of esoterica.[3] Here, blacks

---

[1]Gary S. Becker, *The Economics of Discrimination*, 2nd ed. (Chicago: University of Chicago Press, 1971), pp. 13–17.

[2]Richard Perlman, *The Economics of Poverty* (New York: McGraw-Hill, 1976), p. 68.

[3]This type of prejudice and discrimination has an effect not unlike the exclusion of blacks from certain craft and trade unions. See Peter B. Doeringer and Michael J. Piore, *Internal Labor Markets and Manpower Analysis* (Lexington: D.C. Heath, 1971), pp. 25–26.

tend to be perceived, and subsequently adjudged, as simply not capable of mastering—at least not to a sufficient degree—the full scope of whatever is required. Examples of these groups are: certain investment managers of institutional portfolios; corporate law firms and groups; and other occupational groups operating at the center of a particular firm or industry. While carried out by individual managers, the source, custom, and motive behind employment decisions define the group's interest. This source of exclusion based on racism is strongly related to the notion of occupational discrimination.

Also related to the notion of occupational group value system is the perception by a corporate organization that the entirety of its organization is off limits to blacks. While it is true that equal employment opportunity and affirmative action laws have significantly reduced, for example, the number of large real estate investment corporations and investment banking firms with no blacks, many small organizations—frequently untouched by federal compliance reviews unless answering an employee complaint of discrimination—continue to employ no blacks. The rationale, of course, is that none is "qualified" or qualifiable.

Fourth, basic organizational policies and practices, sometimes of long standing, are "quiet" in their racist impact on black employees but are, nonetheless, a source of racist behavior. Their peculiar characteristic, of course, absolves white managers of the need to make judgements and decisions regarding black employees. That is to say, such policies and practices are self-operating.

The final major source of racism is institutional in character. Essentially, "racism cannot be eliminated just by moral suasion; nor will it gradually disappear because of market forces. Racism has become institutionalized and . . . its elimination will require more than a change of attitudes; a change in institutions is necessary."[4] The practice of this form of racism does not require either a taste for discrimination on the part of white managers, or the imposition of occupational group value systems. Rather, it reflects the interplay of institutional forces in society. As Perlman has hypothesized:

> A department store recruits management trainees among recent graduates of a college business administration curriculum. It loudly and proudly announces that race, creed, etc., will play no part in its employment decisions. There is no overt discrimination here; it is not the store's fault that there are few blacks who can meet its minimum hiring standard of business degree attainment. The college is not practicing overt discrimination if

---

[4]Michael Reich, "The Economics of Racism," in *Problems in Political Economy: An Urban Perspective*, 2d ed., ed. David M. Gordon (Lexington: D.C. Heath, 1977), p. 185.

it receives few such black applications. Is it to be blamed because weak prior schooling and insufficient financial resources foreclose college to blacks? Early schooling was inadequate because the public schools that blacks attend are weakly financed and are thus often poorly staffed and equipped. Their education is further handicapped by a home environment preoccupied with the problems of economic survival and a neighborhood in which all are beset with the basic monetary problems of maintaining life rather than in preparing for a livelihood—a way of life in keeping with the old proverb that man must eat before he can philosophize.[5]

The five major sources of racism which deny employment and relegate blacks to positions of underemployment not only work in conjunction with each other but assume important roles at different points in the employment process. Their interplay depends on: 1) the demand factors; 2) the supply factors and worker qualifications; 3) types of position or promotion being applied for; 4) the degree of a manager's taste for discrimination; and 5) the specific organization to and in which the black employee makes application and seeks upward mobility opportunities.

BECKER AND THE NEOCLASSICISTS

The neoclassical or orthodox models seek optimal states of equilibria flowing from a predictable economic rationality brought to bear on the various decision-making processes by employers. These models further assume that economic behavior and decision-making motivated by racism are consistent "rational behavior," and that the resulting wage rate differences for black and white workers are logical and stable consequences of equilibria. Further, the neoclassical models used to explain the dynamics of racial discrimination in labor markets and workplaces have tended to view that particular racism which gives economic meaning to the concept of race as a sort of benign and exogenous force—benign in the sense that the insidiousness of racism is neither recognized nor accounted for, and exogenous in the sense that these models generally assume given units of black

---

[5]Perlman, *Economics of Poverty*, p. 69. In addition, Thurow has categorized seven broad types of racial discrimination consistent with Perlman's description of institutional racism. His categories include employment, wages, occupations, investment in human capital, costs of acquiring capital, exclusion from organizations with monopoly power, and price discrimination. For a full discussion, see Lester C. Thurow, *Poverty and Discrimination* (Washington: The Brookings Institution, 1969), pp. 117–26.

and white labor to be homogeneous in the production process (i.e., perfect substitutes), but possessed of different marginal utilities based on race.[6]

Empirical data point to the conclusion that the dynamics of the corporate employment process as applied to blacks—including the decisions to hire, terminate, promote, transfer, give merit and training pay increases, and encourage career path development—are not sufficiently explained by neoclassical paradigms. In general, neoclassical models have concentrated on discriminatory wage rates arising from differences in black and white supply functions and from differences in employers' utility functions for black and white workers. In fact, these differences would likely have their greatest impact on the *hiring* phase of the employment process, to the exclusion of other important employment elements. Moreover, wage rate differences in contemporary corporate organizations tend to be diminished by: 1) heightened employee awareness regarding pay scales; 2) less willingness on the part of black employees to accept clearly discriminatory wages; 3) the gigantic size of many corporations, which requires wage and salary administration programs for thousands of employees and in turn dampens the desire and opportunity for "group" wage rate discrimination; 4) the presence of collective bargaining agreements or the threat of unionization; 5) federal wage and hour legislation and affirmative action laws. In other words, the heretofore unbridled impact of employer utility (and disutility) on wage rate differences is currently a less clear reflection of employers' racist behavior.[7]

These neoclassical wage rate discrimination models rest on the purportedly rational assumption that black and white labor is homogeneous in production and on the assumption of "irrational" utility formation based on employer racism.[8] Thus, it is through the employer's

---

[6]This assumption can be noted throughout the neoclassical literature. See Gary S. Becker, *Economics of Discrimination*; Kenneth J. Arrow, *Some Models of Racial Discrimination in the Labor Market* (Santa Monica: The Rand Corporation, RM–6253–RC, Feb. 1971); and Anne O. Krueger, "The Economics of Discrimination," *Journal of Political Economy*, 71 (October 1963), 481–86.

[7]See Perlman, *Economics of Poverty*, p. 68.

[8]The concept of utility is indeed rooted in *subjectivity*. Moreover, to term a utility function shaped by racism as "irrational" is to impose one's value system on another. One argument for progressive taxation assumes that interpersonal comparisons can be made and leads to the conclusion that a dollar shifted from a rich man to a poor man would increase aggregate consumer satisfaction, i.e, the increase in utility to the poor man increases by more than the decrease in utility to the rich man. Similarly, arguments for equal employment opportunity and affirmative action legislation raise questions concerning the social appropriateness and the economic legitimacy of equilibria resting on a manifest racism which produces and justifies a black wage rate below the black marginal product, and a white wage rate above the white marginal product. While these equilibria may be mathematically sound, they are

utility function that racist behavior is introduced into the economics of the dynamic employment process. The utility function is viewed as continuous and decreasing as the number of black workers is increased. This is to say that the cost of compensating white and black workers is some function of W/L and/or B/L where W is the number of white workers, B is the number of black workers, and L is the number of workers in the firm's work force. These relative costs then determine the equilibrium number of blacks and whites employed in individual firms and the wage rate differences.

Essentially, the neoclassical models of employment discrimination based on race do not adequately explain or describe contemporary corporate managers' racist behavior or the significant results of that behavior.[9] Rather, they concentrate on determined wage rate differentials and generalized optimal levels of black employment to the exclusion of some important and observable ways in which blacks are additionally victimized in the corporate arena. Moreover, it is not sufficient to ascribe to employers a taste for discrimination, since the various employment decisions involving blacks also reflect other sources of racism.[10] Nonetheless, Becker, and the neoclassicists, contend that white employers play a major role in creating an employment market imperfection through an expression of utility for labor power based on racial differences. Further, white workers, through labor unions and refusals to work alongside black workers, virtually control the supply side of the labor market. In essence, then, the taste for discrimination, which influences decisions and behavior patterns of white employers and employees, creates the labor market imperfection.

Becker's theoretical model is developed on the assumption that except for the taste for discrimination the labor market is a purely competitive market comprising two racial societies. As such, each society is free to trade with the other. Given the two societies, one is assumed to be black with a relatively abundant labor supply, and the other is assumed to be white with capital as its abundant factor.

---

empirically reprehensible and are irrational to the extent that racism is irrational. The employment decisions of white corporate managers, which are thought to be based on a rational evaluation of factors, are responses, in part, to racism.

[9]Neoclassical models are more concerned with logic machines of discrimination, which explain the determination of different wage rates applied to homogeneous factors of production with dissimilar non-economic characteristics (e.g., sex, religion, race). The economics of racism—in contrast to the economics of discrimination—requires a model which, at least: 1) recognizes the institutionalization of the perverse economic and social objectives of racism that extend beyond the utility map of a specific employer, but which influence the shape of that map; 2) identifies the various results seemingly satisfying the objectives; and 3) evaluates the salient variables and their relationships.

[10]Gary S. Becker, *Economics of Discrimination.*

The model is developed on two bases, namely, the price theory of labor in a purely competitive labor market and the international trade model, in which each society would export its product freely with high comparative advantage until the marginal products of the factors were equal in both societies.

Becker's model assumes that units of black and white labor are homogeneous and that, under conditions of perfect competition, any labor input performing the same job and producing the same marginal physical product should receive the same wage. Thus:

$$W_b = \text{MPP} (P_x) \tag{1}$$
$$W_w = \text{MPP} (P_x) \tag{2}$$

where W_b and W_w are money wages for black and white labor units, respectively, and P_x is the price of the product.

In the real world, this assumption of labor homogeneity does not hold because introduction of the disutility, or taste for discrimination, into the market creates an imperfect market. Such disutility causes the employer to undercompensate black workers and/or overcompensate white workers. Under these circumstances, the new equations become:

$$W_b^* (1 + d) = \text{MPP}(P_x) \tag{3}$$
$$W_w^* \qquad = \text{MPP}(P_x) \tag{4}$$

and therefore:

$$W_w^* = W_b^* (1 + d) \tag{5}$$

where d is the disutility coefficient and by assumption is greater than zero. The quantity $W_b^*(d)$ is the exact money equivalent of the non-monetary cost caused by the disutility. Dividing equation (5) by W_b^* yields:

$$\frac{W_w^*}{W^*_b} = (1 + d) \tag{6}$$

Expressing equation (6) in terms of d,

$$d = \frac{W_w^* - W_b^*}{W_b^*} \tag{7}$$

Equation (7) expresses the relative differential of the two wage rates and is labeled by Becker the Market Discrimination Coefficient (MDC). It can be concluded that a reduction in the taste for discrimination by both white employers and employees could reduce the relative wage differentials between the two races.

In the trade model, it is assumed that two independent societies exist, one black (b) and the other white (w). Further, it is assumed that the black society is relatively well-endowed with labor (L) compared to its capital stock (K), and that the white society is relatively capital rich compared to its labor endowment—i.e., $(K/L)_b < (K/L)_w$. Each society exports its relatively abundant factors; therefore, the black society exports labor and the white society exports capital. Under conditions of the trade model, there are no tariff protections or quota limitations, and transportation costs are zero. Further, it is assumed that one good is being produced in each society and that the production functions are homogeneous.

Introducing the taste for discrimination, the white society imposes a tariff on imports and a quota on capital being exported. That is, free trade no longer prevails. The change in terms of trade causes a shift in demand for exports and imports. The result is a reduction in the amount of capital flowing from the white society to the black society and a reduction in the flow of labor from the black society to the white society.

Becker stipulates four major propositions regarding the effects of discrimination:

1. In a purely competitive society with two groups of people, the effect of a taste for discrimination against one group as reflected in a positive Market Discrimination Coefficient against the group is to reduce the per capita real incomes of both groups;
2. Discrimination will harm the group discriminated against (black) more than the discriminating group (white);
3. When there is discrimination against blacks as labor sellers, the effect is to raise the wage rate for white workers, and to harm white capitalists by causing them to pay more than otherwise for labor input;
4. If blacks attempt to retaliate, they will lower their own income by more than they will lower incomes of the white group.

Becker's first and second propositions imply that the positive Market Discrimination Coefficient produces imperfect trade flows in which the amount of capital exported by whites would decrease as would the amount of labor exported by blacks. A result would be less labor to combine with white capital such that the net return to that capital would be reduced. Clearly, the return to black labor would be reduced also. The amount of goods produced would be less in each society, and the per capita income of blacks would be reduced by the change in the price ratios induced by changes in the terms of trade. Thus, total aggregate income earned by blacks would be smaller than that which would be earned in the free trade market.

The third proposition implies that discrimination against black labor causes a rise in the wage rate of white workers and thereby negatively affects white capitalists by causing them to pay more than they otherwise would for their labor. Here, Becker is dealing with the widely held belief that white capitalists are the major beneficiaries of prejudice and discrimination in a competitive capitalistic economic system. Becker demonstrates, however, that a taste for discrimination on the part of white capitalists against black workers tends to lower profits.

The fourth proposition states that if blacks attempt to retaliate, they will lower their income further and by more than they will lower the income of whites. On the surface, this would not appear to be completely valid, for if blacks refused collectively to deal with discriminators, they might raise the marginal cost of discrimination sufficiently to alter the relative demand for their labor services and thereby increase their incomes. However, if the retaliation insisted on such conditions as the hiring of black workers on the same terms as white workers, at the penalty of black withdrawal from the labor force, then, given the magnitude of the discrimination coefficient, the total labor supply could decrease substantially and thereby further raise white wages.

Closely following Becker's approach is the work of Kenneth Arrow.[11] Arrow is concerned with the "demand determinants of wage differentials," and, consistent with Becker, assumes that a white employer's utility function is:

$$U (p, W, N)$$

where p is the firm's profits; W and N are the numbers of white and black workers respectively; and $U_w > 0$ and $U_n < 0$ reflect a positive marginal utility for white workers and a negative marginal utility for black workers, respectively. Thus, given the market wage rate, a white employer will hire white workers somewhere beyond the point where the wage rate equals the marginal product, and black workers somewhere below that equality. Further, it can be demonstrated that maximization of the utility function implies "higher wages for whites than for Negroes of identical productivity."[12] And, as Arrow points out, "it is elementary that the white community (employers plus white workers) gains in pecuniary terms precisely the gap between the marginal product and the wage for black workers."[13]

The neoclassicists have clearly rested their case and described their findings in terms of marginal analysis. In fact, not only does wage rate discrimination constitute but one form of discrimination

---

[11]This description of Arrow's work is based on Arrow, *Racial Discrimination*.
[12]Ibid., p. 30.
[13]Ibid., p. 31.

in the corporate workplace, it sheds little light on the actual workings of the internal labor market.

AN OVERVIEW OF THE DUAL LABOR MARKET THEORY

This theory is yet another view of labor market dynamics. It recognizes socioeconomic market characteristics which lead to differences in the demand and supply for labor. Essentially, the dual labor market theory segments labor market demand into *primary* and *secondary* demands; and labor market supply into *primary* and *secondary* supplies. Primary markets control the allocation of the better jobs with "high wages, good working conditions, employment stability, chances of advancement, equity, and due process in the administration of work rules."[14] Needless to say, the types of workers slotted into primary jobs are those whose value systems, education and training, and cultural backgrounds are consonant with institutional and organizational value systems, goals and objectives. Secondary labor markets, on the other hand, are characterized by relatively low wages, poor working conditions, and minimal job security. The supply of labor for this market is thought to come from the disadvantaged population, which exhibits tendencies toward "greater turnover, higher rates of lateness and absenteeism, more insubordination, and [which] engage[s] more freely in petty theft and pilferage."[15]

The labor market segmentation approach does not necessarily depend on race for its validity; rather it depends on behavioral characteristics often exhibited by poor and disadvantaged workers. This notion on which duality rests, including the responses of internal labor markets to various types of employees, is consistent with the "culture of poverty" thesis and its corollary described earlier. (See Chapter II.) Thus, one would be inclined to ascribe employee behavioral characteristics to conditions of social class and to view secondary employees as essentially trapped in that labor market. On the other hand, employees conditioned by the higher socioeconomic class dynamics (i.e., who possess behavioral traits consistent with mainstream institutional values and norms) are generally admitted to the primary markets. Here again, the emphasis would appear to be on class rather than race. A disturbing aspect of such an emphasis,

---

[14]Doeringer and Piore, *Internal Labor Markets*, p. 165. See also Michael Reich, David M. Gordon, and Richard C. Edwards, "A Theory of Labor Market Segmentation," *American Economic Review*, 63 (May 1973), 359–65.

[15]Ibid., pp. 165–66.

however, is that presumably if one successfully alters one's behavior patterns in terms of class norms, then access to primary labor markets should be virtually assured. It should be noted that this simple strategy has worked over and over again for white employees seeking egress from the lower employment ranks, but it has worked significantly less well for blacks. The clear implication, then, is that the dual labor market theory in its fundamental form does not sufficiently recognize the force of racism or explain the inability of blacks to move into primary labor markets and/or experience expected rates of upward mobility.

Race and accompanying employment discrimination enter the model directly when white employers impute secondary characteristics to black workers simply because they are black. Michael J. Piore has written, "certain workers who possess the behavioral traits required to operate efficiently in primary jobs are trapped in the secondary market because their superficial characteristics resemble those of secondary workers."[16] It can be put more strongly: racial dualism in labor markets exists. In addition to income and employment disparities, white and black workers are recruited and hired in separate labor markets, and jobs tend to be allocated along racial lines.[17] Howard M. Wachtel and Charles Betsey have attempted to verify such a duality and the characteristics central to the theory empirically.[18]

Importantly, the dual labor market theory recognizes that wages and incomes and upward mobility are related to specific job groups, on the one hand, and levels of formal schooling and behavioral characteristics, on the other. Buttressed by custom and institutional patterns more so than by merit or productivity, incomes and rates of upward mobility are further differentiated among employees.[19] But how Category II employees are managed in such an internal market is not altogether clear since this differentiation applies to all employees. For black employees specifically, the "racially induced discrimination element" reduces horizontal and vertical mobility relative to

---

[16]Michael J. Piore, "The Dual Labor Market: Theory and Implications," in *Problems in Political Economy: An Urban Perspective*, 2nd ed., ed. David M. Gordon (Lexington: D.C. Heath, 1977), p. 94.

[17]See Harold M. Baron and Bennett Hymer, "Racial Dualism in an Urban Labor Market," in Gordon, *Problems in Political Economy*, pp. 189–90. Also see Ken Gagala, "The Dual Urban Labor Market," *Journal of Black Studies*, 3 (March 1973), 350–70.

[18]Howard M. Wachtel and Charles Betsey, "Low Wage Workers and the Dual Labor Market: An Empirical Investigation," *The Review of Black Political Economy*, 5 (Spring 1975), 288–301. Also see Paul Osterman, "An Empirical Study of Labor Market Segmentation," *Industrial and Labor Relations Review*, 28 (July 1975), 508–21.

[19]David M. Gordon, *Theories of Poverty and Underemployment* (Lexington: D.C. Heath, 1972), pp. 49–51.

white employees. Additionally, identification of the internal labor market *techniques* for effecting reduced mobility, and the roles of non-wage consequences in this process, is essential for a better grasp of this market's mechanisms with respect to black employees.

In broad terms, Piore has defined and described "mobility chains" as paths or lines of progression comprised of "stations" that

> generally include not only jobs but also other points of social and economic significance. Thus, people in a given job will tend to be drawn from a limited range of schools, neighborhoods, and types of family backgrounds.[20]

While this description is typical of the blue-collar internal labor market, it also applies, in the main, to managerial-type jobs in the corporate sector.[21] This particular model of the dual labor market accounts for the impact of socioeconomic factors including the learning process, the role of technology, and others, but not the role of racism explicitly. That is to say, Category II employees—as distinguished from black employees with many secondary market characteristics—are subject to the same internal forces as white employees, but with the additional burden of racism affecting movement along the mobility chains.

THE RADICAL APPROACH

Broadly, the radical approach attempts to define the relationship between capitalists and workers in terms of class structure, modes of production, wages and profits, and the development and maintenance of institutions which give meaning to the capitalist-worker relationship.[22] What does the radical theory reveal with respect to the employment process, and black employees in particular?

First, it is useful to understand that the radical theory puts forth the notion that employers benefit from a divided and stratified work force—i.e., white-collar vis-à-vis blue-collar, black workers vis-à-vis white workers—which delimits the development of class consciousness and its implications for costly demands on employers.[23] Moreover, employers, historically,

---

[20]Michael J. Piore, "Notes for a Theory of Labor Market Stratification," in *Labor Market Segmentation*, ed. Richard C. Edwards, Michael Reich, and David M. Gordon, (Lexington: D.C. Heath, 1975), p. 128.

[21]Ibid., p. 129.

[22]Gordon, *Poverty and Underemployment*, chap. 5.

[23]Ibid., p. 73.

were likely to try to fill the worst jobs with those who were least likely to identify with advantaged workers. Gradually, as the composition of the American labor force changed, it became relatively easy for employers to reserve the most 'secondary' jobs for . . . minority group workers with quite confident expectations that they would not identify with more advantaged workers and develop a common consciousness about the disadvantages of their jobs.[24]

We find an obvious kinship with the dual labor market theory in terms of the notion of primary and secondary markets.

A second important tenet of radical thought is that the role of racism is significantly crucial within the capitalist system: "the divisiveness of racism weakens workers' strength when bargaining with employers; the economic consequences of racism are not only lower incomes for blacks, but also higher incomes for the capitalist class coupled with lower incomes for white workers."[25]

It is clear that the radical theorists share with the dual labor market theorists the notions of market stratification and segmentation, but the former stress the capitalists' need for control over the work force and, hence, profitability as an essential rationale. The use of job groupings (stratification)—and job characteristics within the primary market, in particular—further balkanized by the promotion of racism extends the development of the internal labor market and its facility for determining the allocation of jobs, wage and salary levels, and upward mobility paths. Gordon states:

The importance of job characteristics in determining relative income among workers has undoubtedly grown in importance, . . . for job structures have probably tended increasingly to dominate relative opportunities among workers for skill acquisition. The more that skills must be developed within specific job situations, the more the structure and distribution of those job opportunities tends to affect the distribution of skills among workers. Abstract, generalized individual abilities (like reasoning and reading abilities) become less and less important in determining or explaining variations in labor market status and income.[26]

This important description is consistent with and supportive of the views to be expressed in Chapter VI. Moreover, the concept of mobility chains discussed in the previous section is a logical extension of the radical paradigm—or, conversely, the radical paradigm extends

---

[24]Ibid., pp. 73–74.
[25]Reich, "Economics of Racism," p. 185.
[26]Gordon, *Poverty and Underemployment*, p. 79.

the concept of mobility chains. Both recognize market stratification, the relationship of upward mobility opportunities to those job groups which facilitate skill acquisition, and the role of racism in market stratification and segmentation and in the exclusion of blacks from key job groups.

SUMMARY

The sources of racism are many and probably cannot be subsumed under the concept of *taste for discrimination*, as is done in the neoclassical approach. On the contrary, this neoclassical concept should be viewed as part of the racist schema. Nonetheless, the orthodox approach relies on the marginal product machinery in combination with a taste for discrimination to explain wage differences between white and black workers. However, it offers very little insight into the workings of the internal labor market. Wages are but one aspect of internal control of access to certain job groups or relegation to certain others, skill acquisition, and upward mobility opportunities.

The dual labor market theory and the radical theory present models which contain internal labor market components. Though differing in the bases on which the approaches rest, the concept of *mobility chains*, and its relationship to stratification and segmentation, is embraced by both theories. How black employees—especially those in Category II—are managed, once in the internal market, is not fully addressed by either approach. Even these two theories impute a rationality to the practice of racism in the sense that it serves the requirements of the economic system. In fact, internal labor market decisions are generally made by individual managers who probably do not consciously think of their decisions as supporting the role of racism in the society. Rather, white managers identify with internal customs and patterns which for them as individuals translate into a white superiority–black inferiority mode of practice. The use and encouragement of racism as a divisive force, or to reduce screening costs associated with hiring, may indeed have validity in a *macro* framework; but in a *micro* sense, internal employment decisions regarding Category II black employees are largely governed by a base and irrational racism. It is this micro effect which must be isolated for a fuller understanding of black mobility in the internal labor market.

V

Black Employees in Corporate America: Current Observations

INTRODUCTION

THE VIRULENCE OF contemporary American racism, while often camouflaged and therefore distinguished from the egregiously racist character which marked the period of slavery in this country, is most clearly defined by the relative economic status of black Americans. This status is brought into focus when one examines black/white differences in housing conditions, levels of nutrition and health care delivery, quality educational opportunities, access to capital markets, and, more specifically, the employment picture for blacks and whites, and measures of income functionally related to that employment. With respect to employment, such an examination reveals greater differences over time between black and white workers (in terms of numbers employed, the quality of that employment, and earnings and unemployment rates) than would be expected by chance. Therefore, it would not be unreasonable to attribute some significant portion of these differences to employment discrimination—i.e., management employment decisions based primarily on racial considerations.

A significant part of this overall employment discrimination is directed toward white-collar blacks who are already in corporate work forces. Needless to say, this assertion is supported by the character of observable differences in salaries, occupational categories, and organizational levels between white and black employees. At this point, let us take a somewhat closer view of corporations, in general, and the white-collar employees who work in them.

Corporate white-collar workers, as typically distinguished from plant and factory workers, may be viewed as office workers at various levels—clerical, technical, professional, and managerial—engaged in the administrative and supportive functions, including finance, marketing, and sales, of corporations, rather than in a direct manufacturing process. At the same time, many thousands of white-collar workers are found in the offices of corporations which, indeed, manufacture and deliver services instead of products—e.g., banks, insurance companies, trade associations, many private non-profit organizations. In either case, such offices are hierarchically structured and functionally bureaucratic.

White-collar workers tend to exhibit a strong affinity for upward mobility and the roles of management and supervision. This is not unexpected since the corporate structure and environment encourage competition among workers for management and higher-level positions and for career advancement. But who wins these competitions, unlike blue-collar plant workers whose upward mobility paths are frequently determined by union rules and policies, is decided by a host of factors, the values of which are predetermined or determined by the corporate organization and over which individual employees have little, if any, control. Nonetheless, it is likely that most corporate employees—especially those with appropriate educational and training credentials and background experiences who presume that upward mobility is preordained—assimilate corporate and organizational values, seek organizational experiences and opportunities beyond the boundaries of a current assignment, and attempt to develop in-house political relationships with peers and superiors, all with an eye toward upward mobility and career advancement.

For black employees, in contrast to white employees, upward mobility paths and career advancement are not so easily negotiated. Indeed, while blacks may embrace corporate and organizational values, their efforts in gaining developmental corporate experiences and opportunities and in developing meaningful in-house relationships tend to be subject to the impacts of both individual and institutional racism.

These kinds of racism, while observable in both individual and organizational behavior patterns, emanate from values produced in a societal context and embraced by individuals and organizations. Regarding individual behavior, G. Hugh Russell and Kenneth Black state:

> the core of values held by a particular person may include the value of using *force* to get what he wants, [and] the value of *white supremacy.* . . . With these values as part of the basic core, it would not be surprising to see attitudes develop from them

that include the attitudes that peaceful demonstrations of a contrary view should be beaten back, [and] legislation supporting
racial segregation should be voted for. . . . With these attitudes
prevailing in that person, we would predict his active participation *(behavior)* in swinging a pick handle at the demonstrators,
[and] running for or voting for the segregationist candidate.[1]

Of course, individuals take values into the corporate work place as
employees and managers, and these are translated into attitudes and
behavior.

That corporate and organizational value systems are also shaped
by societal forces and further influence employee and manager
behavior is well known. Specifically, Martha Brown makes the point
that values generated by society and inculcated by organizations,
managers, and employees are quite interdependent despite obvious
differences in impact. (See Figure 5.1) She contends:

while all the variables are to some extent interdependent, the
degree of influence varies, i.e. one manager's or employee's values have little power to change a firm's organizational values or
society's values, while organizational and societal values exert
considerable pressure on a single manager or employee.[2]

Figure 5.1

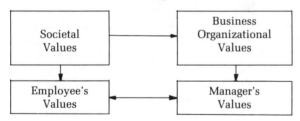

Source: Brown, "Values," p. 17.

To be sure, racism is a likely element in the value systems of white
individuals and institutions, and its resulting impact on black corporate employees is quite clear.

In this volume, concentration is given to an analysis of the
internal labor market for white-collar workers in the corporate sector.
Regarding the interplay of internal and external labor markets, Peter
Doeringer and Michael Piore have stated:

---

[1]G. Hugh Russell and Kenneth Black, Jr., *Human Behavior in Business* (New
York: Meredith Corporation, 1972), pp. 167–68.

[2]Martha A. Brown, "Values—A Necessary but Neglected Ingredient of Motivation on the Job," *Academy of Management Review* (October 1976), p. 16.

The internal labor market, governed by administrative rules, is to be distinguished from the *external labor market* of conventional economic theory where pricing, allocating, and training decisions are controlled directly by economic variables. These two markets are interconnected, however, and movement between them occurs at certain job classifications which constitute *ports of entry and exit* to and from the internal labor market. The remainder of the jobs within the internal labor market are filled by the promotion or transfer of workers who have already gained entry.[3]

In addition to administrative rules as factors of control within the internal labor market, Doeringer and Piore also identify custom as an element of governance and define it as "an unwritten set of rules based largely upon past practice or precedent."[4] As we shall see, these implicit customs, along with administrative rules, broadly reflect the matrix of institutional and organizational values which play a major role in the corporate internal labor market.

A THEORY OF THE CORPORATE INTERNAL LABOR MARKET

The important distinctions between corporate internal labor markets and the more commonly recognized external labor market are ones of substance and form. While it would not be entirely correct to assume that administrative rules and organizational customs and values replace the forces of demand and supply, or the equilibrating processes, it is important to note that such elements establish and define an evaluative context in which demand and supply operate. What is demanded and supplied in the external labor market is significantly different from that demanded and supplied in the corporate internal labor market; moreover, a major function of the external labor market is as a conduit to internal labor markets where jobs and salaries actually exist. The former is characterized by a *corporate* demand for workers with varying skill levels, experiences, and backgrounds for specific jobs or specific assignments. The corporate internal labor market, on the other hand, is characterized by *worker* demand for career opportunities and advancement—i.e., promotions, training opportunities, salary increases, and the like. Workers use the initial employment position as a base from which to begin or continue career development and advancement.

---

[3]Peter B. Doeringer and Michael J. Piore, *Internal Labor Markets and Manpower Analysis* (Lexington: D.C. Heath, 1971), p. 2.
[4]Ibid., p. 23.

Typically, markets may be seen as comprised of groups offering products, services, or resources (suppliers) and groups willing to buy such products, services, or resources (demanders). Markets will clear at a value (price) both buyers and sellers agree upon—namely, where the marginal cost of production equals unit price. The external labor market may be thought to generally operate in this manner at least under conditions of perfect competition. Specifically, corporate bureaucracies have demands for unskilled labor (e.g., recent high school graduates); generally skilled labor (e.g., an accountant); and experienced labor (e.g., a financial manager with several years of experience gained elsewhere). The demand and supply process operates such that for some workers the salary and position offered are equal to or greater than an acceptable minimum salary and position. When this equilibrium is established, *ceteris paribus*, workers transfer from the external labor market to the corporate internal labor market, and corporate labor demand is satisfied.

Once inside the corporate structure, two interesting processes go on, and these add to the complexities of the internal labor market, tend to obscure some of its important dynamics, and, finally, distinguish it from the external counterpart.

Demand for Career Opportunities

Unlike the external labor market which allocates labor on the basis of corporate demand and worker supply, the internal labor market is comprised of sub-markets which allocate career opportunities and govern the rates of career advancement. In a reversal of labor market roles, employees establish the demand and corporations create and control the supply. Specifically, there exist separate but related demand and supply functions for two general categories of personnel actions which give rise to career advancement. First, there are those actions that provide *preparation* for advancement—e.g., training, attendance and participation in organizational meetings, membership in certain communication networks, opportunities for significant discussions with superiors, and meaningful task force and committee assignments. Second, there are actions that *result* in advancement—e.g., promotions, salary increases, higher organizational titles, additional responsibilities and authorities, and certain transfers within the organization. Until an employee is the beneficiary of key personnel actions in sufficient abundance and quality, the experiential base will not be notably expanded, and management's evaluation of overall performance is not likely to be significant. Thus, as we shall see, career advancement depends on both performance evaluation and personnel actions.

In any of these separate submarkets, equilibrium is established at the point where employee demand, related to a particular personnel action, is equal to the corporate supply of that personnel action.[5] The employee demand facing corporate managers is perfectly elastic, and its level is determined by "overall employee performance." In general, managers are continually evaluating employee performance, in terms of assigned tasks and in terms of the degree to which employees reflect a consonance with organizational values. Moreover, management perceptions of these are themselves influenced and shaped by organizational values and customs. Thus, within the internal labor market context, employees have little, if any, direct control over the level of demand as measured by "overall employee performance."

Figure 5.2 describes a submarket for an individual corporate worker. The demand curve (D_1) facing the corporation is perfectly elastic and supports the employee's infinite demand for the personnel action in this submarket. "Overall employee performance" (OP) determines the level of the demand curve and is constant in the short run: that is, measures of overall performance tend to be rigid in the short run. At OP_1, the quantity or quality of the personnel action is PA_1. If the employee's overall performance index improves, the demand curve facing the corporation will rise to OP_2, for example. The supply of personnel actions in this submarket is described by S_1, and its positive slope implies availabilities in greater quantity and/or quality to employees with high levels of overall performance

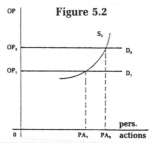

OP | Figure 5.2

5Quite apart from the earlier description of the external labor market, Professor Lloyd L. Hogan has pointed out in discussions that this particular use of the market concept is strained and tends to be violative of the basic notions that: 1) employers *purchase* labor services; and 2) *money* is essential for market exchanges. More specifically, Hogan has written: "An essential condition of market relations is that members of one of the classes must be owners of money; members of the other class must be owners of non money commodities. The money owners are called buyers; . . . The non money commodity owners are called sellers." See his *Principles of Black Political Economy* (unpublished manuscript, 1982), chap. 2, pp. 29–30. In our special context, however, the mechanics of the corporate internal labor market turn on elements other than the direct purchase of labor and money exchanges, and it is these elements that distinguish the internal from the external labor market.

than to employees with relatively low levels of overall performance. Thus, as "overall employee performance" increases from OP_1 to OP_2, the quantity or quality of personnel actions increases from PA_1 to PA_2, thereby increasing opportunities for career advancement.

Simultaneous Demand and Supply

The second interesting process within the internal labor market relates to the role of those with corporate management and supervisory responsibilities. Facing the external labor market, managers and supervisors with hiring authorities reflect the corporate demand for workers. But, internally, members of this group simultaneously demand career advancement opportunities for themselves and supply such opportunities for subordinates. The complexity broadens when it is recognized that managers are themselves subordinate and have reporting relationships to higher-level managers. The consequence of this development is that managers, in the process of directly estimating measures of overall performance for subordinates and thereby impacting the availability of career opportunities, are engaging at the same time in an act which forms part of the basis on which they themselves are evaluated. Thus, the simultaneity. Incidentally, what better technique for enforcing institutional values and custom than tying managerial upward mobility to subordinate evaluation?

Given organizational norms and custom and institutional values, it is probable that managers perform their simultaneous tasks in ways supportive of their own candidacy for continued upward mobility and career advancement. Clearly, managers are evaluated by their superiors in a fashion similar to that for nonmanagement employees. There are important differences, however. Lower-level nonmanagement employees, for example, are evaluated heavily on day-to-day performance on the job and on the mastery of required duties. On the other hand, managers generally tend to have principal responsibilities for resources and their allocation in terms of organizing, coordinating, planning, and meeting objectives consistent with major organizational objectives. Interestingly enough, the successful undertaking of these responsibilities requires not only cognizance and sensitivity, but an allegiance to institutional values. A major question, perhaps unspoken, is whether these managerial responsibilities, including the various employment decisions, are carried out in a manner consistent with institutional values. Of course, if the answer is in the affirmative, and institutional racism is part of the organizational value matrix, then a general result is that black employees will be denied certain roles and assignments and are likely to be evaluated as if to discount their performance. The result notwithstanding, managers will have succeeded in serving their own career interests.

Summary

This general theory of the corporate internal labor market puts forth the notion of a set of internal submarkets not for labor services per se, but rather for the *personnel actions* that comprise career development and advancement. Employees create the demand for promotions and salary increases, and corporations, through managerial responsibilities, create the supply. However, corporate managers establish the level of employee demand through their estimates of "overall employee performance"; corporations also determine the shape and position of the supply curves for personnel actions. Thus, corporations virtually control the internal labor market and its submarkets and effectively decide the beneficiaries of career opportunities and advancement.

Since managers seek additional upward mobility, they are simultaneously in the submarkets as demanders and suppliers. The manner in which managers satisfy employee demands impacts the level of their demand curve for career opportunities. Succinctly, organizational and institutional customs and values influence management decisions regarding employees, which, in turn, influence management decisions regarding other managers.

CORPORATE MANAGERS AND THE INTERNAL LABOR MARKET

In view of the pivotal manager role in the dynamics of the corporate internal labor market, it is important to briefly examine manager characteristics impacted by institutional values and customs and their potential effect on the allocation of black employees. By no means exhaustive, two central management postures—independent and dependent—can be identified.

A general distinction between corporate managers who may be grouped as independent or those who are dependent concerns the role of "risk-taker." While most managers tend to view themselves as risk-takers—ascribing to that label's implications for independent thought, judgement, and action; creativity; daring; innovativeness; the willingness to challenge and deviate from accepted practices— the real likelihood is that most managers, in fact, are not risk-takers.

Rather, their tendency is to imitate and perform in ways consistent with perceived organizational values and customs, and expectations. How and to what extent individual managers are perceived to be imitating and performing determine the level of respect and the span of influence accorded each by the organization. Obviously, each manager strives to maximize respect and influence since they undergird career paths and future positioning in the organization, whether the base is one of independence or dependence.

Very simply, and without attempting to distinguish the numerous variations in manager characteristics, Figure 5.3 describes four categories into which corporate managers may be grouped: 1) those tending toward independence—i.e., risk-takers who operate near the fringes of organizational norms, customs, and values, who are respected by peers and superiors, and who have developed an influence capability; 2) those tending toward independence but who are *not* organizationally respected and influential; 3) those tending toward dependence—i.e., not risk-takers, but managers who play it "close to the vest," who are more heavily dependent for guidance and direction on organizational norms and customs, and who have earned levels of respect and acquired bases of influence; and 4) those tending toward dependence but who are *not* organizationally respected and influential.

Those managers tending toward dependence are far greater in numbers than those who operate at the other end of the spectrum. The choice of the terms *many* and *few* in Figure 5.3 provides some sense of group sizes.

The groupings in Figure 5.3 provide a basis for three conclusions. First, whether a manager's style is toward independence or

Figure 5.3 Some Manager Characteristics within the Corporate Organization

Characteristics	Managerial Independence	Managerial Dependence	Probable Level of Organizational Success
Respected and Influential	(1) Few Managers	(3) Many Managers	High
Not Respected and Not Influential	(2) Few Managers	(4) Many Managers	Low

dependence, the acquisition of organizational respect and influence is essential for enhancing the probability of a successful career pattern, Groups (1) and (3). Second, a great number of managers achieve some level of organizational success via Group (3) characteristics than Group (1) characteristics. Lastly, managers in Groups (2) and (4) are not likely to be organizationally successful beyond current levels. The point is that the dynamics of the corporate internal labor market may be significantly influenced by manager responses to institutional values.

Briefly, let us examine each of the four management groups in terms of broad implications for black employment.

Group (3)

This group, which constitutes the majority of the success-oriented managers, is highly dependent on perceived organizational values and customs for guidance with respect to appropriate postures, reactions, and decisions. Given that institutional racism is an element in the set of values, norms, and customs, black employees assigned to a unit headed by a white Group (3) manager are likely to find upward mobility opportunities scarce. Of course, this does not preclude the reality of "tokenism" or the presence of black employees whose credentials and performance are compelling. Basically, black employees will likely be managed in accordance with accompanying reputations and performance appraisals since Group (3) managers have no strong inclination toward deviating from actual organizational assessments, or expected ones. More importantly, white Group (3) managers can be expected to manage black employees in a fashion consistent with the values of institutional racism which generally predict specific occupational exclusion and a rate of upward mobility that is lower than that for white employees in similar circumstances. After all, the white Group (3) managers are neither prepared nor willing to jeopardize continued managerial success by deviating from perceived norms and customs.

Group (4)

In many instances Group (4) managers tend to be in charge of organizational units, or in positions, viewed by the organization as relatively less critical to the accomplishment of overall goals and objectives than other units and positions. Given that the probability of notable upward mobility for this group is relatively low, some managers in this group are bitter, frustrated, and resentful; others are indifferent or resigned to their fate and straightforwardly carry out their responsibilities while looking forward to retirement; and still others remain hard working, optimistic, and intent on improving their lot. An unfortunate personnel action which undermines quality length-of-service experiences and upward mobility opportunities for black employees is to assign them to white Group (4) managers. The result is disastrous, since it is extremely difficult to develop positive organizational credentials in an environment which is neither respected by the organization nor capable of exercising influence within that organization. Moreover, many of these managers, taking advantage of opportunities to be reevaluated and relying on norms and customs for operational inputs, tend to relegate blacks to the lesser positions and to assign them the least important tasks. While they provide little basis for career development, through these decisions Group (4) managers hope to evidence a sense of team membership and to further demonstrate that the character of their decisions is indeed consonant with overall organizational values.

Group (2)

There are relatively few managers in this group. They, like Group (4), do not command adequate levels of respect and influence, but they tend to be somewhat confounded by the organization's indifference toward them and its apparent lack of appreciation for their "special" skills and talents. Consistent with their spirit of independence, some of these managers may behave in ultra-conservative ways relative to corporate employment norms, and some others in liberal ways. An example of the ultra-conservative posture is the white manager who has concluded that Equal Employment Opportunity laws, for example, and the corporation's affirmative action commitment are so reprehensible that he (she) dares to not only openly voice dissent but plainly refuses to comply fully with the organization's directives. Such managers tend not to hire blacks under their own volition; and if black employees are placed in their charge, the work experience is often negative for the employee, the psychic costs are extortionately high and termination a likely inevitability. The liberal white managers in this group often tend toward the opposite extreme, but since they command no respect and have little influence, their positive evaluations and performance appraisals for black employees create a discounted stir.

Group (1)

This group of independent, respected, and influential managers is frequently thought of as the elite of the management corps. Like Group (2), it has members who could be labeled ultra-conservative

or liberal. Generally, black employees who are viewed as good performers and outstanding performers tend to fare well under liberal
white managers in this group.

The above is a brief attempt to better understand how corporate
managers generally function in the internal labor market with particular reference to the employment process for black employees.
However, the reader should recognize the simplicity of its development. In fact, a sufficiently complex discussion would account for
a manager's personal attitudes and reactions regarding race, and the
organization's reward-punishment system; a manager's rank or position within the organization, whether the unit is viewed as *line* or
staff, its perceived proximity to profit centers, and the manager's
prospects for advancement; and the nature of a manager's relationship with peers and employee groups. But such a discussion must
wait for a more appropriate opportunity.

In the meantime, an additional consideration deserving of special mention is the matter of employee job and/or position assignment. While there are organizational and circumstantial exceptions,
most managers are expected to fill their vacancies from either the
external or internal labor markets subject to, perhaps, peer review
and the approval of superiors, depending on the level of the vacancy.
But the selection and approval processes, in any event, are impacted
by organizational values and customs, as previously discussed. Thus,
regarding black personnel for vacancies, white managers may satisfy
one or more possible motivations depending on their own level within
the organization, the character of the organizational unit, the existing
proportions of white and black employees, and the relative "positioning" of vacancies to be filled. For example, the decision not to
place a black employee in a particular vacancy (or unit) under any
circumstances might reflect a white manager's need to satisfy personal feelings of racism—perhaps heightened by institutional values—and/or a perception that white employee group reactions may
be negative. Or, the assignment of black employees to Group (2) and
Group (4) managers may be persuaded or induced, if these employees
are viewed as relatively less productive. A third case concerns an
organization, or a manager, who wants to be rid of a particular black
employee but does not choose direct termination. Job assignment
and manager selection could be critical to that objective. Similarly,
if the objective was to "test" the black employee, assignment and
manager selection could be an important technique. Clearly, such a
technique may also be utilized in appropriate situations involving
white employees. The fundamental difference between its application to black employment situations, on the one hand, and to white
employment situations, on the other, may be the difference between

ruse and "legitimate evaluation." For the ruse may be motivated, to a large extent, by institutional and individual racism, while the legitimate evaluation is presumably motivated by an adherence to some standard managerial practice.

Obviously, the possible variations are many. Nonetheless, the identification of four distinct manager groups and the likely impact of institutional values and customs on their employment decisions is important for an extended understanding of the corporate internal labor market. How that market allocates black employees is the core of this work.

INTERNAL COMMUNICATION SYSTEMS

The communication of all sorts of information at many levels and in many ways is essential to and characterizes the functioning of the corporate internal labor market.[6] Present-day managers broadly understand the need to communicate and the role of information as it relates to the coordination of an organization's goals and objectives. Also, employees depend heavily on the communication of certain kinds of standard information from managers and others for the decision-making processes regarding career opportunities and advancement, and for carrying out assignments. Managers depend on information from employee groups and individuals for purposes of improving control, and for instituting indicated changes and corrections in the management process. Of importance here is the extent to which institutional values and custom determine who receives what information, the quality of that information, and, in particular, the role of communication networks.

An organization's broad plans and objectives, its policies and practices, specific kinds of work force data, personnel vacancies, financial results, the competitive picture, relevant notices and directives, planned training sessions—these are all examples of information generally available and often *formally* communicated to corporate employee groups. These kinds of information flow from downward communication systems—i.e., from the top of an organization downward. As often as not, the vehicles for transmission

---

[6]Theoretically and empirically, communications specialists have developed frameworks for analyses of organizational communication systems which include upward and downward communications, and the concepts of intergroup, intragroup, and interpersonal relations. While these are far more complex and extensive than the framework discussed herein, the interested reader is referred to Howard H. Greenbaum and Raymond L. Falcione, *Organizational Communication: Abstracts, Analysis, and Overview*, vol. 6 (Beverly Hills: Sage Publications, 1981).

may be bulletin boards; memoranda; policy handbooks; staff, departmental, and other meetings; annual statements; and in-house news organs.

Other kinds of formal downward communications are those directed to individual employees rather than to groups. Typical of this kind of communications is the performance appraisal review wherein an employee and supervisor meet to discuss on-the-job performance, assignments and responsibilities and perhaps salary increases and possible promotions and advancements.

Upward communication systems generally refer to the flow of information from employees to management. An employee "attitude survey," for example, is a flow of information from employee groups to management, and the now classic "suggestion box" provides an opportunity for individual employees to communicate with management.

Formal communication systems are fairly standard in corporate organizations and facilitate the flows of information basic to a coordinated and efficient functioning of internal labor markets and organizations as a whole. But of singular importance to the internal labor market itself are the informal communication systems comprised of networks and structured in consonance with institutional values and customs. Not only are they networks of communication, but also networks of *action*. Such communication networks likely embrace everyone in the corporation. Thus, networks may be large or small; significant or insignificant; made up of lower-level employees, middle- and upper-level employees, upper-level women, middle-level blacks, and/or certain managers. Clearly, the possible combinations of network members, and the extensiveness, or lack thereof, of networks may vary exponentially, even though networks tend to be comprised of employees with similar interests, values, and goals. Information moving through the networks ranges from banal and inaccurate gossip to the highest levels of sensitive organizational plans. The key observation here is that corporations assign different values to each of the communication networks.[7] The values assigned to each network reflect corporate values and customs and, in a significant sense, define the acceptable interpersonal, intergroup, and intragroup relations. While organizational information of many sorts may be transmitted, networks categorize workers such that when corporate needs are to be met, or some personnel action is required, organizations look to that network (or group) which, based on its assigned value,

---

[7]This observation may likely produce some disagreement since, in some quarters, it is felt that the plight of black employees could be effectively addressed if black networks were better structured and expanded. This notion, in our view, probably has limited viability.

can best meet the need or facilitate the desired personnel action. That networks have a communications bond is a valuable observation at this point because corporate needs can be translated into information which is then communicated.

Most corporate employees understand this very well and as a result strive to become members of higher-valued communication networks. Doubtless, organizational reputation and subsequent opportunities for upward mobility and career advancement depend on gaining membership. Therefore, employees evince value matrices (e.g., dress and appearance, subjects and issues discussed as well as the intellectual position taken, job commitment and hard work) which they hope will signal their readiness to join and consonance with the institutional values cherished by a particular network or networks.

For black employees, however, the problem is that racism is a likely institutional value embraced by these organizational networks—certainly, by the higher-placed and more highly valued networks. Consequently, black employees often find the simplest and most fundamental of techniques for gaining entry out of reach. For example, countless black employees describe the difficulty of engaging white managers and other superiors in serious discussions beyond the scope of their immediate job assignments, discussions which might involve information reserved for more highly placed audiences. Likewise, not being invited to certain meetings or, if invited, not being given a role is a common occurrence. In other words, the simplest of opportunities for evidencing appropriate levels of knowledge, concern, competence, commitment, interest, and desired involvement may be broadly denied. Generally, as black employees strive for higher levels within organizations, they are taken less seriously by white network members. The obvious consequence, of course, is that certain network memberships are rarely, if ever, made available to black employees. This limitation reduces the kinds of qualifying experiences essential for higher-level organizational responsibilities and negatively impacts not only rates of upward mobility but the availability of specific positions and the nature of assignments.

A final comment regarding communication networks and the role of performance appraisal is in order. Ideally, a principal function of the performance appraisal process is to provide an employee with the supervisor's reasonably confidential assessment of overall performance, including counsel regarding areas in need of improvement, prospects for advancement, and other data and information presumably required by an employee for career development. Whether carried out orally, in writing, or both, the appraisal conclusions tend to reach certain communication networks and, in some measure, identify prospective members. To communicate to and through

particular networks that the employee is "outstanding," "high potential," and a "top manager for the future," for example, is tantamount
to describing the employee favorably in terms of institutional values.
Higher-value networks become accessible to that employee. On the
other hand, if what is communicated to networks is that an employee
is "average" and possesses "little potential for higher level responsibility," higher networks tend not to take that employee's candidacy
seriously. Thus, in addition to the formal performance appraisal
process, an informal evaluation of performance is on-going and so
is the flow of information to networks.

Most employees can be easily victimized by these formal and
informal evaluation processes if such is the intent of management.
Black employees, in particular, are subject to this victimization since
institutional racism generally predicts an inferior performance and
white managers, as discussed earlier, tend to embrace perceived organizational values for their own survival and career advancement.
However, "victimization," in this sense, does not necessarily mean
that a black employee is inaccurately rated, even most of the time.
What it does mean is that the performance, at whatever level, tends
to be discounted to the extent that acceptance for membership in a
higher-value communication network may be unlikely.

This concept of networks is not inconsistent with J. E. Cairnes's
nineteenth-century description of "noncompeting" occupational
groups. His analysis led to the conclusion that industrial worker
groups were formed on socioeconomic class bases which generally
precluded movement from one broad occupational category to
another.[8] In a more recent analysis, Clark Kerr found that "institutional rules in the labor market . . . establish more boundaries between
labor markets and make them more specific and harder to cross. They
define the points of competition, the groups which may compete,
and the grounds on which they compete."[9]

In the corporate internal market, it is clear that networks are
structured on the basis of institutional and social values, reflect class
and race considerations, and communicate manager preference for
specific employee characteristics. What is more, clerical and management groups may be described as generally noncompeting groups;
and even *within* occupational categories, it is likely that noncompeting groups exist. To carry this a step further, "Negro jobs" and
female jobs are readily seen as examples of such noncompeting groups.
In the final analysis, communication networks mirror internal labor
market segmentation; both contribute to the likelihood that the general upward mobility of black corporate employees will be stalled.

---

[8]J. E. Cairnes, *Political Economy* (New York: Harper, 1874), pp. 67–68.
[9]Clark Kerr, *Labor Markets and Wage Determination* (Berkeley: University of
California, 1977), p. 37.

TWO BASIC CATEGORIES OF BLACK EMPLOYEES

While it would be unpardonable to oversimplify a rather complex dynamic—especially if the result is misleading—it is desirable, at this point, to generalize two readily discernable categories of black employees in corporate offices.

Category I Employees

The first, and by far the largest, category (Category I) is comprised of black employees with fairly minimal educational achievements (e.g., high school graduates), with neither extensive nor intensive work experiences, and often with few generally acceptable and conventional communication skills (e.g., reading, writing, and speaking). This group is typically relegated to the lower-paying and menial corporate assignments such as those found in mail rooms, duplicating services, basic clerical and typing operations, supply units, and the like. Even when not placed in these areas, black employees in Category I still tend to be assigned to the relatively lower-paying and lower-positioned jobs.

Obviously, white employees with similar characteristics are also assigned to lower-level jobs, but important differences are evident. Frequently, lower-level jobs and positions assigned to whites would appear to be broader in scope and potentially cut across the base of the organization. This spells some degree of enhanced opportunity for upward mobility. Moreover, the broader opportunity for job assignments to some extent widens salary and wage scales so that relatively fewer white than black employees receive lower and lowest pay. Secondly, white managers and supervisors tend naturally to encourage, support, and select for promotion white employees with whom they feel a kinship—a kinship which is strengthened by the presence of black employees.[10]

In significant contrast, most blacks in Category I appear to constitute a "quasi-caste" within many corporate offices as regards job classifications and opportunities for advancement. Once so categorized, the probability of progressing from that group, while not nil, seems to be much lower for black employees than for white employees. Even those who try to adopt accepted institutional behavior

---

[10]This is related to the notion of an employer's "taste for discrimination" used initially in the 1957 work of Becker, and subsequently by others in the neoclassical school. See Gary S. Becker, *The Economics of Discrimination*, 2nd ed. (Chicago: University of Chicago Press, 1971).

patterns of attire, everyday attendance in a timely fashion, and good performance find their egress blocked, for the most part.

Many ambitious black employees in Category I recognize their educational handicaps as chinks in the armor of qualifications. They may devote several years to the achievement of two- and four-year college degrees and other educational and training credentials, only to be rebuffed partially, if not totally, at the caste gate. Typically, the rebuff takes the form of specifying additional qualifications, ignoring the employee's achievement, or simply downgrading the achievement. It should be pointed out that this tends to be truer for those employees receiving liberal arts degrees than for those earning educational credentials in areas such as computer science, for example. As we have seen from our discussion of internal labor markets, this is more than simple discrimination; rather, it reflects institutional values and internal labor market customs supported by communication networks.[11] One common solution employed by some ambitious black employees in this Category is to seek improved opportunities in other organizations; thus, turnover rates for this group tend to be significantly higher than for the work force as a whole.[12] Of course, in most instances, the hoped-for improvement continues to be largely frustrated by both individual and institutional racism.

Category II Employees

The second category (Category II) of black employees in corporate offices is made up of individuals who tend to have higher educational credentials and/or considerably more work experience of a professional and managerial sort. Included in this group are recent college and graduate-school graduates who are generally recruited for trainee jobs designed to produce lower and middle management types. Black employees in this Category tend to view themselves as upwardly mobile and, in fact, maintain staff and line positions in *technician* job categories, and predominantly staff functions in the higher *professional* and *officials and managers* job categories.

Actually, the presumed upward mobility potential of blacks in

---

[11]Doeringer and Piore view these networks and their role as an adherence to internal labor market customs through the formation of both employee and manager groups within the work force. *Internal Labor Markets*, pp. 22–23.

[12]It can be demonstrated that in times of economic recession, turnover rates for black employees who would voluntarily terminate employment in corporate offices are typically low, for obvious reasons.

Category II is largely mythical. On the one hand, there is not only a narrowing of upward mobility channels and an artificial ceiling on career paths, but certain kinds of jobs appear to be generally closed to blacks; or, to put it conversely, certain kinds of jobs appear to be reserved for Category II blacks. On the other hand, the caste character of Category I is not clearly discernable in Category II, and thus a feeling of "having made it" when one is in the latter group serves to provide hope and, ironically, an intensification of social and economic class stratification between the categories. From one point of view, this latter phenomenon relates to membership differences in networks, as discussed earlier.

The mythical character of upward mobility for those in Category II is further confirmed by the relatively low degree of management utilization and the quality of job assignments. If one has not been utilized in a significantly intensive (and extensive) manner or assigned important and/or challenging work activities, then the upward mobility channels are narrowed on the grounds that the employee has not had sufficient experience; or the employee has not really been "tested"; or the employee does not really understand the business. (Incidentally, for white employees with similarly limited experiences, upward mobility is often based on "potential"!) Disproportionate numbers of blacks in Category II face this circumstance, and a contrived legitimacy is thereby attached to the artificial ceiling.

Over the past few years, it has become fashionable in some corporate organizations with relatively large black work forces and/or black customers to appoint one or two black vice presidents, and a few managers. While not always the case, it generally is true that in order for an organization to benefit from such appointments, black corporate officials must be visible both internally and externally. Therefore, it is not uncommon to find such employees positioned in public and community relations, personnel, special markets, equal employment opportunity, and other staff-type jobs. Exceptions to this observation, while existing and growing, are relatively rare.

INTERNAL LABOR MARKET DYNAMICS

Within a corporate framework established by institutional values and customs, and powered by communication networks, management decisions to hire blacks, and those internal labor market decisions affecting the allocation of blacks, are generally buttressed by a host of secondary considerations which emerge as *prima facie* rationales for those decisions and which, presumably, embrace some objective concepts of qualification. (See Chapter VI.) Ostensibly, the most common of these are education, training, and job experience. At least three important observations ought to be made about this preliminary conclusion.

First, in an analytic sense, a factor of discrimination based on racism is difficult to isolate from all other factors which form the usual basis for a management employment decision. To be sure, education and training, experience and its qualitative character, age, previous affiliations, references, level and type of position sought, personality and attitude (insofar as they can be and are assessed), attire, speech patterns—all to a lesser or greater degree shape the decision to hire, promote, or undertake other actions central to the employment process. But these factors tend to be weighted and evaluated differently for blacks than for whites: for blacks they tend to carry a discount value.[13] Thus, the pervasiveness of racism, on the one hand, and its camouflaged character, on the other, make difficult the process of analyzing the employment decision in a way that isolates the racially induced discrimination element (the discount value) contained in the management evaluation process. Moreover, this "racially induced discrimination element" exists to varying degrees. Thus, depending on the personnel decision-maker and the specific organization, as well as demographic and economic factors,[14] black workers will be employed *at* labor market levels of availability, *below* or *above* labor market levels of availability, or *not at all*. This result is also linked to the rates at which the internal labor market allocates promotions, salary increases, and job assignments to black workers. For it is clear that black employees have fewer in-house informal training opportunities than white employees, less access to the variety of career assignments available to white employees, and earn less than white employees, on the average. And the presence of black employees in upper-middle level jobs and above, relative to their numbers in lower-level jobs, might lead one to believe that the corporate internal labor market ceases to function for blacks beyond a certain organizational level. That is, as black employees rise in the corporate organization, so does the discount value.

Second, past acts of racial discrimination must be distinguished from, but recognized as impacting, current acts of discrimination in employment. The entire history of black slavery in America and its

---

[13]This view is similar to that of Welch. See Finis Welch, "Labor Market Discrimination: An Interpretation of Income Differences in the Rural South," *Journal of Political Economy*, 75 (June 1967), 227.

[14]For example, blacks as a percentage of the community population; the types of jobs being applied for; the degree of organizational commitment to equal employment opportunity laws; the geographical location of the firm; the specific firm or industry; the number of blacks already employed.

aftermath shape contemporary race relations in terms of employment, education, nutrition and health care, housing, ownership of capital, and the general participation in and exposure to all levels of American life. The result has been that black Americans for the most part have shared, and continue to share, minimally in the benefits produced by the various sectors of the society, including cultural interchange and intercultural familiarity. The transition from plantation to ghetto colony[15] sets the stage, then, for the current employment of black America in the private sector: either black America is victimized by institutional racism and racist employers; or it is victimized by "objectively determined" job qualifications which it is not given much of an opportunity to acquire; or both.

One of the most important qualifications for upward mobility is job experience, and the quality of that experience. It is interesting to note that while employees have a large degree of control over the qualifications associated with academic and training pursuits, employers enjoy control over the intrinsic value and quality of the job experience qualification. To the extent that this latter qualification is the cornerstone of career development and advancement, employers (managers) play a major role in determining the rates of upward mobility of employees. Black employees in corporations tend to be excluded from those activities which provide the quality experiences undergirding upward mobility.

Last, racist employment practices tend to label black workers acceptable for the relatively lowest-paying jobs, the unpleasant and "dirty" jobs, the jobs white workers find least desirable. Thus, depending on the types of skills required, one finds proportionately greater numbers of corporate blacks in lower-level clerical and technician functions and in laborer and service worker groups, rather than in higher job categories. This is principally a problem of occupational mobility, and what occurs in corporations is simply a denial of access to certain organizational units and/or certain jobs within those units.

Beyond these broad observations, the dynamics of the corporate internal labor market are clothed in a varied and subtle web of organizational values and customs, as was earlier discussed. With particular reference to Category II employees, a rather interesting dichotomy describes an important employment dynamic which serves

---

[15]See William K. Tabb, *The Political Economy of the Black Ghetto* (New York: Norton, 1970), pp. 21–27. See also August Meier and Elliott Rudwick, *From Plantation to Ghetto*, 3rd ed. (New York: Hill and Wang, 1976); and Arthur M. Ross, "The Negro in the American Economy," *Employment, Race and Poverty*, ed. Arthur M. Ross and Herbert Hill (New York: Harcourt, Brace and World, 1967).

to legitimatize the upward mobility discrimination experienced by these employees, especially at higher organizational levels.

One branch of the employment dynamic involves what may be termed the "Super-Black" syndrome. Here, white managers tend to insist on hiring or promoting only blacks who possess credentials (e.g., those who are affable and have academic degrees from prestigious institutions, appropriate levels of dress and self-confidence, standard communication skills, and who appear competent, alert, intelligent) beyond those normally specified or required for the position in question. An interpretation of this *modus operandi* is that white managers, who are subscribers to the white superiority–black inferiority myth, assume that black employees must be "Super-Black" in order to perform *adequately*. This effect is often seen in work situations, for example, where the lone black may have earned a graduate degree while white colleagues performing the same or similar tasks may have earned bachelor degrees or less; where the black employee's overall experience level is higher; where the black employee's communication skills are excellent; and where the employee's management potential for creative thinking, problem solving, and personnel management is perceived as high. More often than not, such employees tend to be relatively underutilized and underchallenged in their work.

The other branch of this employment dynamic may be labeled the "Hire to Fail" syndrome. This management syndrome leads to the choice of a black employee whose skills and/or experiences and perhaps capabilities are weak and insufficient for a particular position. One observes that the "work assets" of the employee are frequently overtaxed and lead to unsatisfactory performance results. Often times, the orchestration of this result is deliberate and satisfies a white manager's need to confirm, once again, the myth of white superiority–black inferiority.

These two approaches are curiously consistent with the role of institutional racism and lay the foundation for legitimately denying upward mobility opportunities. For example, one possible scenario describes a black employee with qualifications beyond those required (as seen in the general qualifications possessed by white incumbents in a work unit) who is asked to work alongside whites having fewer qualifications. The black employee senses a pointed discrimination. When this sensing develops into frustration, which can become increasingly bitter, the black employee may act out the negative feelings. This acting out will be perceived by whites as a change—i.e., the black employee may be perceived as having a reduced sense of humor or an unwillingness to fraternize as before; or having developed a general disinterest in broad participation or a "chip-on-the-shoulder" attitude, or other manifestations of psychic discomfort. A likely result is that this employee will be passed over for promotions, new career assignments, and training opportunities; will be transferred laterally; or will leave the organization in search of the elusive discrimination-free environment. In this regard, Richard F. America and Bernard Anderson suggest that "black managers . . . need to be alert against behaving or opening up suddenly in any markedly different manner. Such a change can unsettle, and perhaps threaten, superiors and coworkers."[16] In any event, management will have unwittingly—and in a context of qualifications—blocked the upward path of the employee.

It should be noted that this particular result is not necessarily the intent of management; rather, it flows from an adherence to the racist belief in white superiority–black inferiority, which was the basis for inappropriately positioning the black employee in the first instance. And, in the minds of white managers, the black employee is blamed for his failure to comport with behavioral norms of the organization. For example, this quote from a white manager is typical:

> "I have noticed a tendency to be more emotional in black managers," observes a Philadelphia manager. "They allow gripes and concerns to surface and deal with them overtly. Also, they are somewhat more caustic in confrontations."[17]

Not only will the perceived aberrant behavior of a particular black employee be communicated to key networks and, at the same time, evidence the white manager's consonance with institutional values, but it will also serve as a basis for possibly denying future upward mobility opportunities.

Of course, there are blacks who successfully maintain a sufficiently balanced perspective based on an understanding of this dynamic and, through great effort, make limited progress. To some extent, such progress will depend on whether the position of the black employee is line or staff. Given the generally accepted definitions of *line*, which describe that hierarchy of positions having direct responsibility for corporate operations, and *staff*, those positions that provide administrative support and which are not directly related to production, it is clear that higher-level Category II black employees tend to be positioned in staff (e.g., personnel, EEO) more frequently than in line positions. And the evidence suggests that progress for blacks is more likely to occur at higher rates in the former

---

[16]America and Anderson focus on black managers, but their observations are relevant for many Category II nonmanagers. See Richard F. America and Bernard Anderson, "Black Managers: How They Manage Their Emotions," *Across the Board* (April 1979), p. 81.

[17]Quoted in America and Anderson, "Black Managers," p. 81.

than in the latter positions. The relatively unprepared black employee in Category II, while often able to maintain employee status through the skillful development of acceptable postures, experiences little, if any, upward mobility. In general, the movement tends to be lateral—or none at all.

These experiences are not as frequently endured by Category I employees since their upward mobility path generally is bound by the caste-like circumstances in which they find themselves. Of course, the frustration level rises as some of these employees with maturity and talent, who are intelligent, eager to learn, and willing to work hard, see white employees moving out and ahead, leaving them behind to perform the same tired and unrewarding tasks often with no real prospects in sight.

SUMMARY

A broad description of the corporate internal labor market reveals that the major values allocated therein are represented by career development opportunities and career advancement. Importantly, these allocations are made largely on the basis of institutional and organizational values and custom. Depending on organizational level, and posture and position, managers reflect their perceptions of these values in the management of career opportunities and advancement for subordinates and, in so doing, influence their own career paths.

Critical elements in the functioning of the corporate internal labor market are the communication networks. Numerous and varied in size and composition, communication networks are informally but hierarchically arranged based on their significance derived from organizational values and custom. Membership in networks determines the distribution of quality assignments, the organizational perception of employees, and, ultimately, career advancement and upward mobility. Moreover, networks translate corporate needs into information and career actions for their members and, further, communicate employee performance appraisal in ways that determine membership.

Institutional racism is an element in the set of organizational values that control internal labor markets; thus, it influences management decisions regarding the career development opportunities and career advancement for black employees. To be sure, individual and institutional racism subscribes to and perpetuates the notions of black inferiority, or white superiority, or both; hence, racism provides a fundamental rationale for the relegation of blacks to staff and other support-type jobs and for their exclusion from significant line jobs and/or key manager positions. The result, then, is that black corporate employees, whether in Category I or in the more credentialed Category II, tend to be positioned in the relatively lower-paying jobs requiring minimal skills, or in lower mid-level line jobs, or in the higher professional and managerial job groups peripheral to corporate line operations and profit centers.[18]

---

[18]See John P. Fernandez, *Black Managers in White Corporations* (New York: John Wiley, 1975); and John W. Work, "Management Blacks and the Internal Labor Market: Responses to a Questionnaire," *Human Resource Management* (Fall 1980), pp. 27–31.

VI

Black Corporate Employees:
Key Aspects of Utilization

INTRODUCTION

LET US TAKE a closer look at the corporate internal labor market for black employees. Given that we will find differences in the wages and salaries accruing to black and white workers, differences in the occupational patterns of the two groups, and differences in their upward mobility patterns, what factors and forces, manipulated in a racial context, shed light on these differences? White managers tend to cite cultural differences and the lack of qualifications as reasons for the relatively inferior positioning of blacks; blacks, on the other hand, cite racial discrimination as the appropriate explanation for their not evidencing progress equivalent to that of white employees. Interestingly, some white managers also subscribe to the racial discrimination view.[1] This chapter attempts to identify and describe such factors and their roles in the internal labor market process—recognizing not only the techniques used in limiting upward mobility, but the non-wage consequences which form a basis for discrimination.

---

[1]John P. Fernandez, *Black Managers in White Corporations* (New York: John Wiley, 1975), pp. 77–79.

HUMAN CAPITAL THEORY AND THE SUPPLY OF BLACK WORKERS

The proponents of the human capital theory might well argue that the previous discussion in Chapter V has ignored the qualitative aspects of the supply of black labor.[2] Essentially, human capital theory argues that the role of and the economic return to a unit of labor are determined by the investment in that labor as reflected in the educational and training processes in the society. Thus, a prime explanation of wage and salary differences between white and black workers, and evident occupational discrimination, concerns the different levels of investment in white and black human capital. Specifically, this approach determines that black and white workers have attained different skill and capability levels through the educational and broader societal training processes. These, then, purport to explain differences in productivity, and, hence, in wages and income.[3]

Sowell argues that human capital is "the vital accumulation of knowledge, skills, and organizational experience."[4] Others categorize the components of human capital as "native ability, formal education, vocational education, on-the-job training, and on-the-job experience,"[5] and conclude that blacks have less investment in these than whites and are, therefore, less productive and less well-compensated. Sowell adds a cultural dimension to this view of human capital:

> The pattern of cumulative inequalities in human capital investment in formal schooling is repeated in the other forms of human capital. The whole way of thinking and behaving appropriate to the more lucrative and responsible occupations is something which comes freely, and even unconsciously, to people reared in families where such occupations have been common for generations, whereas such human capital comes to the low-income person only slowly, imperfectly and with great deliberate efforts to break his natural patterns. Such basic traits as punctuality, efficiency and long-run planning are of little use to people who have been limited to menial jobs for generations as with most

---

[2]Among those who have contributed to the development of the human capital theory are Gary Becker, *Human Capital* (New York: National Bureau of Economic Research, 1964); and *Human Capital and the Personal Distribution of Income* (Ann Arbor: University of Michigan Press, 1967); Lester C. Thurow, *Investment in Human Capital* (Los Angeles: Wadsworth, 1970); Bennett Harrison, *Education, Training and the Urban Ghetto* (Baltimore: Johns Hopkins University Press, 1972); Thomas Sowell, "Economics and Black People," *The Review of Black Political Economy*, 1 (Winter/Spring 1971), 3–34.

[3]For a summary of this thesis, see David M. Gordon, *Theories of Poverty and Underemployment* (Lexington: D.C. Heath, 1972), pp. 27–32.

[4]Sowell, "Economics and Black People," p. 4.

[5]Gordon, *Poverty and Underemployment*, p. 31.

black Americans. Everyone can understand the economic value of such traits as an abstract intellectual proposition but to understand such qualities abstractly and to have such *habits* in reality are very different things. Those black people who have such traits have typically acquired them through persistent, and sometimes painful, adjustment which would be difficult to explain to people who grew up with these patterns as a free cultural inheritance.[6]

While these descriptions of the human capital theory sound cogent, in fact the corporate employment process is generally devoid of techniques for objectively evaluating candidates presenting themselves for general hire, specific hire, or promotional opportunities— whether white or black. Of course, many corporate managers would never admit that the calculus for selecting employees is arbitrary and subjective, at best.[7] Thus, the evaluation of an employee after some period of on-the-job work is done with inexactitude, and a general bias, Sowell's observations notwithstanding.

What is more likely, in the case of blacks, is that the attributes of relatively lower human capital levels are *presumed*. For example, the strict neoclassicists argue that managers have a "taste for discrimination" directed toward black people which translates into a presumption of low human capital acquisition and relatively low marginal productivity; the dual labor market theorists contend that such a presumption is linked to socioeconomic class and behavioral traits which reflect minimal investments in human capital. The human capital theorists relate productivity directly to education, training, and other kinds of acquisitions, and since the evidence is that blacks, on average, have less of these than whites, the presumption is that blacks are generally less productive. Finally, the statistical discrimination theorists, relating nonwhite color to relatively low productivity, argue that the *blackness* of black employees serves as an inexpensive screening device for excluding presumably less productive employees.

These theories, which, incidentally, contribute to the conventional wisdom, inherently rest on a perceived black inferiority, whether based on innate, social, or environmental factors. From the standpoint of practice, it makes little difference that a white manager is under the influence of one or another of these theories, since, in

---

[6]Sowell, "Economics and Black People," p. 7.

[7]"Hiring decisions are often made on the basis of both objective criteria, such as education, and in interviews where more subtle criteria such as speech and deportment are applied. Even the managers find such standards difficult to specify, and their informality permits racial discrimination to be practiced." See Peter B. Doeringer and Michael J. Piore, *Internal Labor Markets and Manpower Analysis* (Lexington: D.C. Heath, 1971), p. 138.

any case, they all promote the broad presumption that blacks possess less human capital, on average, than whites.[8] In the corporate internal labor market, specifically, the evidence for this presumption is found in occupational exclusion and in differing rates of upward mobility for black and white employees. As will be seen in later chapters, the lower upward mobility rates for blacks are some function of discrimination in in-house training activities and a general resistance to providing black employees with those corporate experiences critical to assuming higher-level organizational responsibilities.

The tautalogical character of the human capital theory robs it of much of its viability and essential usefulness. For example, theorists might say that blacks are poor because of a relatively smaller investment in their human capital through inferior educational systems, substandard housing, minimally proper diets, poor health care delivery systems, low-level community development, and the value systems of a restrictive ghetto culture. These inadequacies and failures produce workers whose values in the productive process are relatively low. Thus, following the neoclassical notion of an equality between wage rates and the marginal product, black workers earn less than white workers since they produce less. And since they produce and earn relatively less, their command over society's goods and services remains limited, and their consignment to a ghetto environment ensured. Such reasoning is similar in structure to that which deduces that poor people are poor because they are poor! The cycle completes itself, and this concept of human capital spawns a profound sense of hopelessness for black people.[9]

While the human capital theory purports to describe and explain the supply of black labor—as well as the supply of white labor—the role of racism is, at best, underplayed. The implication, of course, is that labor flows are determined by an objective and impersonal market mechanism. But, considering custom, this simply is not so. Moreover, the theory is strained to explain the mechanics of the internal labor market and the virtual underemployment of the vast

---

[8]For a sample of the literature, see Gary S. Becker, The Economics of Discrimination, 2nd ed. (Chicago: University of Chicago Press, 1971); Kenneth J. Arrow, Some Models of Racial Discrimination in the Labor Market (Santa Monica: The Rand Corporation, Feb. 1971); Michael J. Piore, "Notes For a Theory of Labor Market Stratification" in Labor Market Segmentation, ed. Richard C. Edwards, Michael Reich, and David M. Gordon (Lexington: D.C. Heath, 1975); Finis Welch, "Human Capital Theory: Education, Discrimination, and Life Cycles," American Economic Review, 65 (May 1975), 63–73; Lester C. Thurow, Generating Inequality (New York: Basic Books, 1975); and Dennis J. Aigner and Glen G. Cain, "Statistical Theories of Discrimination in Labor Markets," Industrial and Labor Relations Review, 30 (Jan. 1977), 175–87.

[9]Interestingly, this human capital theory "cycle" is akin to the cycle often used to describe the workings of institutional racism. See Richard Perlman, The Economics of Poverty (New York: McGraw-Hill, 1976), pp. 68–70.

majority of well-credentialed and well-trained blacks in the corporate sector.

An important contribution to a general explanation of the unemployment and underemployment of blacks, which human capital theorists largely have ignored, is that of *statistical discrimination*.[10] This concept is an outgrowth of the dual labor market theory which segments the external labor market into primary and secondary sectors. The primary sector generates the demand for the "better" members of the labor force, and the secondary sector utilizes the "poorer" workers and assigns them the least attractive employment opportunities. Since these sectors are defined and described in terms of worker behavior, the introduction of racism to the dual market model consigns disproportionate numbers of black workers to secondary jobs on the basis of readily observable characteristics—e.g., race, dress, speech. The result is statistical discrimination.

Though black and white corporate workers, for the most part classified as white-collar, are considered primary sector workers, this sector can be viewed as being made up of two groups of employees. Earlier, we labeled these groups Category I and Category II. (Others have labeled these groups differently; see Chapter VIII.) In any case, the concept of statistical discrimination applies to black workers generally and its inclusion in an analysis of corporate internal labor markets is quite appropriate. However, the human capital theorists do not account sufficiently for this form of discrimination when in fact its role is of major importance in the allocation of labor and jobs in both the external and internal markets.

FACTORS INFLUENCING THE DEMAND FOR BLACK LABOR

Figure 6.1 is a generalized model of black-white employment dynamics based on the foregoing discussion.[11] Assuming that blacks and whites with minimal work experiences are hired into Category I or Category II jobs, the figure depicts the likely kinds of upward mobility paths descriptive of corporate career growth. Though the two categories are separated initially by qualification differentials, the model does show how employees may progress eventually from

---

[10]For a discussion of this concept, see Michael J. Piore, "The Dual Labor Market: Theory and Implications," in *Problems in Political Economy: An Urban Perspective*, 2nd ed., David M. Gordon (Lexington: D.C. Heath, 1977), p. 94; Aigner and Cain, "Statistical Theories," pp. 175–87; and Thurow, *Generating Inequality*, pp. 170–77.

[11]Doeringer and Piore have used similar diagrams to describe the flow of labor in internal labor markets. See Doeringer and Piore, *Internal Labor Markets*, pp. 140–45.

Figure 6.1 Relative Personnel Flow Tendencies

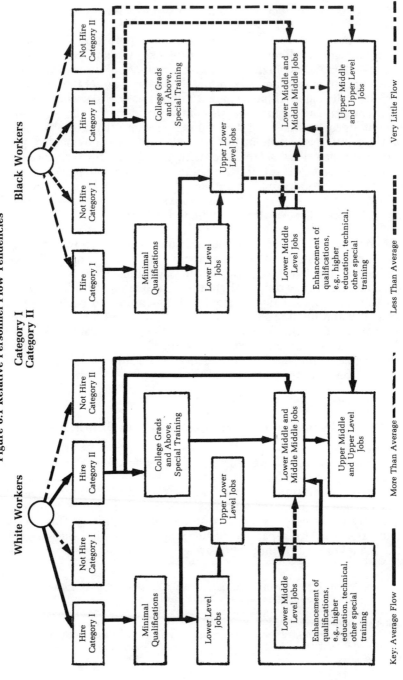

Category I
Category II

White Workers

Black Workers

Hire Category I · Not Hire Category I · Hire Category II · Not Hire Category II

Minimal Qualifications

Lower Level Jobs

College Grads and Above, Special Training

Upper Lower Level Jobs

Lower Middle Level Jobs

Enhancement of qualifications, e.g., higher education, technical, other special training

Lower Middle and Middle Middle Jobs

Upper Middle and Upper Level Jobs

Key: Average Flow ▬▬▬   More Than Average ▬ ▬ ▬   Less Than Average ▪▪▪▪   Very Little Flow ▪—▪—▪

Category I positions to Category II positions. Note that black employees have fewer opportunities for this kind of progress than white employees—even if qualifications are enhanced. Generally, the upward mobility of black employees, though less than that of white employees, compares favorably in the lower parts of the organization. However, significant differences in the flows of black and white employees are revealed as the paths of upward mobility reach middle-level jobs. Even for black employees in Category II, flow patterns become relatively differentiated as job levels rise.

Specification of model parameters with respect to the flow of black labor into and within the corporate sector tends to be some function of black labor as a percentage of the total labor force in an employment area, modified to reflect relative education and training levels, age, and other factors. Further specification requires a broad categorization of corporate organizations by the character of resource utilization, the nature of labor costs, and the rates of profit, as shown in Figure 6.2. These factors relate to the distributions of relatively low-paying clerical jobs requiring minimal skills versus relatively high-paying, technically oriented and professional positions typically requiring considerably more education, training, and skills. Thus, it may be hypothesized that the degree to which a corporate organization depends heavily on labor input, and the character of that input, will determine the extent of black representation in its work force.

Figure 6.2 Key Economic Factors Influencing the Flow of Black Labor— The Corporate Sector

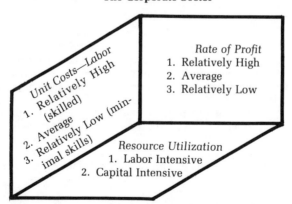

Corporate offices which are relatively large in terms of numbers of employees (labor intensive) may tend to have higher percentages of black employees than organizations which have relatively smaller work forces and which may or may not tend to be capital intensive. This situation is affected by the general character of skills required by organizations. For example, in a labor intensive organization where the average skill level is relatively high (and unit costs for labor are relatively high), blacks will tend to be poorly represented in the work force. On the other hand, given a similar corporate organization wherein the preponderant labor activity is clerical in nature (and unit costs for labor are relatively low), blacks will likely be better represented. (See Table 6.1.) Undergirding these two influences is the rate of profit, which appears to guide management behavior and determines, in large measure, the degree of black representation in work forces.

In the final analysis, however, the corporate demand for black workers will be largely determined by factors internal and external to the firm. Table 6.1 lists three additional and important factors: 1) labor market; 2) potential market growth; and 3) organization size. It summarizes likely outcomes with respect to the hiring and upward mobility dynamics confronting Categories I and II black employees. What the table does not attempt to do at this juncture is consider the combined impact of the six factors on the black employment picture.[12]

Though something less than a solid empirical base is offered in direct support of Table 6.1, other researchers have pursued the relationship of black employment to factors listed in the table. Not surprisingly, our studies of corporate employee mobility are consistent with many of their conclusions. For example, as early as 1964, Dale L. Hiestand observed that the patterns of black employment in occupations and/or industries were some function of the rate at which occupations/industries grew:

> When a field is new, it is likely to grow quite rapidly. During its initial period it is likely that very few or no Negroes will be employed in it. As it grows, some Negroes will be employed. As its growth rate slows down, more and more Negroes will be employed. Because of the original very small number of Negroes, these additions may represent a very high growth rate for the group, but compared to the total field and its net growth the number of Negroes employed continues to be almost insignificant. . . . Later, when the field is growing relatively slowly, the employment of Negroes may still increase fairly rapidly, and they come to represent a larger and larger share of the net growth.[13]

---

[12]An important exogenous impact not included in Table 6.1 is that of government regulations, especially affirmative action and equal employment opportunity laws. An assumption is that these fall equally upon all employers and need not be explicitly dealt with here.

[13]Dale L. Hiestand, *Economic Growth and Employment Opportunities for Minorities* (New York: Columbia University Press, 1964), p. 76.

Table 6.1 Some Factors Affecting the Demand for Black Labor in Corporate Organizations

Factor	Corporate Characteristic	Hiring Tendencies	Upward Mobility Tendencies
(1) Production Inputs	Labor Intensive	Organization needs many workers; normally this tends to include Categories I and II black workers.	Category I black employees may achieve first-line supervisory positions but rarely go much higher. Category II black employees achieve middle management positions and occasionally upper-level positions in primarily staff functions.
	Capital Intensive	Organization utilizes few Category I or Category II black workers depending on type of labor skills required.	Not much upward mobility.
(2) Labor Costs (Unit)	High Costs	Relatively high cost organization implies highly skilled, technical, and professional work force. Category I and Category II black workers are relatively few.	Category II blacks experience little upward progress, and then, in personnel, special marketing, public relations, etc.
	Low Costs	Relatively low cost organization implies preponderance of lesser-skilled workers in the work force, e.g., clerical. Organization hires many Category I black workers.	Category II black employees make progress into middle management levels faster here as supervisors of areas with high proportions of Category I black employees. Even Category I black employees achieve first line supervisory positions.

107

Table 6.1 Some Factors Affecting the Demand for Black Labor in Corporate Organizations (continued)

Factor	Corporate Characteristic	Hiring Tendencies	Upward Mobility Tendencies
(3) Profit Rate (Relates strongly to 1 and 2)	Relatively High	Inclusion of blacks in the workforce, say racists, tends to lower profits since they are relatively unproductive. On the other side is the attractiveness of cheap labor (Category I black workers) in low-cost labor intensive organizations.	Upward mobility rates for Category II black employees are low and practically non-existent for Category I black employees beyond the limits imposed on that group.
	Relatively Low	If low-cost and labor intensive, organization hires Category I and Category II blacks for lower-level jobs. If high cost and labor intensive, presumption of relatively low productivity tends to be strong. Few black workers hired.	If large numbers of Category I blacks are hired, the upward mobility rates will be relatively high for lower-level jobs.
(4) Labor Market	Relatively Large Black Representation	Tend to hire large numbers of Category I black workers, and available Category II black workers.	Upward mobility rates for Category II black employees not as high as might be assumed. Category I black employees move upward toward the limits imposed on that group.
	Relatively Small Black Representation	Mostly Category I black workers are hired.	Token upward movement for Category II black employees characterizes this type of labor market. Limited upward mobility for Category I black employees up to limits imposed on that group.

(5) Potential Market Growth	Matured Industry	Often characterized by marginal profits and minimal growth potential. Category I black workers tend to be numerous. Available Category II workers are hired.	Whether cost is high or low determines rate of upward mobility.
	Infant or Developing Industry	Often characterized by high profit rates and high growth potential. Tend to hire fewer blacks (relatively) than matured industry.	New opportunities and potential high growth rate do not work in favor of upward mobility for Category I or Category II black employees, as might be expected.
(6) Organization Size	Relatively Large	The larger the organization, the more *likely* it is to hire Categories I and II black employees.	Whether upward mobility for black employees takes place and at what rates depends on other factors, especially nos. 1, 2, and 3.
	Relatively Small	The smaller the organization, the *less likely* it is to hire especially Category II black employees.	Neither Category I nor Category II black employees experience significant upward mobility rates.

More recently, in terms of employment discrimination within industry groups, Lloyd Hogan and Harry Harris found that of fifty-two such groups, black employees tended to be significantly over-represented in seventeen of those groups which contain many lower-level and low-paying jobs traditionally held by blacks and severely underrepresented in twenty-seven groups which tend to be relatively more capital intensive and which employ relatively more high cost labor.[14] In another study, William S. Comanor computed coefficients of employment discrimination and estimated their relationship to industry profit rates and firm size. The study concluded that employment discrimination is: 1) greater for skilled blacks than for unskilled blacks; 2) heightened when profit rates increase; 3) affected by firm size, the particular industry, and location.[15]

When the existence of employment discrimination is theoretically modeled, evidence of the impact of factors shown in Table 6.1 remains. In one such model, David H. Swinton demonstrates that "black workers will not generally be able to find employment in high-wage firms in proportion to their numbers in the population with 'qualifications'." Conversely, black workers "will be concentrated in low-wage firms . . . [which] . . . have no choice but to hire . . . [black] . . . workers, since they cannot compete with the high-wage firms for the scarce . . . [white] . . . workers."[16] In another model, Duran Bell also finds a relationship between employment discrimination and firm size and cost structure.[17]

These findings have profound implications for the operation of the corporate internal labor market, which mirrors the factors influencing the demand for workers and translates the various impacts into job assignments, promotions, salaries, and training and career opportunities. While schools of economic thought may have constructed explanations for occupational and salary differences between black and white workers, the thesis here is that these differences, and the black-white differences in the rates of upward mobility, are functions of *perceived* low black productivity rooted in the white superiority–black inferiority mentality and functions of a *real* low black productivity resulting from insufficient in-house training and job experiences doubtless growing out of an institutional racism.

[14]Lloyd Hogan and Harry Harris, "The Occupational-Industrial Structure of Black Employment in the United States," *The Review of Black Political Economy*, 6 (Fall 1975), 14–26.

[15]William S. Comanor, "Racial Discrimination in American Industry," *Economica*, 40 (Nov. 1973), 363–78.

[16]David H. Swinton, "A Labor Force Competition Model of Racial Discrimination in the Labor Market," *The Review of Black Political Economy*, 9 (Fall 1978), pp. 36–37.

[17]Duran Bell, "Occupational Discrimination as a Source of Income Differences: Lessons of the 1960's," *American Economic Review*, 62 (May 1972), 363–72.

An appropriate postulate, then, is that white corporate managers associate relatively low productivity with black workers, and this association is at the center of the discrimination process and its impact on job assignments and upward mobility. Interestingly enough, this association is broadened in the minds of white managers as wage rates rise. That is, the higher the job level and its wage rate, the more pronounced the perceived gap between white and black productivity.

Figure 6.3 Hypothetical Perception of the Relationship Between Wages and Productivity for White and Black Workers

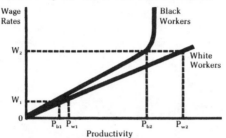

Figure 6.3 shows a hypothetical perception by white corporate managers of the relationship between wages and productivity for white and black workers. At low wage rates (W_1), perceived black productivity (P_{b1}) is less than that of white workers (P_{w1}) but not significantly so. Thus, when the demand for labor is high in a labor intensive and low unit cost organization, Category I black workers will be used to satisfy the demand. This is especially true when the supply of white workers for the lowest-level and lowest-paying jobs in the organization is inadequate. At higher wage rates, e.g., (W_2), the perceptions of white corporate managers are that the differences in productivity between white and black workers are relatively great, i.e., ($P_{w2} - P_{b2}$). Hence, relatively few blacks ascend to the higher wage levels. As was noted earlier, when Category II black workers are paid (W_2) wages, they are more often than not assigned to staff jobs away from profit centers.[18]

Beyond (W_2), as the hypothetical function for black workers bends upward, the productivity gap between white and black workers widens at an increasing rate and identifies those job levels and wages which white corporate managers perceive blacks as never being fit to command.

It appears, then, that labor intensive corporate organizations which benefit from low unit costs for labor tend to exhibit a greater

---

[18]Survey results would tend to support this conclusion. See John W. Work, "Management Blacks and the Internal Labor Market: Responses to a Questionnaire," *Human Resource Management* (Fall 1980), pp. 27–31.

demand for black labor—especially Category I workers—than corporate organizations with different production functions. While racism portrays blacks as relatively unproductive, corporate organizations tend to select Category I blacks for their lowest-level and lowest-paying jobs, which are in abundance in labor intensive, low unit cost firms. These employment decisions stem from the following motivations, among others: 1) a reduced willingness on the part of white workers to accept certain low-level and low-paying jobs; 2) proportionate increases in the black labor forces in major cities; 3) government affirmative action requirements; 4) *real* black productivity—in contrast to *perceived* productivity—which contributes to corporate profitability when blacks are underemployed and their productivity is higher than the wages paid; and 5) the corporate observation that total exclusion of blacks is no longer in vogue.

THE QUALIFICATIONS CONCEPT

The concept of qualifications may be divided into three essential parts: 1) Basic—education, training, experience, performance evaluation, and tests; 2) Secondary—references and internal and external corporate relationships; and 3) Superficial—mode of dress, speech pattern, personality, overall appearance, and the like. The Basic qualifications tend to be *objectively* determined, the criticism of tests and testing procedures notwithstanding. The Superficial qualifications tend to be *subjectively* determined within some context of societal, institutional, and individual values. The Secondary qualifications are primarily *political* in nature and are determined on the basis of a particular relationship or set of relationships. While these kinds of qualifications may be determined in the manner suggested, they may be subjectively evaluated by an employer in a manner which tends to discriminate.

Consider two candidates who are vying for an available middle-management position. Objectively, an employer can determine that each candidate, for example, has a four-year liberal arts degree and similar previous experiences in terms of specific job assignments and activities. In order to reach a decision, the employer likely will bring personal value judgements to bear on the qualitative aspects of the candidates' credentials which, in fact, may have little to do with predicting on-the-job performance and future success.[19]

---

[19]This observation has been made by others. For example: "The criteria upon which hiring decisions are based are surrogates for . . . [on-the-job] . . . performance, and there is little evidence of a causal relationship between the two. . . . Instead, the

Whether an individual is being hired or being considered for promotional opportunities, his or her candidacy will be filtered through the three qualification sectors. Clearly, an individual being hired generally will be subject to a different emphasis in the evaluation of qualifications process than the already hired employee seeking advancement and promotional opportunities. The latter has added, by his or her presence in an organization, to the broad base on which some qualifications are evaluated. This seems to be especially true for Superficial qualifications, but it is also true for such things as performance evaluation and corporate relationships.

As was stated earlier, the qualifications of black employees—and those seeking employment in the corporate sector—are more often than not "discounted" to some degree by corporate employers. And, of course, the discount factor reveals its widest range when applied to the Superficial qualifications and its narrowest range when applied to Basic qualifications.

More specifically, a young black person seeking employment and an upward career path, with a seemingly appropriate degree and other necessary credentials from a black college, is likely to generate less interest in his or her candidacy for the entry-level positions than that generated by young whites with similar backgrounds. This appears to be the case especially for those jobs under the broad rubric of "management trainee." While there are exceptions, many blacks hired as management trainees are that in title only. On the other hand, blacks with specific technical skills (e.g., engineers, computer programmers, and undergraduate accountants) will find the employment door more widely open. The fact is that white managers—dare I say most white people—view black colleges as generally inferior to white colleges. It is a small step to conclude that black college graduates are generally inferior to white college graduates. Thus, some discount factor is applied to the Basic qualifications of many Category II employees.

A probable scenario for a black graduate of a white college rests on an evaluation of his or her transcript and, perhaps, faculty references. If a transcript reflects below average performance, for example, then the inferiority of the black graduate is conveniently viewed as having been established by objective criteria outside the employer's purview. Such a job seeker, if employed, will likely command neither a favored position nor a handsome salary offer. On the other hand, if the transcript reflects well above average performance, the white manager's inclination may be to review the courses under-

---

screening criteria (like hiring standards) are based upon the subjective judgements of line supervision and personnel managers whose perceptions may be distorted by prejudice." Doeringer and Piore, *Internal Labor Markets*, p. 139.

taken. Often times, the ploy is to denigrate specific courses and their content, thereby lessening the candidate's claim to superior academic performance.[20] Here again is an example of the discount phenomenon.

It should be noted that the easiest hiring and/or upward mobility decisions are made when a manager views a candidate, either a new applicant or an employee seeking promotion and advancement, as meeting qualifications in all of the three areas mentioned above. More often than not, black candidates, by dint of racism and corporate exclusion heretofore, rarely meet Secondary qualifications—i.e., relationships with those in centers of power and influence or those who comprise important communication and in-house political networks. Of course, one might counter that many whites being employed and promoted in corporate offices also do not meet the politically characterized Secondary qualifications. On the contrary. Their mutually recognized "whiteness" and their relationship through cultural values are intrinsically valuable to the overall employment process even in the absence of important cultivated relationships. As a matter of fact, the former can give rise to the latter. For blacks, race obviates the former and racism significantly reduces opportunity for the latter.

For black and white employees seeking upward mobility opportunities, Superficial qualifications may be as important as Basic and Secondary qualifications. One reason is that this part of the qualifications matrix allows a quick and easy *subjective* evaluation of on-the-job performance. A truly sound and reasonably *objective* performance evaluation technique is not only difficult to find but its administration is often complex and time-consuming. Thus, many managers and corporations, while experimenting from time to time with supposedly objective and validated performance evaluation models, end up using the tried and true personal assessment method. A second reason is that Superficial qualifications possessed by employees reflect the degree to which their value systems coincide with those of managers in the corporation. What better mechanism than a protective manager's personal assessment? A final reason probably relates to a manager's ego needs with respect to those employees seeking advancement. Many managers take great pride— in some instances, rightfully so—in pointing to a former subordinate, generally recognized as a valued member of the corporate team, as an individual whom "I trained and developed." Needless to say, an element of control is also introduced since an employee knows that the position is owed, in some sense, to the manager.

---

[20]Additionally, I have known managers to presume that white professors, under the duress of affirmative action, have awarded higher grades than deserved in order to facilitate the achievement of a requisite grade point average, and to avoid anticipated confrontation.

Racism's infamous dimension of paternalism notwithstanding, most black applicants and employees in the corporate arena simply cannot meet subjective qualifications with sufficient success to ensure career advancement at rates similar to white employees with equivalent Basic qualifications. First, there are cultural differences which managers often view as signs of racial inferiority. Second, white managers often labor under preconceived notions about the work habits and attitudes of black employees. The extent to which these views are held determines the extent to which the performance of blacks, as well as other presumedly important qualifications, is subject to a discount factor.

In a speech at a Work In America Institute Conference in 1977, the Institute president, Jerome M. Rosow, had occasion to describe the positive and negative forms of individual behavior at the work place:

Positive factors:

— Motivation to work at optimum levels
— Involvement and commitment to the product or service
— Optimum output in quantity and quality of product
— Interests and work goals which are linked to the goals of the organization
— Healthy competitiveness to succeed and achieve on the job
— Interpersonal and group or team efforts which support cooperative achievement and reinforcement of combined efforts
— An achievement–reward–performance loop
— Creativity, initiative, innovation, willingness to change, and the use of personal talent to make new ideas work
— Loyalty, honesty and integrity, personal standards which are a credit to the organization

Negative factors:

— Absenteeism disruptive of work scheduling and output
— Turnover, with replacement and training costs
— Grievances, with stress, anxiety and interpersonal friction
— Defiance of rules, policies or authority
— Militant union activity with slowdowns, stoppages or extended strikes
— Sabotage of equipment, materials or product
— Theft or dishonesty in dealings with fellow workers or customers
— Accidents and work related injuries
— Wastage of materials, supplies, equipment, space or energy

— Interpersonal conflict with coworkers or supervisors
— Poor quality of work
— Noninvolvement or subtle withdrawal from the goals of the organization
— Malingering or killing time on the job
— Hostility or disinterest in the goals of the organization[21]

While the descriptions, as presented, are generally applicable to any and all workers, it is clear that the task of white job seekers and employees is to prove by some means, including demonstration, that their behavior will (and does) exemplify the desired positive behavior traits. Black job seekers and employees in the corporate sector, on the other hand, have exactly the opposite task: namely, to prove that their behavior will not (and does not) mirror the undesired negative behavior traits. For black employees, this sometimes can be a more difficult undertaking than it appears to be on the surface. One important reason is that racism shapes the expectations of white managers with respect to black performance and behavior, and these expectations are often negative. Such burdens, when the negative expectations are particularly strong, are onerous for black employees. Their attempts to perform in a manner which vitiates such expectations and at the same time merits upward mobility may develop into feelings of frustration, bitterness, and, perhaps, defeat. This state, indeed, can affect one's work; finally, the negative expectations may be realized.

SUMMARY

The perceived productivity of black employees by white managers is purportedly explained by human capital theory and manifested in the internal labor market demand for black employees. The result is that black corporate employees experience rates of occupational and upward mobility that are significantly lower than those experienced by white employees. However, the breadth of this discrimination, the roles of custom and tradition in the internal labor market, and the persistence of a white superiority–black inferiority mentality supported by institutional racism point less to legitimate issues of productivity and more to issues of employment racism. Specifically, by reason of race and cultural differences, the qualifications discount phenomenon, and economic factors related to the

---

[21]Jerome M. Rosow, "Quality of Working Life and Productivity," an address delivered at a Work In America Institute Conference, Chicago, April 28, 1977; reprinted in *Vital Speeches of the Day*, 43 (June 1, 1977), 496.

demand for black labor, black corporate employees find themselves relegated to lower-level jobs requiring the least skills (Category I), middle-level and upper middle-level jobs peripheral to the major corporate activities (Category II), and relatively low upward mobility rates constrained by the boundaries of the caste and the limits imposed by the artificial ceiling, respectively.

PART 2
Empirical Investigation

VII

The Corporate Organization:
An Empirical Description

INTRODUCTION

PART 1 DESCRIBED the effects of the corporate internal labor market on Category I and Category II employees in terms of an historical racism. In addition, current economic theories of discrimination were examined for their relevance to the observed wage and income differences between white and black corporate employees, and the observed differences in rates of upward mobility for the two groups.

Part 2 examines the internal labor market of a major U.S. corporate bureaucracy in terms of the hypotheses and conclusions presented in Part 1. A basic profile of white-collar employees in this corporation has been made available for use in this volume with the assurance of anonymity. Though the data base lacks information regarding occupational categories, it describes the work force in terms of salary, salary grade in the organization, race, sex, length of service, and educational attainments.

There are three general reasons for using this data base with confidence. First, this data base is descriptive of a Fortune 500 headquarters white-collar facility. It is a major firm in its industry, has a recognized equal employment opportunity and affirmative action program, and is engaged in extensive corporate social responsibility efforts.

Second, in analyzing corporate internal labor markets, the need to actually look inside these giants is paramount. While inside data are sometimes difficult to obtain, not to mention the fact that examining a single firm has its methodological risks, such efforts remain worthwhile when compared with the alternatives.

Finally, when a single corporation is studied, the term "case study" is often applied. But the term is narrow and frequently implies the study of organizational characteristics that are unique to the case. But employment discrimination based on race is practiced extensively throughout corporate America. From the standpoint of internal labor market analysis, our studies reveal such discrimination to be reasonably consistent with respect to upward mobility even when considering the demand factors in Table 6.1. Therefore, the concept of case study is not utilized; rather, the results are viewed as generalizable. Only if the results fail to conform to the important social and economic realities should we dismiss the single corporation data base as inappropriate for establishing generalizations.

Some important facts about the data and the structure of the corporation: first, the data identify only *white* male and female employees and *nonwhite* male and female employees. Since the proportions of black and other minority employees are unknown within the nonwhite category, the analyses assume that the majority of such employees are black in the interest of the study's objectives and interpret that category as representing black employees. Second, the corporation's employees are organized by salary grades 1 through 10, with 10 being the highest salary grade and 1 the lowest. However, the data made available for this study were collapsed into five salary grade groupings, viz., 1–2, 3–4, 5–6, 7–8, and 9–10. The corporation's senior management and officer group, which comprises less than 3 percent of the total number of employees, is outside the graded structure, and data on this group were not provided. There were in 1978, however, eighty-one individuals in this top group of whom five were minority and twelve were female. Third, these employee data are for a corporate headquarters office site which is comprised of 2,721 white-collar, nonunion, salaried, and graded employees. Furthermore, these corporate employee data are for the year 1978, i.e., as of December 31, 1978. The Appendix contains data on each of the individual employees.

WORK FORCE DATA

Table 7.1 describes the distribution of the corporation's work force by race and sex. Of the total number of 2,721 graded employees, more than 76 percent are white, while the nonwhite proportion is 23.6 percent. It is interesting to note that in terms of the total work force, the number of nonwhite females is substantially larger than

Table 7.1 Total Corporate Work Force by Race and Sex—1978

Race/Sex	Numbers of Employees	Percent of Total
White Males	1231	45.2
White Females	847	31.1
Nonwhite Males	234	8.6
Nonwhite Females	409	15.0
TOTAL	2721	100.0

the number of nonwhite males; on the other hand, white males are significantly greater in number than white females. These differences may reflect occupational discrimination experienced by nonwhite males; occupational preference expressed for nonwhite females for lower-paying positions; somewhat less occupational discrimination against but substantial occupational preference for white females; and organizational domination by white males.

Table 7.2 shows the organization's total work force by salary grade groups. Clearly, the largest percentage of employees is found in the middle grade group.

Table 7.2 Total Work Force by Salary Grade Groups—1978

Salary Grades	Numbers of Employees	Percent of Total
1–2	244	9.0
3–4	694	25.5
5–6	871	32.0
7–8	569	20.9
9–10	343	12.6
TOTAL	2721	100.0

Table 7.3 reveals the distribution of employees by race, sex, and salary grade. This distribution is highlighted by the dominance of nonwhite females in the lowest salary grade groups, 1–2. In the two top grade groups, viz., grade groups 7–8 and 9–10, white males dominate. White females, while most numerous in the middle grade groups, represent the largest proportion of the work force in the grade group 3–4.

What is clear from Table 7.3 is that white males, as a percentage of each successively higher grade group, are an increasing percentage of the work force. Nonwhite males and females are a decreasing percentage from the lowest to the highest grade group. White females

Table 7.3 Total Work Force by Race/Sex and Salary Grade Groups—1978

| | Salary Grades | | | | | | | | | | |
| Race/Sex | 1–2 | | 3–4 | | 5–6 | | 7–8 | | 9–10 | | |
	Actual	Percent	Actual	Percent	Actual	Percent	Actual	Percent	Actual	Percent	TOTALS
White Males	21	8.6	107	15.4	378	43.4	420	73.8	305	88.9	1231
White Females	85	34.8	268	38.6	352	40.4	113	19.9	29	8.5	847
Nonwhite Males	37	15.2	82	11.8	85	9.8	24	4.2	6	1.8	234
Nonwhite Females	101	41.4	237	34.2	56	6.4	12	2.1	3	0.9	409
TOTALS	244	100.0	694	100.0	871	100.0	569	100.0	343	100.0	2721

Table 7.4 Length of Service—1978

| | Employee Groups by Race and Sex | | | | | | | | |
| Years of Service | White Males | | White Females | | Nonwhite Males | | Nonwhite Females | | TOTALS |
	#	%	#	%	#	%	#	%	
Less than 2 yrs.	122	27.2	169	37.7	68	15.2	89	19.9	448
2–4 yrs.	196	33.9	161	27.9	74	12.8	147	25.4	578
5–9 yrs.	246	37.3	194	29.4	69	10.5	151	22.8	660
10–14 yrs.	172	60.8	85	30.0	14	5.0	12	4.2	283
15–19 yrs.	184	70.8	67	25.8	5	1.9	4	1.5	260
More than 19 yrs.	311	63.2	171	34.8	4	0.8	6	1.2	492
TOTALS	1231		847		234		409		2721

would appear to fare a bit better than nonwhites through salary grade group 5–6 but show significant decreases in the upper grades.

WORK FORCE AND LENGTH OF SERVICE

Dividing length of service into six categories, Table 7.4 shows the distribution of employees by race, sex, and number of years in the company. Reading down the percent columns reveals a pattern of increasing white male representation relative to years of service. For white females, the pattern of percentage distribution seems to display an element of stability. For both nonwhite males and females, the proportions of representation decline markedly from the "Less than 2 yrs." category to the "More than 19 yrs." category.

Tables 7.5, 7.6, 7.7, and 7.8 reveal a relationship between length of service and salary grades for white males, white females, nonwhite males, and nonwhite females, respectively. Neither the white males nor the nonwhite males appear to stay in the lowest salary grade category beyond the "5–9 years" category. Females, on the other hand, show a somewhat different pattern—especially nonwhite females. As percentages of the total numbers of nonwhite females in the three longest service categories (see Table 7.8), nonwhite females in salary grades 1–2 are significantly represented. On the other hand, the numbers of white males as percentages of the total numbers of white males by salary grades and length of service show a domination of the higher salary grades as length of service increases.

LENGTH OF SERVICE AND EDUCATIONAL LEVEL BY RACE, SEX, AND SALARY GRADE

Before examining the upcoming tables which display length of service, salary grade, and levels of education for the corporate work force, it would not be unreasonable to presume, for example, that employees with the least amount of education would tend to be in the lower salary grades of the organization and that employees with the highest educational accomplishments would tend to be in the upper salary grades. Such a presumption ought to be tempered by a recognition of the leveling effect of length of service as a great teacher and trainer. Thus, it might be expected to find relatively few employees with long service in the lower grades, and more employees with long service in the upper salary grades.

Table 7.5 Length of Service and Salary Grades—1978

White Males	Salary Grades										
	1–2		3–4		5–6		7–8		9–10		
	Actual	Percent	Actual	Percent	Actual	Percent	Actual	Percent	Actual	Percent	TOTALS
Less than 2 yrs	13	10.7	24	19.7	42	34.4	24	19.7	19	15.6	122
2–4 yrs.	5	2.6	39	19.9	87	44.4	44	22.5	21	10.7	196
5–9 yrs.	3	1.2	10	4.1	99	40.2	77	31.3	57	23.2	246
10–14 yrs.	–	–	10	5.8	47	27.3	79	45.9	36	20.9	172
15–19 yrs.	–	–	8	4.4	45	24.5	68	37.0	63	34.2	184
More than 19 yrs.	–	–	16	5.2	58	18.7	128	41.2	109	35.1	311
TOTALS	21		107		378		420		305		1231

Table 7.6 Length of Service and Salary Grades—1978

White Females	Salary Grades										
	1–2		3–4		5–6		7–8		9–10		
	Actual	Percent	Actual	Percent	Actual	Percent	Actual	Percent	Actual	Percent	TOTALS
Less than 2 yrs.	44	26.0	69	40.8	37	21.9	15	8.9	4	2.4	169
2–4 yrs.	20	12.4	79	49.1	47	29.2	13	8.1	2	1.2	161
5–9 yrs.	14	7.2	70	36.1	81	41.8	24	12.4	5	2.6	194
10–14 yrs.	4	4.7	18	21.2	45	52.9	14	16.5	4	4.7	85
15–19 yrs.	2	3.0	11	16.4	38	56.7	12	17.9	4	6.0	67
More than 19 yrs.	1	0.6	21	12.3	104	60.8	35	20.5	10	5.9	171
TOTALS	85		268		352		113		29		847

Table 7.7 Length of Service and Salary Grades—1978

Nonwhite Males	Salary Grades										
	1–2		3–4		5–6		7–8		9–10		TOTALS
	Actual	Percent	Actual	Percent	Actual	Percent	Actual	Percent	Actual	Percent	
Less than 2 yrs.	28	41.2	17	25.0	16	23.5	6	8.8	1	1.5	68
2–4 yrs.	8	10.8	39	52.7	21	28.4	4	5.4	2	2.7	74
5–9 yrs.	1	1.5	24	34.8	34	49.3	9	13.0	1	1.5	69
10–14 yrs.	—	—	1	7.1	8	57.1	3	21.4	2	14.3	14
15–19 yrs.	—	—	1	20.0	2	40.0	2	40.0	—	—	5
More than 19 yrs.	—	—	—	—	4	100.0	—	—	—	—	4
TOTALS	37		82		85		24		6		234

Table 7.8 Length of Service and Salary Grades—1978

Nonwhite Females	Salary Grades										
	1–2		3–4		5–6		7–8		9–10		TOTALS
	Actual	Percent	Actual	Percent	Actual	Percent	Actual	Percent	Actual	Percent	
Less than 2 yrs.	49	55.1	29	32.6	8	9.0	2	2.3	1	1.1	89
2–4 yrs.	38	25.9	97	66.0	9	6.1	2	1.4	1	0.7	147
5–9 yrs.	10	6.6	103	68.2	33	21.9	4	2.7	1	0.7	151
10–14 yrs.	2	16.7	5	41.7	4	33.3	1	8.3	—	—	12
15–19 yrs.	1	25.0	1	25.0	1	25.0	1	25.0	—	—	4
More than 19 yrs.	1	16.7	2	33.3	1	16.7	2	33.3	—	—	6
TOTALS	101		237		56		12		3		409

Clearly, when race and sex are introduced, expectations can and will differ. Broad-based discrimination against blacks, other minorities, and women is very much in evidence. There are significant differences, however, in the relative educational achievements of various minority and female groups in a given corporate work force and in the relative experiences, exposures, opportunities, and organizational intentions embodied in the length of service teachings. Therefore, the probability is low that white males, nonwhite males, white females, and nonwhite females would be similarly distributed by "salary grade" category and "length of service" category.

White Males

Tables 7.9, 7.10, 7.11, 7.12, and 7.13 describe the absolute and percentage distribution of white males in the five salary grade categories in terms of length of service and educational levels attained. For example, from Table 7.9, of the twenty-one white male employees in salary grades 1–2, eighteen are high school graduates, and one has had college experience but earned no degree.

Reviewing the five tables in this section, the following observations can be made:

(a) In salary grades 1–2, white males do not constitute an important share of the employee population.

(b) High school graduates in the total white male employee group are better represented in salary grades 5–6 than in lower grades, as might have been expected.

(c) Without regard to educational status, increasing white male representation in the upper salary grade categories (see Tables 7.12 and 7.13) would appear to be highly correlated with increasing years of service. When college graduates are considered, the apparent correlation with years of service remains high.

(d) In salary grade categories 1–2 and 3–4, no white male employees are college graduates; conversely, in salary grade categories 7–8 and 9–10, the number of high school graduates is relatively significant, and these numbers tend to rise with increases in years of service.

(e) In terms of numbers, white males clearly dominate the top salary category.

Table 7.9 Length of Service and Educational Levels, White Males—1978

Salary Grades 1–2
Number of Employees

Length of Service	High School		Training or Spec. Educ.		College But No Degree		College Graduate		Beyond College		TOTALS
	#	%	#	%	#	%	#	%	#	%	
Less than 2 yrs.	12	92.3	1	7.7	—	—	—	—	—	—	13
2–4 yrs.	4	80.0	—	—	1	20.0	—	—	—	—	5
5–9 yrs.	2	66.7	1	33.3	—	—	—	—	—	—	3
10–14 yrs.	—	—	—	—	—	—	—	—	—	—	—
15–19 yrs.	—	—	—	—	—	—	—	—	—	—	—
More than 19 yrs.	—	—	—	—	—	—	—	—	—	—	—
TOTALS	18		2		1						21

Table 7.10 Length of Service and Educational Levels, White Males—1978

Salary Grades 3–4
Number of Employees

Length of Service	High School		Training or Spec. Educ.		College But No Degree		College Graduate		Beyond College		TOTALS
	#	%	#	%	#	%	#	%	#	%	
Less than 2 yrs.	18	75.0	4	16.7	2	8.3	—	—	—	—	24
2–4 yrs.	27	69.2	6	15.4	6	15.4	—	—	—	—	39
5–9 yrs.	7	70.0	2	20.0	1	10.0	—	—	—	—	10
10–14 yrs.	7	70.0	2	20.0	1	10.0	—	—	—	—	10
15–19 yrs.	5	62.5	1	12.5	2	25.0	—	—	—	—	8
More than 19 yrs.	11	68.8	3	18.7	2	12.5	—	—	—	—	16
TOTALS	75		18		14						107

Table 7.11 Length of Service and Educational Levels, White Males—1978

Salary Grades 5–6
Number of Employees

Length of Service	High School		Training or Spec. Educ.		College But No Degree		College Graduate		Beyond College		TOTALS
	#	%	#	%	#	%	#	%	#	%	
Less than 2 yrs.	7	16.7	5	11.9	5	11.9	20	47.6	5	11.9	42
2–4 yrs.	26	29.9	9	10.3	18	20.7	31	35.6	3	3.5	87
5–9 yrs.	22	22.2	12	12.1	24	24.2	37	37.4	4	4.0	99
10–14 yrs.	13	27.7	5	10.6	15	31.9	14	29.8	–	–	47
15–19 yrs.	15	33.3	6	13.3	15	33.3	9	20.0	–	–	45
More than 19 yrs.	26	44.8	5	8.6	23	39.7	4	6.9	–	–	58
TOTALS	109		42		100		115		12		378

Table 7.12 Length of Service and Educational Levels, White Males—1978

Salary Grades 7–8
Number of Employees

Length of Service	High School		Training or Spec. Educ.		College But No Degree		College Graduate		Beyond College		TOTALS
	#	%	#	%	#	%	#	%	#	%	
Less than 2 yrs.	–	–	–	–	3	12.5	11	45.8	10	41.7	24
2–4 yrs.	2	4.5	2	4.5	6	13.6	26	59.1	8	18.2	44
5–9 yrs.	8	10.4	8	10.4	14	18.2	40	52.0	7	9.0	77
10–14 yrs.	15	19.0	7	8.9	20	25.3	31	39.2	6	7.6	79
15–19 yrs.	16	23.5	7	10.3	8	11.8	32	47.1	5	7.3	68
More than 19 yrs.	39	30.5	16	12.5	26	20.3	44	34.4	3	2.3	128
TOTALS	80		40		77		184		39		420

Table 7.13 Length of Service and Educational Levels, White Males—1978

Salary Grades 9–10
Number of Employees

Length of Service	High School		Training or Spec. Educ.		College But No Degree		College Graduate		Beyond College		TOTALS
	#	%	#	%	#	%	#	%	#	%	
Less than 2 yrs.	–	–	1	5.3	–	–	15	78.9	3	15.8	19
2– 4 yrs.	2	9.5	2	9.5	–	–	15	71.4	2	9.5	21
5–9 yrs.	5	8.8	3	5.3	–	–	39	68.4	10	17.5	57
10–14 yrs.	2	5.6	3	8.3	1	2.8	26	72.2	4	11.1	36
15–19 yrs.	6	9.5	4	6.4	4	6.4	43	68.2	6	9.5	63
More than 19 yrs.	14	12.8	9	8.3	10	9.2	71	65.1	5	4.6	109
TOTALS	29		22		15		209		30		305

White Females

The positioning of white females in the organization is shown in Tables 7.14, 7.15, 7.16, 7.17, and 7.18. Contrasting patterns begin to emerge when these tables are examined.

(a) The representation of white females in salary grades 1–6 is substantial; however, high school graduates with varying length of service are most numerous in salary grades 1–2 and 3–4.

(b) As years of service increase, the numbers of white females in salary grades 1–2 and 3–4 tend to decrease, as expected. Beginning in salary grades 5–6, on the other hand, the opposite result is noted for non-college graduates and probably indicates fewer opportunities to move to higher salary grades.

(c) The total complement of white females increases steadily through salary grade 6 but, unlike white male representation, begins to decline in salary grades 7–8 and 9–10.

(d) Although the absolute numbers of white females are relatively small, their percentage representation and distribution in the salary grades 7–8 slightly resemble that for white males. Meaningful comparisons vanish in the salary grades 9–10, however.

Nonwhite Males

There are few similarities between the distribution patterns and representation of white males and nonwhite males based on length of service and educational level except in the lowest salary grade categories. Tables 7.19, 7.20, 7.21, 7.22, and 7.23 present a picture of nonwhite males in the corporation.

Key observations about this group are:

(a) In salary grades 1–2, twice as many high school graduates appear in the "Less than 2 year" category than white male high school graduates. In both cases, however, it would be reasonable to assume either their promotion to the salary grade category 3–4, or their termination from the organization after no more than nine years.

(b) Salary grade category 3–4 is virtually devoid of nonwhite male employees beyond the ninth year, in contrast to white male employees in the same salary grade category.

(c) The number of nonwhite males shows no significant increase from the salary grade category 3–4 to salary grade 5–6, as in the case of white males.

Table 7.14 Length of Service and Educational Levels, White Females—1978

Salary Grades 1–2
Number of Employees

Length of Service	High School		Training or Spec. Educ.		College But No Degree		College Graduate		Beyond College		TOTALS
	#	%	#	%	#	%	#	%	#	%	
Less than 2 yrs.	39	88.6	5	11.4	–	–	–	–	–	–	44
2–4 yrs.	15	75.0	3	15.0	2	10.0	–	–	–	–	20
5–9 yrs.	10	71.4	2	14.3	2	14.3	–	–	–	–	14
10–14 yrs.	3	75.0	1	25.0	–	–	–	–	–	–	4
15–19 yrs.	–	–	1	50.0	1	50.0	–	–	–	–	2
More than 19 yrs.	1	100.0	–	–	–	–	–	–	–	–	1
TOTALS	68		12		5		–		–		85

Table 7.15 Length of Service and Educational Levels, White Females—1978

Salary Grades 3–4
Number of Employees

Length of Service	High School		Training or Spec. Educ.		College But No Degree		College Graduate		Beyond College		TOTALS
	#	%	#	%	#	%	#	%	#	%	
Less than 2 yrs.	50	72.5	8	11.6	11	15.9	–	–	–	–	69
2–4 yrs.	58	73.4	6	7.6	13	16.5	2	2.5	–	–	79
5–9 yrs.	45	64.3	10	14.3	12	17.1	3	4.3	–	–	70
10–14 yrs.	12	66.7	3	16.7	2	11.1	1	5.5	–	–	18
15–19 yrs.	7	63.6	2	18.2	1	9.1	1	9.1	–	–	11
More than 19 yrs.	14	66.7	2	9.5	4	19.0	1	4.8	–	–	21
TOTALS	186		31		43		8		–		268

Table 7.16 Length of Service and Educational Levels, White Females—1978

Salary Grades 5–6
Number of Employees

Length of Service	High School		Training or Spec. Educ.		College But No Degree		College Graduate		Beyond College		TOTALS
	#	%	#	%	#	%	#	%	#	%	
Less than 2 yrs.	8	21.6	5	13.5	11	29.7	13	35.1	–	–	37
2–4 yrs.	10	21.3	5	10.6	20	42.6	12	25.5	–	–	47
5–9 yrs.	24	29.6	9	11.1	27	33.3	19	23.5	2	2.5	81
10–14 yrs.	15	33.3	6	13.3	15	33.3	9	20.0	–	–	45
15–19 yrs.	17	44.7	2	5.3	14	36.8	5	13.2	–	–	38
More than 19 yrs.	44	42.3	13	12.5	38	36.5	9	8.7	–	–	104
TOTALS	118		40		125		67		2		352

Table 7.17 Length of Service and Educational Levels, White Females—1978

Salary Grades 7–8
Number of Employees

Length of Service	High School		Training or Spec. Educ.		College But No Degree		College Graduate		Beyond College		TOTALS
	#	%	#	%	#	%	#	%	#	%	
Less than 2 yrs.	–	–	1	6.7	–	–	8	53.3	6	40.0	15
2–4 yrs.	–	–	–	–	2	15.4	8	61.5	3	23.1	13
5–9 yrs.	3	12.5	5	20.8	5	20.8	10	41.7	1	4.2	24
10–14 yrs.	2	14.3	2	14.3	3	21.4	6	42.9	1	7.1	14
15–19 yrs.	2	16.7	2	16.7	5	41.7	3	25.0	–	–	12
More than 19 yrs.	11	31.4	6	17.1	9	25.7	9	25.7	–	–	35
TOTALS	18		16		24		44		11		113

Table 7.18 Length of Service and Educational Levels, White Females—1978

Salary Grades 9–10
Number of Employees

Length of Service	High School		Training or Spec. Educ.		College But No Degree		College Graduate		Beyond College		TOTALS
	#	%	#	%	#	%	#	%	#	%	
Less than 2 yrs.	–	–	–	–	–	–	2	50.0	2	50.0	4
2–4 yrs.	–	–	–	–	–	–	2	100.0	–	–	2
5–9 yrs.	1	20.0	–	–	–	–	3	60.0	1	20.0	5
10–14 yrs.	–	–	1	25.0	–	–	3	75.0	–	–	4
15–19 yrs.	–	–	–	–	1	25.0	2	50.0	1	25.0	4
More than 19 yrs.	1	10.0	1	10.0	1	10.0	7	70.0	–	–	10
TOTALS	2		2		2		19		4		29

Table 7.19 Length of Service and Educational Levels, Nonwhite Males—1978

Salary Grades 1–2
Number of Employees

Length of Service	High School		Training or Spec. Educ.		College But No Degree		College Graduate		Beyond College		TOTALS
	#	%	#	%	#	%	#	%	#	%	
Less than 2 yrs.	24	85.7	4	14.3	–	–	–	–	–	–	28
2–4 yrs.	5	62.5	2	25.0	1	12.5	–	–	–	–	8
5–9 yrs.	1	100.0	–	–	–	–	–	–	–	–	1
10–14 yrs.	–	–	–	–	–	–	–	–	–	–	–
15–19 yrs.	–	–	–	–	–	–	–	–	–	–	–
More than 19 yrs.	–	–	–	–	–	–	–	–	–	–	–
TOTALS	30		6		1						37

Table 7.20 Length of Service and Educational Levels, Nonwhite Males—1978

Salary Grades 3–4
Number of Employees

Length of Service	High School		Training or Spec. Educ.		College But No Degree		College Graduate		Beyond College		TOTALS
	#	%	#	%	#	%	#	%	#	%	
Less than 2 yrs.	15	88.2	2	11.8	–	–	–	–	–	–	17
2–4 yrs.	25	64.1	6	15.4	8	20.5	–	–	–	–	39
5–9 yrs.	15	62.5	3	12.5	5	20.8	1	4.2	–	–	24
10–14 yrs.	1	100.0	–	–	–	–	–	–	–	–	1
15–19 yrs.	–	–	1	100.0	–	–	–	–	–	–	1
More than 19 yrs.	–	–	–	–	–	–	–	–	–	–	–
TOTALS	56		12		13		1				82

Table 7.21 Length of Service and Educational Levels, Nonwhite Males—1978

Salary Grades 5-6
Number of Employees

Length of Service	High School		Training or Spec. Educ.		College But No Degree		College Graduate		Beyond College		TOTALS
	#	%	#	%	#	%	#	%	#	%	
Less than 2 yrs.	3	18.8	1	6.2	6	37.5	6	37.5	—	—	16
2–4 yrs.	5	23.8	2	9.5	6	28.6	8	38.1	—	—	21
5–9 yrs.	14	41.2	2	5.9	12	35.3	6	17.6	—	—	34
10–14 yrs.	3	37.5	2	25.0	3	37.5	—	—	—	—	8
15–19 yrs.	—	—	—	—	1	50.0	1	50.0	—	—	2
More than 19 yrs.	2	50.0	—	—	2	50.0	—	—	—	—	4
TOTALS	27		7		30		21		—		85

Table 7.22 Length of Service and Educational Levels, Nonwhite Males—1978

Salary Grades 7–8
Number of Employees

Length of Service	High School		Training or Spec. Educ.		College But No Degree		College Graduate		Beyond College		TOTALS
	#	%	#	%	#	%	#	%	#	%	
Less than 2 yrs.	—	—	—	—	—	—	3	50.0	3	50.0	6
2–4 yrs.	—	—	—	—	—	—	3	75.0	1	25.0	4
5–9 yrs.	1	11.1	1	11.1	3	33.3	3	33.3	1	11.1	9
10–14 yrs.	—	—	—	—	—	—	1	33.3	2	66.7	3
15–19 yrs.	—	—	—	—	—	—	2	100.0	—	—	2
More than 19 yrs.	—	—	—	—	—	—	—	—	—	—	—
TOTALS	1		1		3		12		7		24

143

Table 7.23 Length of Service and Educational Levels, Nonwhite Males—1978

Salary Grades 9–10
Number of Employees

Length of Service	High School		Training or Spec. Educ.		College But No Degree		College Graduate		Beyond College		TOTALS
	#	%	#	%	#	%	#	%	#	%	
Less than 2 yrs.	—	—	—	—	—	—	—	—	1	100.0	1
2–4 yrs.	—	—	—	—	—	—	1	50.0	1	50.0	2
5–9 yrs.	—	—	—	—	—	—	1	100.0	—	–	1
10–14 yrs.	—	—	—	—	—	—	—	—	2	100.0	2
15–19 yrs.	—	—	—	—	—	—	—	—	—	—	—
More than 19 yrs.	—	—	—	—	—	—	—	—	—	—	—
TOTALS	—		—		—		2		4		6

144

(d) Practically all nonwhite male employees in the salary grade category 7–8 are college graduates or have attended college. This fact compares with a 19 percent white male proportion in the salary grade category 7–8 who have only completed high school. If the forty white male employees shown in the "training or special education" column are added to the high school figure of eighty, then the percentage of white male employees in salary grades 7–8 who are not college graduates rises to more than 28 percent.

(e) Table 7.23 speaks for itself. Nonwhite male representation in the top salary grade category is barely significant when compared with white males in that category and is but approximately one fifth of the number of white female employees in the top category.

Nonwhite Females

Nonwhite female employees in the corporation are described in Tables 7.24, 7.25, 7.26, 7.27, and 7.28. These employees, while more numerous than nonwhite males, are heavily concentrated in salary grade categories 1–2 and 3–4.

Major observations with respect to nonwhite female employees are:

(a) Of the total number of 409 nonwhite female employees, 338 are in salary grades 1–2 and 3–4. Moreover, this group outnumbers white female employees in salary grades 1–2.

(b) The nonwhite female employee group and the white female employee group have *college graduates* in the salary grade category 3–4, and in the lowest salary grade category members who have *attended college*. Neither of the male employee groups in these two lowest salary grade categories is equivalently represented.

(c) In salary grade category 5–6, nonwhite female total distribution by length of service is more akin to the distribution describing nonwhite males than that describing white females. The similarity in distributions is also seen in the levels of education.

(d) Nonwhite female representation in the two upper salary grade categories is practically nil. Of the fifteen employees in both categories, fourteen are college graduates, but only four are long-service employees.

Table 7.24 Length of Service and Educational Levels, Nonwhite Females—1978

Salary Grades 1–2
Number of Employees

Length of Service	High School		Training or Spec. Educ.		College But No Degree		College Graduate		Beyond College		TOTALS
	#	%	#	%	#	%	#	%	#	%	
Less than 2 yrs.	38	77.6	9	18.4	2	4.1	—	—	—	—	49
2–4 yrs.	27	71.0	7	18.4	4	10.5	—	—	—	—	38
5–9 yrs.	6	60.0	2	20.0	2	20.0	—	—	—	—	10
10–14 yrs.	2	100.0	—	—	—	—	—	—	—	—	2
15–19 yrs.	—	—	1	100.0	—	—	—	—	—	—	1
More than 19 yrs.	—	—	—	—	1	100.0	—	—	—	—	1
TOTALS	73		19		9		—		—		101

146

Table 7.25 Length of Service and Educational Levels, Nonwhite Females—1978

	Salary Grades 3–4 Number of Employees											
	High School		Training or Spec. Educ.		College But No Degree		College Graduate		Beyond College		TOTALS
Length of Service	#	%	#	%	#	%	#	%	#	%	
Less than 2 yrs.	22	75.9	4	13.8	3	10.3	–	–	–	–	29
2–4 yrs.	62	63.9	15	15.5	17	17.5	3	3.1	–	–	97
5–9 yrs.	69	67.0	10	9.7	20	19.4	4	3.9	–	–	103
10–14 yrs.	3	60.0	1	20.0	1	20.0	–	–	–	–	5
15–19 yrs.	–	–	–	–	1	100.0	–	–	–	–	1
More than 19 yrs.	1	50.0	1	50.0	–	–	–	–	–	–	2
TOTALS	157		31		42		7		–		237

Table 7.26 Length of Service and Educational Levels, Nonwhite Females—1978

Salary Grades 5–6
Number of Employees

Length of Service	High School		Training or Spec. Educ.		College But No Degree		College Graduate		Beyond College		TOTALS
	#	%	#	%	#	%	#	%	#	%	
Less than 2 yrs.	2	25.0	1	12.5	2	25.0	3	37.5	—	—	8
2–4 yrs.	3	33.3	1	11.1	3	33.3	2	22.2	—	—	9
5–9 yrs.	11	33.3	2	6.1	13	39.4	6	18.2	1	3.0	33
10–14 yrs.	3	75.0	—	—	1	25.0	—	—	—	—	4
15–19 yrs.	—	—	—	—	1	100.0	—	—	—	—	1
More than 19 yrs.	1	100.0	—	—	—	—	—	—	—	—	1
TOTALS	20		4		20		11		1		56

Table 7.27 Length of Service and Educational Levels, Nonwhite Females—1978

Salary Grades 7–8
Number of Employees

Length of Service	High School #	%	Training or Spec. Educ. #	%	College But No Degree #	%	College Graduate #	%	Beyond College #	%	TOTALS
Less than 2 yrs.	–	–	–	–	–	–	1	50.0	1	50.0	2
2–4 yrs.	–	–	–	–	–	–	2	100.0	–	–	2
5–9 yrs.	–	–	–	–	–	–	3	75.0	1	25.0	4
10–14 yrs.	–	–	–	–	–	–	–	–	1	100.0	1
15–19 yrs.	–	–	–	–	–	–	1	100.0	–	–	1
More than 19 yrs.	–	–	–	–	1	50.0	1	50.0	–	–	2
TOTALS					1		8		3		12

Table 7.28 Length of Service and Educational Levels, Nonwhite Females—1978

Salary Grades 9–10
Number of Employees

Length of Service	High School		Training or Spec. Educ.		College But No Degree		College Graduate		Beyond College		TOTALS
	#	%	#	%	#	%	#	%	#	%	
Less than 2 yrs.	—	—	—	—	—	—	—	—	1	100.0	1
2–4 yrs.	—	—	—	—	—	—	—	—	1	100.0	1
5–9 yrs.	—	—	—	—	—	—	1	100.0	—	—	1
10–14 yrs.	—	—	—	—	—	—	—	—	—	—	—
15–19 yrs.	—	—	—	—	—	—	—	—	—	—	—
More than 19 yrs.	—	—	—	—	—	—	—	—	—	—	—
TOTALS	—		—		—		1		2		3

Table 7.29 Salary Ranges—1978
(Weekly)

Salary Grade Category	Minimum	Midpoint	Maximum
1–2	$130	$155	$181
3–4	162	196	230
5–6	229	286	343
7–8	333	417	500
9–10	511	639	767

SALARY RANGES AND EARNINGS

The study has been provided with basic compensation data for members of the work force by salary grade category. Table 7.29 shows the applicable salary ranges for each salary grade category in 1978; Table 7.30 gives the average weekly earnings for that year. An hypothesis stated in an earlier chapter was that wage discrimination was not a major manifestation of employment discrimination. The display of weekly salaries in Table 7.30 by race/sex and a further comparison of Table 7.30 with salary midpoints shown in Table 7.29 would tend to dampen such an hypothesis, length of service notwithstanding for the moment.

Table 7.30 Average Weekly Earnings—1978
(dollars)

| | Salary Grade Category | | | | |
	1–2	3–4	5–6	7–8	9–10
Race/Sex					
White Males	146.05	195.75	308.18	443.91	701.96
White Females	151.07	194.02	297.20	429.03	681.04
Nonwhite Males	144.97	190.18	267.94	401.38	630.00
Nonwhite Females	152.51	190.36	271.25	399.17	566.67

Excepting salary grade category 1–2, the average weekly earnings of white males were consistently highest in all salary grade categories, followed by the earnings of white females. When compared with the midpoints of the salary ranges in Table 7.29, it can be seen that all average weekly earnings in salary grade categories 1–2 and 3–4 are below their respective midpoints, but in the remaining categories white male and female employees are above the midpoint while nonwhite male and female employees are below.

CONCLUSIONS

Based on the corporate data presented in this chapter, white males, in terms of numbers, salaries, and length of service, dominate the organization in the top salary grades. This is an important conclusion since managerial authorities for employment decisions—i.e., hiring, firing, promotions, salary levels and increases, job assignments, and developmental opportunities—are likely quartered with those employees in the higher salary grades. On the other hand, nonwhite employees and white female employees, the latter to a somewhat different extent, are permitted entry at the lowest levels of the organization but are restricted in varying degrees to entry at the higher salary grades.

That the data are not over a period of time significantly delimits an analysis of mobility within the internal labor market. Nonetheless, a review of the "length of service" totals reveals, for example, that the numbers of white male employees in salary grade category 1–2 decline from the "Less than 2 years" category through the "More than 19 years" category. This would imply either that these employees are being promoted to higher salary grade categories, or that they are terminating. The same implication emanates from a review of salary grade category 3–4. However, in salary grade category 5–6, the employee totals over the "length of service" span peak in the "5–9 year" category and then decline for subsequent "length of service" categories, thereby implying promotions or terminations after the five–nine year period. Salary grade categories 7–8 and 9–10 show increasing trends in the "length of service" totals. A conclusion is that white male employees have significant promotional opportunities through salary grade category 7–8.

For nonwhite males, remotely similar patterns emerge from an examination of the "length of service" totals in the five salary grade categories. Strikingly evident, however, is a difference in the magnitude of the numbers. For white males, as was seen, the totals tend to increase; for nonwhite males, the totals associated with "length of service" categories are approximately the same in salary grade categories 3–4 and 5–6 but are consecutively smaller in salary grade categories 7–8 and 9–10. This might lead to the conclusion that nonwhite male employees have far fewer promotional opportunities and that after five–nine years in the corporation in salary grade category 5–6, many terminate voluntarily or involuntarily.

Nonwhite females show an even stronger tendency to terminate than nonwhite males based on the available data. This group of employees peaks in the "5–9 year" category in salary grade category 3–4. The totals in the remaining upper salary grade categories are sufficiently small so as to imply high turnover rates and few promotional opportunities.

VIII

The Corporate Organization: An Analysis of Upward Mobility

INTRODUCTION

DURING THE PAST decade or so, empirical analyses of employee group earnings differentials and rates of occupational mobility have been undertaken and reported. The relevant hypotheses have grown out of human capital or dual labor market theories,[1] and have been evaluated on the basis of earnings and occupational data available largely through government census information and the National Longitudinal Study.[2] However, data descriptive of specific corporate internal markets have not been generally available for analysis.[3] It is this level of data which may provide not only another view of earnings differentials and differing upward mobility paths for black and

---

[1]Summaries of much of this work can be found in Duane E. Leigh, *An Analysis of the Determinants of Occupational Upgrading* (New York: Academic Press, 1978); and Jacob Mincer, "The Distribution of Labor Incomes: A Survey," *Journal of Economic Literature*, 8 (1970), 1–26. Some other analyses not included in these summaries and directed toward black/white differentials are Howard M.Wachtel and Charles Betsey, "Low Wage Workers and the Dual Labor Market: An Empirical Investigation," *The Review of Black Political Economy*, 5 (1975), 288–301; Albert W. Niemi, "Occupational/Educational Discrimination Against Black Males," *Journal of Black Studies*, 9 (1978), 87–92; and David M. Streifford, "Racial Economic Dualism in St. Louis," *The Review of Black Political Economy*, 4 (1974), 63–81.

[2]A description of the National Longitudinal Surveys may be found in H.S. Parnes, B.M. Fleisher, R.C. Miljus, and R.S. Spitz, "The Pre-Retirement Years: A Longitudinal Study of the Labor Market Experience of Men," vol. 1 (Washington, DC: Department of Labor, 1970).

[3]An important exception is the work of Peter B. Doeringer and Michael J. Piore, *Internal Labor Markets and Manpower Analysis* (Lexington: D.C. Heath, 1971).

white employee groups but an enhanced understanding of the dynamics governing the internal labor market.

While virtually all of the analyses mentioned above discern disparate earnings and occupational representation along racial lines, the purpose of this chapter is to examine the corporate data presented in the previous chapter with respect to earnings and upward mobility as a function of length of service, education, and race.

Within the framework of human capital theory, Jacob Mincer has demonstrated that in the absence of longitudinal earnings and schooling data, reasonable assumptions may permit cross section data to approximate developments over time.[4] Following Mincer's line of reasoning, this chapter makes assumptions on which an analysis of upward mobility paths for the four employee groups in Tables 7.5, 7.6, 7.7, and 7.8 is based. The central aim of this analysis is toward a further delineation and comparison of upward mobility paths based on length of service and salary grade, and levels of education and race, rather than an identification of causal factors.

Traditionally, labor economists and other analysts have tended to stress the roles of education and training in the development of explanations of upward mobility. These include the notions of post-school investment and on-the-job training. But viewing "length of service" as a proxy measure of the *quality* of internal labor market experiences, and further observing that black employees appear to have relatively fewer quality experiences than white employees, this chapter examines five hypotheses concerning relationships between upward mobility and education, length of service, race, and point of entry.

Unfortunately, the regression results are not as strongly supportive or as conclusive as one might have hoped. Nonetheless, important insights and qualified conclusions are suggested by the analyses. It would appear that length of service is a more important factor in determining rates of upward mobility in the corporate internal labor market than is level of education. For black employees, however, level of education appears to be relatively more important for upward mobility than length of service. This is not a necessarily unexpected result since its implication is simply that black employees are engaged in relatively fewer organizational activities providing meaningful corporate experiences than are white employees; thus, a higher proportion of upward mobility for blacks is explained by the level of education variable than the length of service variable. Moreover, this finding helps to explain the generally higher rates of

---

[4]Jacob Mincer, *Schooling, Experience, and Earnings* (New York: National Bureau of Economic Research, 1974), pp. 48–51. See also Leo A. Goodman, "Multiplicative Models for the Analysis of Occupational Mobility Tables and Other Kinds of Cross-Classification Tables," *American Journal of Sociology* 84 (Jan. 1979), 804–19.

upward mobility for white corporate employees than rates of upward mobility for black corporate employees.

ASSUMPTIONS

In order to approximate paths of upward mobility based on the grouped data, the following restrictive assumptions are made.

First, assuming the state of the art and technology, major demographic patterns, and the organizational chart to be constant, the pattern of total employee distribution by length of service and salary grade and education level does not change substantially in the short run, and only slightly in the long run. A priori, this important assumption allows us to view employees in Tables 7.5–7.8 as if they had moved from one employment category to another in the longitude, i.e., a proxy measure of upward mobility. This is not an unreasonable assumption given the apparent rigidity of corporate profiles and employee distribution patterns over time.

Second, salary grades define occupational level, and movement from one salary grade level to the next highest salary grade level describes upward mobility and increases in earnings.

Third, entry points are considered to be any salary grade levels where employees have less than two years of employment in the corporation.

Fourth, the likely entry point for Category I employees with no postschool experience is salary grade category 1–2; and the likely entry point for Category II employees with no postschool experience is salary grade category 3–4.

Fifth, the higher the level of entry into the corporate structure, the higher the probable age and number of years of applicable experience.

HYPOTHESES

Growing out of the earlier chapters, and given the available data, the following five hypotheses regarding upward mobility for black and white employees in the corporate internal labor market are testable.[5]

---

[5]The available data describe *whites* and *nonwhites*, the latter group comprised of blacks and other racial minorities. It is assumed that blacks are the substantial majority of the nonwhite category; for the purposes of consistent word usage, and in keeping with the central theme of this study, the word *black* is used throughout.

1. *For whites in Categories I and II, length of service has a more important relationship to upward mobility than level of education.*

Length of service may be viewed as a proxy measure of post-school investment in human capital, i.e., "on-the-job and other forms of training and experience."[6] This is what employers pay and promote employees for, and it is this set of experiences which white employees in either Category I or Category II can have in a far more encompassing way than black employees. Thus, the rate of upward mobility for white employees is likely to be at least high enough to: 1) promote minimally necessary levels of workforce stability; 2) complement expected turnover rates attributable to retirements and terminations; and 3) protect the technical and administrative knowledge bases on which the survival of the organization depends.

2. *For blacks in Categories I and II, upward mobility is more a function of the level of education achieved than length of service.*

Educational achievement is often a kind of screening device and passport. While it serves similar functions for both blacks and whites, relative levels of education are relatively more important for blacks since the full values to be derived from length of service are not likely to be available. That is to say, if upward mobility is some function of postschool investment in human capital, and blacks receive less of this investment than whites, then blacks will likely experience less upward mobility than whites. However, the level of education will separate Category I and Category II employees, and further separate employment levels within Category II.

3. *The rates of upward mobility for blacks are low relative to whites, and sufficiently low so as to preclude reaching upper levels of the corporate structure.*

Since upward mobility for blacks is less related to length of service than to level of education, it is reasonable to think that the rates of upward mobility for blacks will be relatively lower than rates for whites. Considering the typical pyramiding of corporate organizations and the resulting decreasing opportunities in the upper ranks of the organization, it is further reasonable to suspect that the rates of upward mobility are low enough such that black positioning in a given time period would be below that of whites with similar levels of education and lengths of service.[7] The relatively small slope of the upward path for blacks, then, implies that reaching the top

---

[6]Jacob Mincer, *Schooling, Experience, and Earnings*, p. 47.

[7]In this instance, the concept of the *artificial ceiling* discussed in a previous chapter might be viewed as a dynamic rather than static phenomenon. Thus, the relatively smaller slope of upward mobility for blacks is effectively the artificial ceiling.

levels of an organization is virtually obviated by the number of working years typically assumed to be available.[8]

4. *Category I blacks experience fewer obstacles when entering the corporate organization than do Category II blacks and, within the limits imposed by Category I, experience higher rates of upward mobility.*

Given the overall impact of equal employment opportunity legislation and a heightened presence of blacks in major cities and urban centers, the corporate community has responded with few barriers at the low ends of the organizational structure. Relatively large numbers of employees are required at this level of many corporate bureaucracies and the available supply of Category I black labor at minimal wages cannot be ignored.[9] Upward mobility within the internal labor market is probable for this group, but such mobility diminishes drastically as members of Category I begin to approach Category II positions.

Category II blacks, on the other hand, enter the corporate organization at relatively higher levels, but the rate of upward mobility tends to be slow.

5. *Category II blacks have less opportunity for upward mobility than Category II whites.*

The degree to which upward mobility has an earnings equivalent is the degree to which one can examine the relationship between earnings and education and the implications of that relationship for occupational and upward mobility. This relationship has been analyzed extensively by human capital theorists and dual labor market analysts and is not broadly reviewed in this work.

While the dualists argue that educational credentials are screening devices, the human capital proponents see a functional relationship between an earnings path and levels of formal education.[10] A cursory view of an internal labor market would likely vitiate this naive human capital position and give some credence to the dualist notion of screening devices—i.e., that educational credentials serve to distinguish Category I workers from Category II workers.[11] (It should

---

[8]Additionally, it is observable that individuals who reach the top levels of corporate organizations generally tend to exhibit highly sloped upward mobility paths at the beginning of their careers. This is true whether one remains in a specific corporate organization or moves to another. Referred to sometimes as "fast track," blacks have been so categorized occasionally in the lower and middle structures of an organization, but invariably these black corporate employees bump up against the artificial ceiling whereupon the rate of ascent slows perceptibly or stops.

[9]Intensive use of Category I black workers appears to decline as corporate offices increase their distance from urban centers.

[10]See Duane E. Leigh, *Occupational Upgrading*, p. 57.

[11]David M. Gordon, *Theories of Poverty and Underemployment* (Lexington: D.C. Heath, 1972), p. 50.

be recalled that dual labor market theory has as its basis the concepts of primary and secondary labor markets which recognize a funda-mental division of the primary labor market consistent with our notions of Category I and Category II.)[12]

EDUCATION AND POSTSCHOOL INVESTMENT

Our observations lead to the identification of different kinds of educational and training credentials and the roles they play in deter-mining upward mobility. In general, the level of education deter-mines the *entry point*, but different *kinds* and *levels* will impact job assignments, earnings, and the likelihood of a rate ef upward mobil-ity greater or less than some expected average rate. For example, college graduates recruited fresh from campuses with degrees in academic areas not directly applicable to the profitability of a banking institution—e.g., British History, Psychology, Biology—will likely be assigned trainee positions related to some function central to banking activity, or some staff function such as in the personnel department. These will be Category II positions. Evaluation of per-formance during the training period and beyond will largely deter-mine rates of upward mobility and earnings in the short run. On the other hand, individuals beginning their careers with training and education presumed to be readily and directly applicable to the bank's central activity—e.g., graduate degrees in advanced computer and systems analysis, financial and investment analysis—will be viewed differently in terms of immediate earnings and potential rates of upward mobility. Of course, there are those workers who take advan-tage of interfirm mobility opportunities to gain higher entry points.

The point here is that education, used in the broadest sense, probably has more to do with *entering* and less with upward mobility and increasing earnings. And, in any event, the type of education and training and the level of skill mastery—which presumably is correlated with years of schooling—must be looked at relative to the type of corporate organization, the level of technology required, and its industrial classification.

Some human capital theorists go on to say that the abilities and

---

[12]For example, Piore describes the *primary* labor market as consisting of "upper and lower tiers"; Reich, Gordon, and Edwards see the primary labor market in terms of "subordinate" jobs and "independent" jobs. See Michael J. Piore, "Notes For a Theory of Labor Market Stratification" in *Labor Market Segmentation*, ed. Richard C. Edwards, Michael Reich, and David M. Gordon (Lexington: D.C. Heath, 1975), p. 129; and Michael Reich, David M. Gordon, and Richard C. Edwards, "A Theory of Labor Market Segmentation," *American Economic Review*, Proceedings, 63 (May 1973), 360.

learning capacities of workers, sharpened by years of formal schooling, are important determinants of upward mobility and increased
earnings over the long run.[13] The basic implication, of course, is that
upward mobility and increased earnings are functions of merit and
productivity. On the contrary, Gordon states:

> The speed at which workers move through the job structures
> depends primarily on their attitudes and on the state of economic
> conditions, much less on worker merit or productivity in its
> narrow traditional sense. Everything else equal, workers' wages
> will tend to increase with age as the simple effect of institutional
> seniority privileges, fixed through bargaining and custom.[14]

In the corporate internal market, increases in wages and salaries may
increase within limits with age (and length of service), but this is
probably less true for upward mobility or occupational advancement.

In particular, Mincer has put forth the thesis that career earnings
are a function of *postschool* investment in human capital:

> With the same initial earnings capacity, individuals who invest
> more have steeper (earnings) slopes, . . . than those who invest
> less, provided their average rate of return . . . is not excessively
> smaller. This is the basic explanation for the fanning out of
> earnings profiles with age and for increases of variances of earn-
> ings with age, so long as individuals with different investments
> in human capital comprise the earnings distribution.[15]

It is an easy step to the conclusion that if blacks earn less than whites
during and over their working lives, it is simply because blacks
choose, more often than whites, not to forego current earnings in
favor of postschool investments in human capital—i.e., on-the-job
training and other types of training and experiences. Or, knowing or
sensing that innate abilities and learning capacities are limited, blacks
rationally choose not to invest as much as whites in human capital
since the expected returns would be lower than the investment could
earn in alternative uses. Obviously, these conclusions, and others,
diminish employer culpability with respect to discriminatory behavior based on race and impute a general inferiority to blacks.

The development and use of the concept of postschool investment as an explanation of career earnings and upward mobility is

---

[13]See Leigh, *Occupational Upgrading*, p. 10. Also, Christopher Jencks, *Who
Gets Ahead?: The Determinants of Economic Success in America* (New York: Basic
Books, 1979), chap 6.

[14]Gordon, *Poverty and Underemployment*, p. 50.

[15]Jacob Mincer, "The Distribution of Labor Incomes," p. 12.

nonetheless useful in a theoretical context. However, a basic assumption underlying this approach is that "workers are viewed as determining the rate at which current earnings are sacrificed in light of further prospects,"[16] and this assumption robs the postschool investment concept of specific relevancy. More directly, it is this assumption on which a theory of racism in the internal labor market turns: are the career paths, earnings paths, or rates of upward mobility rationally determined by workers' postschool investment in themselves, or by employers and the internal labor market dynamics which govern the work place?

To be sure, many Category I and II workers in the corporate sector return to school for various degrees and other training of one sort or another, but in a significant number of instances such activities are paid for by the corporation under various tuition refund programs. Again, conferences, seminars, training workshops, and the like—generally limited to Category II employees—are for the most part paid for by corporations. Thus, many corporate employees do not spend from current earnings in any substantial way for postschool education and training, certainly not in sufficient numbers (or dollar amounts) to give broad credence to this aspect of postschool investment.[17]

On the other hand, in the matter of interfirm or interindustry mobility and interoccupational mobility, corporate workers in Categories I and II may invest in the kind of education or training which can promote a career change or establish a level of technical facility not especially utilized by one firm but valued by another firm in the same or different industry. Moreover, movement from Category I status to Category II status is often viewed by employees as a function of educational and/or training credentials. (Even here, however, workers are frequently enabled to secure corporate subsidization.)

Probably the most important postschool investment activity is on-the-job training (OJT). In the corporate internal labor market, in

---

[16]Finis Welch, "Human Capital Theory: Education, Discrimination, and Life Cycles," American Economic Review, 65, (1975), p. 63. See also Yoram Ben-Porath, "The Production of Human Capital and the Life Cycle of Earnings," Journal of Political Economy, 75 (1967), 352–65.

[17]One might argue that the opportunity cost of choosing a job with relatively low earnings initially but the prospect of a highly sloped earnings curve vis-à-vis a job with relatively high earnings initially but little prospect of earnings growth is equivalent to an investment in human capital. However, empirical measurement of such opportunity costs would be difficult if not impossible; secondly, in the real world, the process of choosing one job category vis-à-vis another for career pursuits is not generally an open process, but one that is subject to family and cultural influences, specific education and training, internal labor market customs, race, sex, etc. Thurow has looked at the question of who pays for training—employers or employees. The interested reader is referred to Lester C. Thurow, Generating Inequality (New York: Basic Books, 1975), pp. 113–23.

contrast to OJT in a manufacturing plant, for example, the essential training for meaningful upward mobility is not simply mastering the mechanics of an assigned task, but rather understanding the dynamics of the organization and the role and function of management. When given the opportunity(s), an employee must evidence these. Clearly, the individual must learn the management lessons well and, having done so, can promote his or her candidacy for higher-level responsibilities within the organization. This relationship between work, learning, income, and upward mobility has been noted and described frequently.[18] But the extent to which employees may be involved in various kinds of learning processes, or have job assignments which complement those processes, is, more often than not, a management decision. Therefore, managers have major control over the *quality* of internal labor market experiences and the character of those experiences shared by employees.

In summary, then, black employees rarely have critical job assignments or sufficiently lateral job mobility. On the contrary, blacks tend to be constrained by narrowed job opportunities, limited job groups, and "mobility clusters."[19] Therefore, that part of the corporate OJT experience necessary for upward mobility is glaringly absent for most black employees and, in any case, is far less than that afforded white employees.[20] It is for this reason, in large measure, that irrespective of educational credentials, the rates of upward mobility for Category II black employees lag substantially behind those for Category II white employees.

DATA ANALYSIS

Tables 7.5, 7.6, 7.7, and 7.8 in the previous chapter show the distributions of employees by race, sex, salary grade, and length of service. As stated in the section describing assumptions, the assumption is made that each of these tables implies patterns of employee mobility in the longitude. Thus, we can construct a proxy measure of mobility rates.

---

[18]See Lester C. Thurow, *Poverty and Discrimination* (Washington, D.C.: The Brookings Institution, 1969), pp. 67–69; Piore, "Labor Market Stratification," pp. 130–34; Sherwin Rosen, "Learning and Experience in the Labor Market," *The Journal of Human Resources*, 7 (1972), 326–42; and James R. Kluegel, "The Causes and Cost of Racial Exclusion from Job Authority," *American Sociological Review*, 43 (1978), 285–301.

[19]Doeringer and Piore, *Internal Labor Markets*, p. 141.

[20]Thurow, among others, recognizes that broadly blacks receive less OJT than whites. *Poverty and Discrimination*, p. 95. Also, see Doeringer and Piore, *Internal Labor Markets*, p. 177.

If the entry points are along the "less than 2 years" row, then entering employees, over time, will: 1) remain in salary grade, or; 2) move to the next salary grade, or; 3) remain in grade for some period and then move to the next grade, or; 4) move to the next salary grade in the early part of the career and remain in grade thereafter, or; 5) move at an accelerated rate to the next salary grade, or; 6) terminate. For the purposes of this analysis, we assume that only (1) and (2) are operative.

Each table may be viewed as a 6 × 5 cross-classification with a one-to-one correspondence between the rows and the columns. The expected measures of the rates at which employees *remain in grade* or are *promoted to the next salary grade* are of the simple form

$$\text{Aij} = \frac{a_{ij}}{a_{ij}}$$

where a_{ij} ($i = 1, 2, \ldots, 6$; $j = 1, 2, \ldots, 5$) is the ith row and jth column of Tables 7.5–7.8.

Specifically, from Table 7.5, which describes the distribution of white males by salary grade and length of service, measures of white males entering the work force in salary grades 1–2 and remaining in grade are:

$$A_{21,11}^{wm} = \frac{a_{21}^{wm}}{a_{11}^{wm}} \; ; \text{ and } A_{31,21}^{wm} = \frac{a_{31}^{wm}}{a_{21}^{wm}}$$

An interpretation of these measures is that of the thirteen white males who entered the work force in salary grades 1–2 and in time period 1, five remained in grade in time period 2, and three of that five remained in grade in time period 3, *ceteris paribus*.

Similar measures for white males moving to next highest grade when the point of entry is, for example, salary grades 1–2 are:

$$A_{22,11}^{wm} = \frac{a_{22}^{wm}}{a_{11}^{wm}} \; , \ldots, A_{55,44}^{wm} = \frac{a_{55}^{wm}}{a_{44}^{wm}}$$

which depicts movement along the main diagonal, specifically. The interpretation of this measure parallels the one above. Such measures have been constructed for each of four employee groups and are shown in Tables 8.1–8.4 and provide a basis for comparison. Clearly, $A > 0$ in all cases, but $A = 1$ says that the number of employees moving from one cell to another is an equivalence; $A < 1$ means that the number of employees moving from one cell to another is *fewer* than the number available to move; and $A > 1$ means that the number

Table 8.1 White Males

Remaining in Grade

| Length of Service | Salary Grades (ratios) | | | | |
	1–2 / 1–2	3–4 / 3–4	5–6 / 5–6	7–8 / 7–8	9–10 / 9–10
Less than 2 yrs.— 2–4 yrs.	.385	1.625	2.071	1.833	1.105
2–4 yrs.— 5–9 yrs.	.600	.256	1.138	1.750	2.714
5–9 yrs.—10–14 yrs.	–	1.000	.475	1.026	.632
10–14 yrs.—15–19 yrs.	–	.800	.958	.861	1.750
15–19 yrs.—More than 19 yrs.	–	2.000	1.289	1.882	1.730

Moving to Next Highest Grade

| Length of Service | Salary Grades (ratios) | | | |
	3–4 / 1–2	5–6 / 3–4	7–8 / 5–6	9–10 / 7–8
Less than 2 yrs.— 2–4 yrs.	3.000	3.625	1.048	.875
2–4 yrs.— 5–9 yrs.		2.539	.885	1.296
5–9 yrs.—10–14 yrs.			.798	.468
10–14 yrs.—15–19 yrs.				.798

Table 8.2 White Females

Remaining in Grade

| Length of Service | Salary Grades (ratios) | | | | |
	1–2 / 1–2	3–4 / 3–4	5–6 / 5–6	7–8 / 7–8	9–10 / 9–10
Less than 2 yrs.— 2–4 yrs.	.455	1.145	1.270	.867	.500
2–4 yrs.— 5–9 yrs.	.700	.886	1.723	1.846	2.500
5–9 yrs.—10–14 yrs.	.286	.257	.556	.583	.800
10–14 yrs.—15–19 yrs.	.500	.611	.844	.857	1.000
15–19 yrs.—More than 19 yrs.	.500	1.909	2.737	2.917	2.500

Moving to Next Highest Grade

| Length of Service | Salary Grades (ratios) | | | |
	3–4 / 1–2	5–6 / 3–4	7–8 / 5–6	9–10 / 7–8
Less than 2 yrs.— 2–4 yrs.	1.796	.681	.351	.133
2–4 yrs.— 5–9 yrs.		1.025	.511	.385
5–9 yrs.—10–14 yrs.			.173	.167
10–14 yrs.—15–19 yrs.				.286

Table 8.3 Black Males

Remaining in Grade

Length of Service	Salary Grades (ratios) 1–2 / 1–2	3–4 / 3–4	5–6 / 5–6	7–8 / 7–8	9–10 / 9–10
Less than 2 yrs.— 2–4 yrs.	.286	2.294	1.313	.667	2.000
2–4 yrs.— 5–9 yrs.	.125	.615	1.619	2.250	.500
5–9 yrs.—10–14 yrs.	–	.042	.235	.333	2.000
10–14 yrs.—15–19 yrs.	–	1.000	.250	.667	–
15–19 yrs.—More than 19 yrs.	–	–	2.000	–	–

Moving to Next Highest Grade

Length of Service	Salary Grades (ratios) 3–4 / 1–2	5–6 / 3–4	7–8 / 5–6	9–10 / 7–8
Less than 2 yrs.— 2–4 yrs.	1.393	1.235	.250	.333
2–4 yrs.— 5–9 yrs.		.872	.429	.250
5–9 yrs.—10–14 yrs.			.088	.222
10–14 yrs.—15–19 yrs.				–

Table 8.4 Black Females

Remaining in Grade

Length of Service	Salary Grades (ratios) 1–2 / 1–2	3–4 / 3–4	5–6 / 5–6	7–8 / 7–8	9–10 / 9–10
Less than 2 yrs.— 2–4 yrs.	.776	3.345	1.125	1.000	1.000
2–4 yrs.— 5–9 yrs.	.263	1.062	3.667	2.000	1.000
5–9 yrs.—10–14 yrs.	.200	.049	.121	.250	–
10–14 yrs.—15–19 yrs.	.500	.200	.250	1.000	–
15–19 yrs.—More than 19 yrs.	1.000	2.000	1.000	2.000	–

Moving to Next Highest Grade

Length of Service	Salary Grades (ratios) 3–4 / 1–2	5–6 / 3–4	7–8 / 5–6	9–10 / 7–8
Less than 2 yrs.— 2–4 yrs.	1.980	.310	.250	.500
2–4 yrs.— 5–9 yrs.		.340	.444	.500
5–9 yrs.—10–14 yrs.			.030	–
10–14 yrs.—15–19 yrs.				–

of employees moving from one cell to another is *greater* than the number available to move. *A priori*, one should expect white males to have higher relative rates of *moving to next grades*, for example, than the other three groups and lower relative rates associated with *remain in grade* than the other three groups.

Remaining in Grade

In contrast to female employees, neither male group appears to stay in the salary grade category 1–2 beyond the ninth year, as indicated by the *Remaining in Grade* (RG) measures.[21] Comparing the first two time periods in Tables 8.1 and 8.3, however, the ratios for white males are higher than those for black males, and over the nine-year period, they rose for white males and declined for black males. If such differences are not sufficiently explained by the *Moving to Next Highest Grade* (MNHG) measures, then one interpretation might expect higher termination rates, voluntary and involuntary, to explain the downward movement in the black ratio.

Note that the ratios for black and white females through the ninth year also display the opposite RG trends. A *termination* theory would probably address, among other things, employee perceptions of wage discrimination, upward mobility and occupational discrimination (*voluntary*), and employer perceptions of inferior productivity and employee capability (*involuntary*). Since such a theory would have particular relevance for and applicability to black employees, differences in RG ratios become plausible.

We would expect, given the specific data, the RG measures to be dissimilar for the four groups in the early grades and years and to tend toward convergence as opportunities become fewer in the higher grades and as length of service rises. Unfortunately, our approach to measuring RG does not easily reveal clear-cut patterns for black and white employees. In large measure, this shortcoming reflects the differences in employee distribution patterns over time and over the grade ranges and differences in the *absolute* numbers of white versus black employees (see Tables 8.1–8.4). In addition, specific occupational patterns, for which we have no data, would

---

[21]This observation reflects the likelihood that many of the Grades 1–2 (Category I) jobs in this corporate structure are reserved for females—e.g., typists, file clerks, form processors. The fact that some females stay in the same Category I salary grades throughout much of their working careers and that corporate organizations permit and encourage this sexist form of occupational discrimination is further evidence of internal labor market customs, practices, and beliefs being reflective of larger societal values.

likely influence the employee distribution patterns and the RG measures.

From the viewpoint of corporate internal labor market dynamics, it is interesting to note that the RG measure tends to reach its low point in the middle "length of service" category and then rises throughout the remainder of the working years for each of the four groups. Though somewhat less true for white males (Table 8.1), and the lack of data for black males notwithstanding (Table 8.3), the high RG measures generally indicate severely reduced opportunities for upward mobility beyond the fourteenth year for many employees. For the most part, these are employees who have been adjudged probably not capable of higher level responsibility and whose productivity does not warrant a higher salary grade. From the standpoint of many employees in this position, years invested in the corporation, the vested pension benefits, the psychic comfort level associated with familiar people and surroundings, and the fear of being unemployed beyond a certain age all serve to support the RG measures in the later working years. This observation, while described differently here, is generally consistent with the conclusions drawn by those human capital theorists mentioned earlier.

Moving to Next Highest Grades

Estimates of *Moving to Next Highest Grades* (MNHG) are also shown in Tables 8.1–8.4. These estimates attempt to measure employee movement along the diagonals at four possible points of entry. Using the ratio approach, Table 8.1 reveals that Category I white males entering the corporation at the salary grade 1–2 level not only have higher measures than black males and females and white females but that the magnitude of the ratio remains well above unity through the first two "length of service" periods. This should not be surprising in view of the absence and relative scarcity of long-service white males in the lowest grade categories. Note that the values of MNHG for black males are greater than unity in only the first "length of service" category, decline dramatically in the third "length of service" category, are non-existent in the fourth, and considerably lower than for white males throughout. Note, too, that white males and females show stronger tendencies of MNHG than do black males and females.

An interpretation of these trends is simply that white males and females who enter the corporate work force in salary grades 1–2—i.e., Category I employees—have greater access to the next salary grades than do black males and females. (Not so coincidentally, this result squares with the model of employee mobility in Figure 6.1.)

Category II employees, entering the work force at the salary grade level 3–4 and higher, display their initial measures of MNHG along the second diagonal. Again, white males show the dominant trend; and, unlike what was discovered when examining the main diagonal for Category I employees, black males appear to fare better than white and black females. Similar observations follow from an examination of the third diagonal.

White males dominate the upper grade ranks of the corporation. This can be seen from Table 7.5, and from the MNHG measures greater than unity. These measures, when compared with similar measures for the other groups, are all the more emphatic considering the typical pyramiding of an organization.

A MEASURE OF UPWARD MOBILITY

For a given point of entry, e.g., salary grades 1–2, the ratio of MNHG to RG provides a measure of upward mobility (UM). If the value of UM is unity, then the MNHG effect is equivalent to the RG effect; UM > 1 implies a proportionately stronger MNHG effect; UM < 1 implies a proportionately stronger RG effect.

In principle, the UM measure compares MNHG to RG using length of service as the common basis for comparison. Tracing the path of white males, for example, from the entry point at salary grade level 1–2 and from the first "length of service" category through the last category, the procedure may be specified as follows:

$$
UM_{ij}^{wm} = \frac{a_{11}^{MNHG}}{a_{11}^{RG}}, \frac{a_{22}^{MNHG}}{a_{21}^{RG}}, \ldots, \frac{a_{in}^{MNHG}}{a_{nj}^{RG}}
$$

These estimates for the four groups appear in Tables 8.5–8.8.

MODELS OF UPWARD MOBILITY

As was indicated early in this chapter, a number of studies have been undertaken toward an understanding of the relationships between earnings and occupational status, as dependent variables, and education, age, length of service, family background, occupation of head of household, race, sex, and others, as independent variables. Admittedly, I am inclined toward fewer explanatory variables simply

Table 8.5 Upward Mobility
White Males

Ratios of Moving to Next Highest Grade to Remaining in Grade

Length of Service	CATEGORY I				CATEGORY II					
	$\dfrac{3-4/1-2}{1-2}$	$\dfrac{5-6/3-4}{1-2}$	$\dfrac{7-8/5-6}{1-2}$	$\dfrac{9-10/7-8}{1-2}$	$\dfrac{5-6/3-4}{3-4}$	$\dfrac{7-8/5-6}{3-4}$	$\dfrac{9-10/7-8}{3-4}$	$\dfrac{7-8/5-6}{5-6}$	$\dfrac{9-10/7-8}{5-6}$	$\dfrac{9-10/7-8}{7-8}$
Less than 2 yrs.— 2–4 yrs.	7.792				2.231			.506		
2–4 yrs.— 5–9 yrs.		4.232				3.457			1.139	
5–9 yrs.—10–14 yrs.			.798*				.468			.477
10–14 yrs.—15–19 yrs.				.798*						

*Denominator not available

Table 8.6 Upward Mobility
White Females

Ratios of Moving to Next Highest Grade to Remaining in Grade

Length of Service	CATEGORY I				CATEGORY II					
	$\dfrac{3-4/1-2}{1-2}$	$\dfrac{5-6/3-4}{1-2}$	$\dfrac{7-8/5-6}{1-2}$	$\dfrac{9-10/7-8}{1-2}$	$\dfrac{5-6/3-4}{3-4}$	$\dfrac{7-8/5-6}{3-4}$	$\dfrac{9-10/7-8}{3-4}$	$\dfrac{7-8/5-6}{5-6}$	$\dfrac{9-10/7-8}{5-6}$	$\dfrac{9-10/7-8}{7-8}$
Less than 2 yrs.— 2–4 yrs.	3.947				.595			.276		
2–4 yrs.— 5–9 yrs.		1.464				.577			.223	
5–9 yrs.—10–14 yrs.			.605				.650			.153
10–14 yrs.—15–19 yrs.				.572						

Table 8.7 Upward Mobility
Black Males

Ratios of Moving to Next Highest Grade to Remaining in Grade

Length of Service	CATEGORY I				CATEGORY II					
	3–4 / 1–2 / 1–2	5–6 / 3–4 / 1–2	7–8 / 5–6 / 1–2	9–10 / 7–8 / 1–2	5–6 / 3–4 / 3–4	7–8 / 5–6 / 3–4	9–10 / 7–8 / 3–4	7–8 / 5–6 / 5–6	9–10 / 7–8 / 5–6	9–10 / 7–8 / 7–8
Less than 2 yrs.— 2–4 yrs.	4.871	6.976	.088*	—						
2–4 yrs.— 5–9 yrs.					.538	.698	5.286			
5–9 yrs.—10–14 yrs.								.190	.154	
10–14 yrs.—15–19 yrs.										.499

*Denominator not available

Table 8.8 Upward Mobility
Black Females

Ratios of Moving to Next Highest Grade to Remaining in Grade

Length of Service	CATEGORY I				CATEGORY II					
	3–4 / 1–2 / 1–2	5–6 / 3–4 / 1–2	7–8 / 5–6 / 1–2	9–10 / 7–8 / 1–2	5–6 / 3–4 / 3–4	7–8 / 5–6 / 3–4	9–10 / 7–8 / 3–4	7–8 / 5–6 / 5–6	9–10 / 7–8 / 5–6	9–10 / 7–8 / 7–8
Less than 2 yrs.— 2–4 yrs.	2.552	1.293	.150	.500*						
2–4 yrs.— 5–9 yrs.					.093	.418	.049*			
5–9 yrs.—10–14 yrs.								.222	.136	
10–14 yrs.—15–19 yrs.										.500

*Denominator not available

because my observations and studies have led me to think in such terms. Moreover, the explanatory power of many of the models in the literature has not been substantially increased by the wholesale addition of variables.[22]

Taking UM as a dependent variable, it is reasonable to think that length of service and education are important explanatory variables. Thus, at this juncture, the following models were tested:

$$UM_w = f\ (LS,\ Educ) \quad \text{Entry point—Salary Grade 1–2} \quad (8.1)$$
$$UM_b = f\ (LS,\ Educ) \quad \text{Entry point—Salary Grade 1–2} \quad (8.2)$$

$UM_{wm} = f\ (LS,\ Educ,$	Entry points—Salary Grades 1–2,	
EP)	3–4, 5–6, 7–8	(8.3)
$UM_{bm} = f\ (LS,\ Educ,$	Entry points—Salary Grades 1–2,	
EP)	3–4, 5–6, 7–8	(8.4)

The subscripts w, b, wm, and bm denote white, black, white male, and black male, respectively; LS is length of service; $Educ$ is level of education; and EP is entry point.

For this grouped data, the LS variable was assigned the following values:

$$\text{Less than 2 yrs.} — \quad 2\text{–}4 \quad \text{yrs.} = 1$$
$$2\text{–}4 \text{ yrs.} — \quad 5\text{–}9 \quad \text{yrs.} = 2$$
$$5\text{–}9 \text{ yrs.} — \quad 10\text{–}14 \text{ yrs.} = 3$$
$$10\text{–}14 \text{ yrs.} — \quad 15\text{–}19 \text{ yrs.} = 4$$

Values for the $Educ$ variable were derived from data in Tables 7.9–7.28 in Chapter VII. The five educational categories shown there were combined into two categories—namely, "no college" and "college." High school graduates and those employees with other training and special education comprise the "no college" category; and those employees in the remaining categories with varying degrees of higher education were placed in the "college" category. The $Educ$ variable, then, is the ratio of "college" to "no college"—i.e., the ratio of the number of employees in the "college" category to the number of employees in the "no college" category given the appropriate "salary grades" and "length of service" categories.

The EP variable serves to distinguish the different salary grade levels at which employees enter the work force in equations 8.3 and 8.4, i.e., entry points. The variable was assigned the following values:

---

[22]See Jacob Mincer, "The Distribution of Labor Incomes," p. 17; also Larry Lyon and Troy Abell, "Social Mobility Among Young Black and White Men," *Pacific Sociological Review*, 22 (April 1979), 208.

Entry Points
Salary Grades 1–2 = 1
Salary Grades 3–4 = 2
Salary Grades 5–6 = 3
Salary Grades 7–8 = 4

REGRESSION RESULTS

Assuming that linear relationships exist between UM and the selected independent variables, the four equations are summarized in Table 8.9. While the tests of significance are not broadly consistent, the regression results are nonetheless interesting and merit a qualified discussion.

1. For Category I employees, i.e., those entering the corporate work force at the salary grade level 1–2, equation 8.1 appears to be a better model for white employees than 8.2 for black employees. Neither model exhibits satisfactory t scores for the explanatory variables, but 8.1, with an F significant at the .10 percent level, explains approximately .54 percent of the variation in UM. Moreover, the constant term is significant at the .05 percent level. On the other hand, 8.2 purports to explain about .13 percent of the variation in UM for black employees, but the F and t values are much too low for a reasonable level of confidence.

The significance of the constant term in 8.1 gives us confidence that it is probably greater than zero when the length of service and education variables assume zero values. Thus, an interpretation of the constant term is that it measures an *expected* level of UM for employable whites in the "no college" category.

In 8.2, the level of significance associated with the constant term is unacceptable, thereby requiring its rejection as a meaningful measure. However, since from 8.1 we can be reasonably certain of the likelihood of a positive constant term and its implications for an expected rate of UM, then it would not be unreasonable to assume a value greater than zero for the constant term in 8.2. A further assumption would be that the value of the constant term in 8.2 is probably less than the value of the constant term in 8.1. Thus, whites entering the work force as Category I employees with a high school education are more likely to begin their corporate careers with higher-level jobs, more responsibility, and implied higher incomes than blacks entering the corporate work force under similar conditions. Moreover, the difference in constant terms is likely due to management perceptions of black and white workers, their skills, and their probable contributions to productivity.

Table 8.9 Regression Results
Key Factors Influencing Upward Mobility

Category	Entry Point	Regression Coefficients (t Statistics in parentheses)				Adjusted R^2	F	Beta Coefficients			N
		Constant	Length of Service	Education	Entry Point			Length of Service	Education	Entry Point	
I	Gr. 1–2			*Males and Females*							
(8.1)	White	7.8177* (2.908)	−2.4783*** (1.308)	.8853 (.391)		.542	5.141**	−1.140	.341	—	8
(8.2)	Black	3.6016 (.832)	.3084 (.095)	−2.7518 (.568)		.135	1.467	.129	−.774	—	7
I and II	Gr. 1–2, 3–4, 5–6, 7–8			*Males*							
(8.3)	White	10.8413* (4.849)	−1.9803* (3.524)	.1370 (.816)	−2.5649* (2.988)	.632	6.149*	−.878	.274	−1.137	10
(8.4)	Black	11.5986* (2.708)	−2.1304** (1.608)	.6648*** (1.290)	−3.8156* (2.185)	.356	2.289	−.600	.877	−1.625	8

*Significant at the .05 percent level
**Significant at the .10 percent level
***Significant at the .15 percent level

172

8.1 and 8.2 carry opposite signs for length of service and education. Specifically, the coefficients of length of service are negative for whites and positive for blacks; and the coefficients of education are positive for whites and negative for blacks. But the level of confidence in 8.2 is practically nil; in addition, the signs are similar in 8.3 and 8.4 where our confidence is higher. Therefore, the implications of 8.1 should not be taken seriously.

With respect to whites entering the organization as Category I employees in salary grades 1–2, a negative length of service coefficient is expected, since it reflects not only competition for UM opportunities but competition in an organizational structure which tends toward a pyramid—i.e., opportunities become fewer with higher salary grades. Thus, lower UM rates at higher salary grades for white employees.

The education variable is positive for Category I white employees indicating a positive relationship between UM and education. While the length of service variable appears to be substantially more important than the education variable, the latter variable takes on the expected sign in 8.1.

2. Equations 8.3 and 8.4 examine the impact of length of service, education, and entry point on UM for black and white males in salary grade groups 1–2, 3–4, 5–6, and 7–8. Again, the F is significant for the white male model 8.3, and the three variables explain approximately 63 percent of the variation in UM for Categories I and II. In the black male model 8.4, the F value is not statistically significant, but the variables explain .35 percent of the variation. Broadly, the t values in 8.3 and 8.4 improve the reliability of these coefficients relative to 8.1 and 8.2.

Immediately, one notes contrasting results between 8.1 and 8.2, and 8.3 and 8.4. The F values are consistently significant for white employees, but not so for black employees; and the explanatory power of the models is far greater for white UM than for black UM. An obvious interpretation is that UM for white employees is better understood in terms of commonly agreed upon employment factors than UM for black employees. Clearly, the dynamics affecting the black employment process have not been well described by 8.2 and 8.4. In this regard, an improved model will be developed and presented in the next chapter.

The above observation notwithstanding for the moment, important differences in the four models of black and white UM are worth summarizing:

1. The magnitude of the constant terms is similar in 8.3 and 8.4 and quite different in 8.1 and 8.2;

2. The signs of the coefficients are the *same* for black and white
employees in 8.3 and 8.4, and *opposite* in 8.1 and 8.2;
3. In addition to establishing *entry point* as the most influential
variable in 8.3 and 8.4, the beta coefficients reveal that education is the most important variable for black employees, while
length of service is the most important variable for white
employees.

These models, as formulated, beg the question concerning the role
of sex differences in determining the magnitude and direction of the
regression coefficients. While sexism is a recognized force in the
internal labor market, I do not believe that the inclusion of female
workers in 8.1 and 8.2, and their exclusion in 8.3 and 8.4, distort
beyond the bounds of reality the picture of racism that emerges from
the data.

Brief comments regarding these three differences in the four
models are in order. First, to the extent that the constant term reflects
a management perception of potential employee ability and of
expected contribution to productivity, 8.3 and 8.4, which comprise
Category I and Category II male employees, imply that black and
white male employees are perceived similarly. These models are
heavily weighted toward Category II male employees, since the data
in Tables 7.5–7.8 reveal relatively few males in salary grades 1–2.
Second, the sameness of signs in 8.3 and 8.4 indicates that changes
in length of service and education impact black and white employees
similarly. Third, the introduction of *entry point* turns out to be the
most important variable in the models in terms of its beta coefficients.
Clearly, as an individual enters the work force at the higher salary
grade levels—i.e., 5–6, 7–8, and 9–10—the relative prospects for UM
tend to decline. On the other hand, only the most experienced and
skilled workers would be presented opportunities for entering the
work force at high salary levels. Fourth, and finally, education appears
to have a stronger influence on UM for black employees than length
of service. In part, this result is a function of the fact that relatively
few blacks are found in the higher "length of service" categories. The
beta coefficients indicate the opposite effect for white employees;
that is, length of service is the key influence.

AN ALTERNATIVE MODEL

For our purposes, an optional model explicitly includes a race
variable. Thus:

$$UM_{all} = f \, (Race, \, LS, \quad \text{Entry point—Salary Grade 1–2} \quad (8.5)$$
$$Educ)$$
$$UM_{all} = f \, (Race, \, LS, \quad \text{Entry points—Salary Grades 1–2,}$$
$$Educ, \, EP) \quad 3\text{–}4, \, 5\text{–}6, \, 7\text{–}8 \quad (8.6)$$
$$UM_m = f \, (Race, \, LS, \quad \text{Entry points—Salary Grades 1–2,}$$
$$Educ, \, EP) \quad 3\text{–}4, \, 5\text{–}6, \, 7\text{–}8 \quad (8.7)$$

where the subscript *all* denotes black and white employees of both sexes; the subscript *m* denotes black and white males; *Race* is a dummy variable where white = 1, black = 0; *LS* is length of service; *Educ* is level of education; and *EP* is entry point.

Regression results are summarized in Table 8.10. It is interesting to note that the coefficients of race and education are not statistically significant in these models, but the coefficients of race carry the expected positive signs. Length of service and entry point in 8.6 and 8.7 continue, as in the previous models, to be the most influential variables with respect to UM.

A brief comment regarding entry point. Most corporate offices embrace, to a greater or lesser extent, the practice of *promotion from within*. Simply stated, this means that as vacancies occur throughout the work force at levels other than traditional and well understood entry points, employees already in the corporate work force are given primary consideration for such vacancies depending on their current level within the organization, length of service, performance evaluations, skills portfolio, and the "mentor" system. Therefore, unless there is some overriding reason, individuals are infrequently brought into the corporate work force from the outside and placed in positions generally reserved for beneficiaries of the promotion from within policies. But when such an event does occur, it is highly probable that the individual has, or at least is perceived to have, relatively unique qualifications and experiences which merit an exception to the policy. The higher the entry point, presumably, the higher the qualifications and the more intensive and extensive the relevant experiences.

The fact that few blacks find entry points at nontraditional and high corporate levels suggests that either blacks in fact do not possess the qualifications and skills in the amounts required, or that such black employees are perceived by white management as not being sufficiently endowed. The difference in the entry point coefficients for white males and black males in 8.3 and 8.4 further suggests that the rate of upward mobility is higher for whites than blacks with similar length of service and educational credentials. An important implication is that management *perceptions* of blacks at higher levels are different from that of whites, and that the number of blacks who

Table 8.10 Regression Results
Key Factors Influencing Upward Mobility

Category	Entry Point	Regression Coefficients (t Statistics in parentheses)					Adjusted R^2	F	Beta Coefficients				N
		Constant	Race	Length of Service	Education	Entry Point			Race	Length of Service	Education	Entry Point	
		Males and Females											
I (8.5)	Gr. 1–2	5.7138* (2.451)	.5903 (.553)	−1.3497 (.876)	−.3954 (.198)	—	.396	4.062*	.120	−.598	−.137	—	15
I and II (8.6)	Gr. 1–2, 3–4, 5–6, 7–8	6.3261* (5.843)	.4732 (.978)	−1.1903* (4.122)	.0544 (.830)	−1.5340* (4.284)	.413	7.518*	.126	−.609	.145	−.831	38
		Males											
I and II (8.7)	Gr. 1–2, 3–4, 5–6, 7–8	10.0576* (5.187)	.6891 (.856)	−1.9305* (3.639)	.2209*** (1.311)	−2.7018* (3.691)	.544	6.072*	.145	−.733	.375	−1.172	18

*Significant at the .05 percent level
**Significant at the .10 percent level
***Significant at the .15 percent level

176

can expect even to reach the highest levels of corporate organizations is small or virtually non-existent.[23]

CONCLUSIONS

Hypothesis 1: The beta coefficients in 8.1, 8.3, and 8.5–8.7 tend to encourage acceptance of this hypothesis. Upward mobility, in the final analysis, is a function of length of service during which time employees learn, develop, and become members of subpolitical groups and networks within the corporate internal labor market. For white males and females in either Category I or Category II, the opportunities inherent in length of service assure upward mobility for those capable of handling increasing responsibilities. Educational credentials tend to serve more as passport into Category I or Category II status and less as direct contributors to upward mobility.

Hypothesis 2: For blacks in Categories I and II, the beta coefficients in 8.2 and 8.4 support the acceptance of this hypothesis. Blacks tend to be denied the full range of benefits associated with length of service but are admitted to Category I or Category II status on the strength of educational achievement. Thus, upward mobility is limited not only in terms of the higher organizational levels but, we suspect, in terms of various job groups. Of additional importance here is the relative sameness of the constant terms for black and white males in 8.3 and 8.4, and the constant term for all males in 8.7. These imply that the *expected* levels of upward mobility for white and black males are probably equivalent when based on educational and other credentials. The differences in rates of upward mobility for white and black males, then, must be attributable to differences in the impact of the independent variables on upward mobility.

Hypothesis 3: The unacceptable F value associated with 8.4 reduces significantly the confidence in a broad comparison of black and white rates of upward mobility derived from 8.3 and 8.4. From Table 8.10, however, the improved F value in 8.7, the relative magnitudes of the coefficients in 8.3, 8.4, and 8.7, and the sameness of expected signs permits a cautious and considered judgement. Assuming similar values for length of service, education, and entry point, 8.3 and 8.4 estimate rates of upward mobility for black and white males in the corporate internal labor market. The results clearly point to not only higher *absolute* values of upward mobility for white

---

[23]For critical values of EP, LS, and Educ, the values of UM remain positive for white employees but become unrealistically negative for black employees.

males but also higher *rates* of upward mobility for white males than black males. Actually, the values of upward mobility decline with increasing values of length of service and entry, and they do so at faster rates for black males than white males. The analysis also reveals that at higher-level entry points, the values of upward mobility for black males take on negative signs earlier than the values for white males. Again, this suggests the notion of artificial ceiling.

Hypothesis 4: This analysis fails to address a major aspect of this hypothesis, namely, that Category I blacks face fewer obstacles to entering the corporate internal labor market than Category II blacks.

Hypothesis 5: This hypothesis is supported by the qualified analysis of 8.3 and 8.4 and is discussed above.

IX

The Corporate Organization: An Alternative Analysis of Upward Mobility

INTRODUCTION

IN THE PREVIOUS chapter, we attempted a measure of upward mobility on the basis of grouped data. The models better described the paths of upward mobility for white employees than for black employees. Despite weak measures of statistical significance, these measures of UM were explained more accurately by the *length of service* variable than by the *education* variable. A key interpretation of this result should be in terms of the *quality* of an employee's length of service rather than the quantity. For white employees this often means enhanced on-the-job training opportunities, broader organizational exposures, higher valued networks, and potential inclusion in the organization's political life—all of which are supported by *expected* upward mobility paths based on whiteness. For black employees, the quality of length of service tends to be relatively lower.

The role of education in this process, while important, probably has less to do with upward mobility over some period of time than length of service. Its importance can be seen in the allocation of various entry-level positions and in the establishment of an employee's knowledge base, which contributes to skill acquisition.

In this chapter, we propose to examine upward mobility of white and black employees in terms of available individual data by salary grade levels. (See Appendix.) To facilitate the analysis, a measure of Gary S. Becker's *market discrimination coefficient* (MDC)[1] is developed, based on salary data for each of the 643 black employees in the data base. Broadly, the analysis will have as its objective the assessment of the impact of race, education, and length of service on the MDC.

A reasonable set of expectations, consistent with the hypotheses stated in the previous chapter, would be:

1. the MDC for black employees increases with increases in salary grade levels. In other words, as blacks move upward in the organization, the upward mobility paths narrow more quickly than for whites;
2. the MDC for black employees increases with increases in length of service. If the *quality* of length of service for black employees is relatively lower than for white employees, then an important implication is that black productivity is also relatively lower; this inferior quality may be manifested in wages and salaries as well as in promotions, training opportunities, and the like. Thus, increasing the quantity of length of service without quality tends to support an increasing MDC;
3. the level of education attained by black employees has a relatively minimal impact on the MDC. The educational process presumably creates a knowledge base and contributes to intellectual development which, in turn, facilitates skill acquisition. However, for black and white employees, educational credentials—as distinguished from skills mastery—appear from the preceding chapter to have relatively little to do with upward mobility per se, and should not be expected to significantly relate to the MDC.

THE MARKET DISCRIMINATION COEFFICIENT (MDC)

Becker states that if black workers are perfect substitutes for white workers in production under conditions of perfect competition in the labor market, and if W_w and W_b are the wage rates of white and black workers, respectively, then:

$$\text{MDC} = \frac{W_w - W_b}{W_b}$$

---

[1]Gary S. Becker, *The Economics of Discrimination*, 2nd ed. (Chicago: University of Chicago Press, 1971), pp. 17–18.

Clearly, in the absence of discrimination, the equilibrium wage rates for black and white workers would be equal, and the MDC would equal zero.

Placed in our framework, the major portion of employment discrimination based on race finds its significance in the quality of the length of service which characterizes the career longevity of white and black workers in the corporate internal labor market. Becker's "taste for discrimination" concept, which is imputed to individuals in varying degrees, reflects white employer and employee *disutility* with respect to black employees and ultimately results in wage differences. Thus, it is possible to imagine that black corporate employees are perfect substitutes for white corporate employees, and therefore any differences in wages (or rates of promotion and training opportunities) are due to white managers' tastes for discrimination rather than marginal productivity. A more realistic approach would emphasize institutional racism and not the taste for discrimination of individuals. The forces that preclude quality length of service for black employees relative to white employees stem from organizational patterns of behavior (institutional racism) and they are likely to better explain wage and income differences, and differences in rates of upward mobility, than do individuals' tastes for discrimination. Moreover, if, in fact, the quality of length of service for black employees is significantly below that of white employees, then the marginal product of black employees would generally tend to be smaller than the marginal product of white employees over time, especially at the higher corporate levels. Thus, earnings and upward mobility differentials may reflect real differences in the levels of productivity.

This is consistent with our earlier view that differences in black/white wages and salaries in the corporate internal labor market are not the principal tool of employment discrimination. Therefore, the reliance on the MDC should not signal an embracing of Becker's approach to employment discrimination. Rather, in lieu of a broader and better specified data base, the MDC generates earnings comparisons, which otherwise might go begging, as well as evidence of upward mobility growing out of a comparison of salary grade categories.

To approximate this measure for our purposes, the individual salaries of white employees in the corporation in each salary grade category—ie., salary grades 1–2, 3–4, . . ., 9–10—were averaged,[2] and this average was substituted for W_w. Within the salary grade groupings, then, each individual black salary was compared with the white average in the following formulation:

---

[2]This average is a composite of the salaries for white males and the salaries for white females weighted accordingly.

$$MDC_b = \frac{W^*_w - W_b}{W_b}$$

where MDC_b is the market discrimination coefficient estimated for each black male and female employee; W^*_w is the weighted average of white male and female weekly earnings; and W_b is the earnings per week of each black male and female employee. The MDC for black employees is *positive* when black salaries are less than the white average and *negative* when black salaries are greater than the white average.

THE MODEL

To specify the relationships between the MDC and race, education, and length of service over the five salary grade categories, the following model is tested:

MDC_b	$= f(RACE_{all}, EDUC_{all}, LS_{all}) + e_1$	(9.1)
MDC_{bm}	$= f(RACE_{all\ m}, EDUC_{all\ m}, LS_{all\ m}) + e_2$	(9.2)
MDC_b	$= f(EDUC_b, LS_b) + e_3$	(9.3)
MDC_{bm}	$= f(EDUC_{bm}, LS_{bm}) + e_4$	(9.4)

where the subscript b designates black employees; bm designates black male employees; *all* identifies black and white males and females; *all m* is black and white males; and e_1, e_2, e_3, and e_4 are error terms. The explanatory variables are as follows:

1. Race

Race (RACE) is entered as a dummy variable taking the values: Black = 1, White = 0.

2. Education

The education variable (EDUC) is assigned the following values:

high school graduate	= 0
training or special education	= 1
college–no degree	= 2

college graduate   = 3
beyond college   = 4

3. Length of Service

Length of service (LS) is assigned the following values:

Less than 2 years   = 1
2–4   years   = 2
5–9   years   = 3
10–14 years   = 4
15–19 years   = 5
more than 19 years   = 6

This regression analysis is based on the 2,721 employee observations summarized in Chapter VII. These data, including the market discrimination coefficients and the income data from which they were estimated, appear in the Appendix.

REGRESSION RESULTS

Tables 9.1, 9.2, 9.3, and 9.4 summarize equations 9.1, 9.2, 9.3, and 9.4 specified in the model. Generating the regression coefficients for each of the five salary grade groups reveals the relative impact of each variable on the MDC for black employees in Category I and Category II, and in salary grades 1–2 through 9–10.

The F and t values shown in the four tables are consistently impressive for each equation, and the race and length of service variables, respectively. Note, too, that the R^2 values not only tend to rise with higher salary grades, but the percents of explanation attributable to the model for salary grades 5–6—9–10 are substantially above those generated by earlier *schooling models*[3] based on data from the 1/1000 sample of the U.S. Census, 1960. This is especially true for black employees described in Tables 9.3 and 9.4.

In the previous chapter, and reaffirmed here, is the observation that the level of education has a minimal impact on upward mobility

---

[3]For a summary, see Jacob Mincer, "The Distribution of Labor Incomes: A Survey," *Journal of Economic Literature*, 8 (1970), 1–26, esp. p. 8; also, Mincer, *Schooling, Experience, and Earnings* (New York: Columbia University Press, 1974), pp. 43–45 and 53–54.

Table 9.1 The Effects of Race, Education, and Length of Service on the Market Discrimination Coefficient—1978 Black Males and Females

Equation	Category and Salary Grades	Regression Coefficients (t values in parentheses)				Adjusted R^2	F	Beta Coefficients			N
		Constant	Race	Education	Length of Service			Race	Education	Length of Service	
9.1a	Category I Sal. Gr. 1–2	.0634	−.0020 (.274)	.0019 (.297)	−.0356* (9.081)	.258	29.228*	−.015	.017	−.523	244
9.1b	Category II Sal. Gr. 3–4	.0433	.0236* (6.063)	−.0042* (1.824)	−.0155* (10.076)	.187	54.244*	.210	−.063	−.349	694
9.1c	Sal. Gr. 5–6	.0254	.1268* (37.414)	−.0023* (2.235)	−.0060* (7.713)	.657	556.414*	.762	−.046	−.161	871
9.1d	Sal. Gr. 7–8	.0202	.1087* (21.336)	−.0014 (1.363)	−.0042* (5.121)	.487	180.675*	.657	−.045	−.169	569
9.1e	Sal. Gr. 9–10	.0064	.1617* (22.547)	−.0001 (.100)	−.0014* (1.956)	.618	185.648*	.773	−.004	−.068	343

*Significant at the .05 percent level or better

Table 9.2 The Effects of Race, Education, and Length of Service on the Market Discrimination Coefficient—1978 Black Males

Equation	Category and Salary Grades	Regression Coefficients (t values in parentheses)				Adjusted R^2	F	Beta Coefficients			N
		Constant	Race	Education	Length of Service			Race	Education	Length of Service	
9.2a	Category I Sal. Gr. 1–2	.0730	.0283* (2.074)	−.0050 (.370)	−.0473* (4.280)	.315	9.754*	.233	−.042	−.491	58
9.2b	Category II Sal. Gr. 3–4	.0393	.0216* (2.695)	−.0094* (1.837)	−.0123* (4.473)	.164	13.324*	.186	−.123	−.309	189
9.2c	Sal. Gr. 5–6	.0345	.1330* (26.298)	−.0022* (1.396)	−.0091* (7.056)	.646	281.887*	.743	−.040	−.204	463
9.2d	Sal. Gr. 7–8	.0157	.1049* (19.338)	−.0011 (1.123)	−.0032* (3.855)	.499	148.050*	.671	−.041	−.142	444
9.2e	Sal. Gr. 9–10	.0058	.1243* (16.517)	−.0003 (.318)	−.0011 (1.734)	.484	97.748*	.686	−.013	−.073	311

*Significant at the .05 percent level or better

Table 9.3 The Effects of Education and Length of Service on the Market Discrimination Coefficient—1978 Black Males and Females

Equation	Category and Salary Grades	Regression Coefficients (t values in parentheses)			Adjusted R^2	F	Beta Coefficients		N
		Constant	Education	Length of Service			Education	Length of Service	
9.3a	Category I Sal. Gr. 1–2	.1294	.0062 (.767)	−.0790* (13.628)	.583	96.743*	.044	−.777	138
9.3b	Category II Sal. Gr. 3–4	.2195	−.0026 (.874)	−.0812* (25.824)	.682	341.792*	−.028	−.823	319
9.3c	Sal. Gr. 5–6	.3528	.0165* (5.153)	−.0729* (21.659)	.770	234.925*	−.213	−.896	141
9.3d	Sal. Gr. 7–8	.3562	−.0070 (.808)	−.0784* (14.634)	.861	109.474*	−.052	−.941	36
9.3e	Sal. Gr. 9–10	.4137	.0097 (.417)	−.1165* (11.366)	.943	66.838*	.036	−.972	9

*Significant at the .05 percent level or better

Table 9.4 The Effects of Education and Length of Service on the Market Discrimination Coefficient—1978 Black Males

Equation	Category and Salary Grades	Regression Coefficients (t values in parentheses)			Adjusted R^2	F	Beta Coefficients		N
		Constant	Education	Length of Service			Education	Length of Service	
9.4a	Category I Sal. Gr. 1–2	.1750	−.0062 (.385)	−.1052* (6.874)	.575	25.367*	−.043	−.764	37
9.4b	Category II Sal. Gr. 3–4	.2241	−.0045 (.717)	−.0894* (14.307)	.728	109.597*	.043	−.847	82
9.4c	Sal. Gr. 5–6	.3654	−.0141* (3.473)	−.0767* (19.670)	.821	193.673*	−.164	−.929	85
9.4d	Sal. Gr. 7–8	.3799	−.0143* (1.969).	−.0871* (14.903)	.906	111.414*	−.128	−.972	24
9.4e	Sal. Gr. 9–10	.3708	.0178 (.905)	−.1163* (13.847)	.974	96.035*	.065	−.997	6

*Significant at the .05 percent level or better.

187

and MDC. However, it has been shown that the education variable does carry the expected negative sign in most instances. Nonetheless, the relative sizes of the regression coefficients and the absolute values of the beta coefficients clearly point to more important influences on the MDC.

Race

The race variable is positively correlated with the MDC in Tables 9.1 and 9.2, as expected. Moreover, the values of the coefficients tend to be high for black males and females in salary grades 5–6—9–10, and for black males in those grades as well.[4] Specifically, the values of the race coefficient in 9.1c, 9.1d, 9.1e, 9.2c, 9.2d, and 9.2e are significantly higher than those in 9.1a, 9.1b, 9.2a, and 9.2b. Thus, black male and female employees are subject to much higher MDCs (due to race) in the upper part of the corporate organization than in the lower part. In addition, it is probably arguable that this racial impact on employment decisions should be described more in terms of a pattern of institutional behavior than in terms of an individual manager's behavior.

Length of Service

The regression values for this variable are inversely related to the MDC; that is, as length of service increases, the magnitude of the MDC decreases. This would seem logical since employees presumably become more productive as increases in length of service make possible new and more training opportunities, enhanced understanding of the organization and its goals, potential promotions, and an improved knowledge and sense of employee growth and skill acquisition on the part of managers. From Tables 9.1 and 9.2, the negative magnitudes of the length of service coefficients consistently fall as salary grades rise, thereby implying that length of service has a decreasing impact on a rising MDC for black employees in the upper salary grades.

---

[4]Though Category I employees were somewhat arbitrarily defined earlier as constituting salary grades 1–2, this outcome would appear to modify that definition.

Joint Relationship

In Tables 9.1 and 9.2, the regression coefficients for race are positive and increase with higher salary grades, while those for length of service are negative and decrease with higher salary grades. Given the relatively small education coefficients and the declining constant terms as salary grades increase, it can be demonstrated that the values of the MDC are extremely low for salary grades 1–2 and 3–4 but rise dramatically for salary grades 5–6 and above.

The beta coefficients in 9.1a, 9.1b, 9.2a, and 9.2b point to the importance of the length of service variable relative to the race variable in the lower salary grades, i.e., salary grades 1–2 and 3–4. This changes, however, for those black employees in salary grades 5–6—9–10. Here, the beta coefficients—as do the regression coefficients—indicate that *race* has a far greater impact on the MDC than either *education* or *length of service*. These results are consistent with the relevant hypotheses and support the general notion that in the corporate internal labor market race and racism have relatively minimal impact at the lower salary grades (Category I) and heighten as black employees move into Category II positions.

Race as an Implicit Variable

Tables 9.3 and 9.4 describe equations 9.3a–9.3e and 9.4a–9.4e in the model. These regressions are generated on the basis of length of service and education data for black employees only. Again, the length of service variable clearly exerts the preponderant influence on the MDC for black employees. While the magnitude of the coefficients appears somewhat more stable than in 9.1 and 9.2, the significant coefficients are the constant terms. These become higher in value as the salary grade increases, indicating that, under appropriately specified conditions, the MDC for black employees rises with salary grades.

Table 9.5 shows derived values of the MDC for black males based on assumed values for EDUC and LS inserted in equations 9.4a, 9.4b, and 9.4d. The assumed values combine high school graduates (0) and college graduates (3) with no length of service (0), less than two years of service (1), and five to nine years of service (3). From the first column, which assumes no length of service and therefore is roughly representative of black males either seeking employment or applying for employment in the corporation, it is estimated

**Table 9.5 Estimates of MDC for Black Males
Based on Assumed Values for EDUC and LS**

		Length of Service			
E		*0*	*1*	*3*	Equation
d	0	.1750	.0698	−.1406	9.4a
u	3	.1564	.0512	−.1592	
c					
a	0	.2241	.1347	−.0441	9.4b
t	3	.2106	.1212	−.0576	
i					
o	0	.3799	.2928	.1186	9.4d
n	3	.3370	.2499	.0757	

that the expected values of the MDC for black males, in either Category I or Category II, increase as the salary grades increase. It should be noted, however, that changes in educational status from high school graduate to college graduate do have a dampening influence on the values of the expected MDC.

Reading down the second column, where length of service is less than two years, the upward pattern of the MDC is similar to that of the first column except that the values are significantly smaller, as might be expected.

A length of service of five to nine years is assumed in the third column. Here, the MDC takes on negative values for black males in salary grades 1–2 (Category I) and 3–4 (Category II). An interpretation is that black males who stay in the lower salary grades for substantial periods of time reach the upper parts of their earnings range. A review of the basic data presented earlier reveals that white males have much less longevity in the lower salary grades and apparently more opportunity for promotion to higher salary grades than black males. Thus, given relatively long lengths of service in the lower grades, it is not surprising to find black male earnings that exceed the average of white earnings, thereby producing a negative MDC.

Examining the rows of Table 9.5 provides another angle from which to view the MDC for black males. Essentially, as length of service increases, the MDC decreases. In 9.4a and 9.4b (salary grades 1–2 and 3–4), the values of the MDC are relatively close, irrespective of educational status. Moreover, as was postulated early on, discrimination is *less* for blacks in lower salary grades than in higher salary grades. This does not appear to be the case in 9.4d. Here, while education has a more significant effect on the MDC, the MDC remains positive throughout.

CONCLUSIONS

Whether treated explicitly or implicitly, race is an important factor in the employment process facing blacks. One cannot be certain as to just how race impacts the employment process. However, our analysis does seem to point more to an institutional pattern of influence than to variegated individual tastes for discrimination. In any event, the constant terms in Tables 9.1 and 9.2 decline as salary grades rise; and in Tables 9.3 and 9.4, the constant terms rise with increases in salary grades. The strong implication is that race is a positive factor with respect to employment discrimination and upward mobility for black employees. Specifically, then, the analysis tends to confirm the expectation that the MDC for black employees increases with increases in the salary grade levels.

The second expectation, namely, that the MDC for black employees increases with increases in length of service, is not supported without qualification. Viewing Table 9.5 as if it depicted the paths of the MDC over time, the raw values highlight a strong decline in the MDC as length of service increases. However, this pattern assumes that black employees remain in grade over the time period in question. If the main diagonal for high school graduates and college graduates is traced so as to portray promotion from the lowest salary grade to the highest salary grade, then the MDC still declines as length of service increases. On the other hand, a tracing of the minor diagonals reveals that the MDC may increase with increases in length of service.

The third expectation was in terms of the educational attainment of black employees and its impact on the MDC. In the lower salary grades, the differences in the MDC for high school graduates vis-à-vis college graduates do indeed appear minimal relative to either length of service or race. Broadly, the data suggest that factors of race and length of service are important determinants of upward mobility for black employees—and these are factors over which no employee has direct control. It is something of a disappointment to learn, then, that the one factor which black employees can largely determine—namely, educational attainment—tends to have the least impact on their career development and upward mobility.

X

Summary, Conclusions, and Recommendations

INTRODUCTION

AS THIS WORK is brought to a close, I feel compelled to make certain that the reader has not interpreted the foregoing as a thesis that promotes the notion that black and white corporate employees are, in every individual instance, absolute economic equivalents in the corporate workplace. On the contrary, any observer can note the disproportionate conditions of poverty which afflict large numbers of blacks: the wage, income, and occupational differences between black and white employees; differences in educational opportunities and their quality; and lack of substantive internal labor market training and other corporate experiences. Obviously, under such circumstances many blacks do have less than fully developed skills and other qualifications. But the point is that deficiencies are produced by socioeconomic phenomena that are not only self-reinforcing but reinforcing to each other and which are fueled by a racism characterized by a white superiority-black inferiority syndrome. Importantly, this racist line of thinking ascribes to blacks low-status behavior (e.g., "culture of poverty" and social class considerations) and/or innate inferiority (e.g., relatively low IQs and educational achievement) such that institutional discrimination against a black presence may be rationalized if not justified.

In the face of evidence to the contrary, important mainstream writers continue, in often subtle ways, to give an undeserved credence to the presumed reality of white superiority–black inferiority.

193

For many economists—neoclassicists in particular—the strength of racist values, which they all would disavow, impels them toward a conventional wisdom that serves to feed and maintain racism, generally, and rationalize internal labor market discrimination based on race, in particular. The intent of this work has been to demonstrate that it is *racism* which has constructed and maintains a "culture of poverty" as well as notions of inferiority, and that the implicit or explicit inclusion of these ideas in neoclassical economic theories of employment discrimination tends to render such theories as useless as the racist ones that have influenced them.

It would not be possible for this volume to undertake the identification and explanation of even a significant number of the conditioned assertions that pass as knowledge from scholarly hands to the public at large, and especially to managers in the various internal labor markets. But, to make the point clearer, let us cite, in a bit more detail than in earlier chapters, one example of the kind of assertion that purports to explain differences between black and white educational achievement and resulting employment and occupational progress.

There is no deficit of reference in the literature to the issue of "quality education"—or the lack of it—accruing to blacks. It is thought by many writers, and more often than not stated as if it were a foregone conclusion, that blacks "may have less education . . . because of having anticipated discrimination against their education."[1] Again:

> Nonwhite students who anticipate discrimination against their education might be absent a higher proportion of the time, and, while in school, a higher proportion of their time may be devoted to leisure activities. Hence, the effort expended in learning may be less because of the lower value of schooling.[2]

Though Kenneth J. Arrow, to some extent, questions the notion of black preoccupation with the present relative to the future, he states:

> It is frequently held that blacks have, because of cultural and historical conditioning, a stronger tendency to discount the future and, because of this, a lower propensity to make investments in themselves.[3]

And, later on, he writes:

---

[1]Finis Welch, "Labor Market Discrimination: An Interpretation of Income Differences in the Rural South," *Journal of Political Economy*, 75 (June 1967), 225.

[2]Ibid., p. 233.

[3]Kenneth J. Arrow, *Some Models of Racial Discrimination in the Labor Market* (Santa Monica: The Rand Corporation, 1971), p. 4.

The fact that discrimination against blacks increases with the level of education implies that the rate of return to the investment in human capital is lower for blacks than for whites, explaining in turn why the proportion of blacks in college is lower than that of whites.[4]

Noting that there are educational differences between whites and nonwhites, Christopher Jencks observes that:

the desire for higher earnings has been a major reason for seeking education in modern societies. We cannot measure the non-monetary costs or benefits of continuing education for either whites or nonwhites. In the absence of such information, we must assume that lower monetary benefits mean lower overall returns and, hence, lower incentives to continue one's education.[5]

These sample statements, and others akin to them, all exhibit and communicate, beyond their similar content, racial value judgements and ideas and supports for racism.

First, one notes that each statement promotes an idea that is relatively simple and easily understood. In the best tradition of effective propaganda, simplicity is essential for mass communications and general institutional adoption. Here, we have statements and thoughts about black/white education and earnings differentials consistent with that tradition.

The second similarity to be noted in the statements is that each structures rationalizations for differences in education and earnings based on race through a system of contrived incentives and desires, which accordingly motivates whites to higher-level achievements than blacks. Racists might say, "Can white people be held responsible if blacks decide that high educational achievement is relatively unimportant?"

Third, these presumed explanations of education and earnings differentials give credence to the belief that, in fact, blacks, conditioned by their history and culture, are quite content with their existence and lives. For if they were not, then they, like whites, would spend more serious time in those education and training pursuits which could lead to an improved livelihood. Therefore, one need not be overly concerned about the socioeconomic status of blacks since they themselves do not seem to be all that concerned.

A fourth similarity is the implication that blacks exhibit a lack of foresight with respect to the future, i.e., a propensity for current

---

[4]Ibid., p. 9.

[5]Christopher Jencks, *Who Gets Ahead?: The Determinants of Economic Success in America* (New York: Basic Books, 1979), p. 208.

gratification relative to future rewards. Such a notion is clearly related to concepts of "ability" and "outlook." Everybody knows that it is the lower animals that seek only present gratification and have no facility for (or interest in) anticipating the future.

Related to this characteristic, a fifth observation is that these quotations promote the notion that black people have inferior intellectual abilities. If it is suggested that higher levels of black education are discriminated against, or that returns to higher education are lower for blacks than for whites—a state of affairs described by the statistical analyses in Chapters VIII and IX—then one clear implication is that higher levels of educational attainment exceed the intellectual grasp of blacks. Of course, this is consistent with the white superiority–black inferiority view of American whites.

The sixth way in which these statements are similar is in their view of the *oneness* of blacks; that is, black people tend to be viewed in a monolithic way, if you will, in contrast to the range of characteristics exhibited by members of white society. In part, this is the result of the pervasiveness of racism and the imputing of inferior traits and characteristics to blacks irrespective of socioeconomic class affiliation.[6] This approach accommodates, on behalf of racism, a simple and uniform standard for the application of racist principles, which any societal institution can embrace with ease and which the lowliest practitioner can comprehend. Thus, accomplished blacks, too, are victimized by racist thought and practices.

Finally, the ideas contained in these statements, as has already been indicated, serve to absolve whites of social responsibility for the socioeconomic condition of black Americans and, at the same time, promote feelings of white superiority. Whether in the work force or in other of society's institutional arrangements, economic and social outcomes are endogenously determined, while racism is viewed as outside the system.

These implications are really quite subtle. For example, it is one thing to suggest that blacks may be discouraged from seeking advanced education because of racial discrimination, in the manner of Arthur M. Okun,[7] but quite another to imply inferiority with respect to mental capacity and judgement and, in the final analysis, to excoriate blacks for their socioeconomic conditions.

---

[6]See J. K. Vardaman's comment in our Chapter III regarding Booker T. Washington, quoted in John Hope Franklin, *From Slavery to Freedom* (New York: Alfred A. Knopf, 1947), pp. 337–38.

[7]For example, unlike some other writers, Okun assumes the following position: "Moreover, unequal opportunity at one point in time generates unequal opportunity over time. Once people are excluded from good jobs, they are deprived of the incentives and opportunities to develop the skills that would otherwise qualify them for good jobs." See Arthur M. Okun, *Equality and Efficiency: The Big Tradeoff* (Washington: The Brookings Institution, 1975), p. 77.

With reference to education, this is a particularly bitter pill when for decades white society has been saying to blacks that the acquisition of education could doubtless lead to a state of racial "integration" and a presumed absence of racial discrimination. Rather, blacks find that either barriers to quality education persist or that higher levels of education are discriminated against.

Nonetheless, these kinds of assertions grow and develop in every sector of the society, and their influence is felt throughout. While the primary emphasis in this book has been toward a furthered understanding of the corporate internal labor market, needless to say, that market is not spared the influence of such assertions.

MAJOR CONCLUSIONS AND HIGHLIGHTS

As regards the corporate internal labor market, the analyses in Part 2 attempt to explain and confirm the observations and discussion presented in Part 1. Since the personnel data from a single corporation were the basis for the empirical analysis, one would be advised against an overly liberal interpretation of the results when broadly viewing the corporate sector. Doubtless, degrees of employment discrimination based on race vary by type of industry and firm and depend on factors such as location, the size and character of a given minority labor force and work force, the quality of the work force required by the firm, and capital intensive versus labor intensive production techniques. That racial discrimination in employment markets—internal and external—exists is a well-documented fact, and I hope this work adds to the credibility and understanding of that fact.

The broad concept of upward mobility can be brought to measure in many ways—e.g., absolute or relative earnings rates, rates of progress along defined career ladders, movement from lower to higher organizational levels, changes in levels of responsibility. A chosen measure would likely reflect sought-after appropriateness and a consistency with objectives. Further, such choices would be influenced by whether an analysis was aimed at estimating the upward mobility paths for individual employees or employees as a group. In this work, relative rates of group progress were estimated in terms of absolute numbers of black and white employees in cross section by salary grade groups, where the patterns were presumed, for analytical purposes, to comparatively measure upward mobility over time. A second measure of upward mobility estimated differences in black/white earnings via Becker's Market Discrimination Coefficient for each of the five salary grade groups.

Though the data made available for this study do not include explicit measures of employee performance, which could have been used as explanatory variables, estimates of upward mobility and the MDC represent, to some degree, implicit evaluation of employee performance. It is probable that the influence of the performance evaluation process for black employees is felt in the RACE and LS coefficients. This is not a difficult conclusion to reach when the concepts of *statistical discrimination* and the *quality* of length of service are brought to bear. Given that employee performance in the corporate internal labor market is often nonquantifiable and, at best, nearly impossible to measure, the perceptions of white employers and employees tend to discount black employee performance. And such perceptions are often undergirded by the denial of a high quality length of service for black employees generally—hence, a self-fulfilling prophecy.

On the other hand, in a period promoting equal employment opportunity and subscribing to the notion that racial discrimination is no longer a significant factor in the corporate employment process, many white managers do not like to admit or think of themselves as being prejudiced or as making personnel evaluations and decisions on other than objective bases. In fact, as a minimal point of reference, many managers evaluate all employees for upward mobility opportunities in terms of themselves; that is, they seek those who share their own value systems and cultural identity. Most black employees, then, find that their chances for upward mobility become slim relative to white employees as they move toward the middle and upper parts of the organization. This result appears to relate to the major conclusions of this study.

First, Category I black employees experience generally less discrimination than Category II black employees. *Entry* into the corporate internal labor market is relatively easy for Category I black employees, but less easy for Category II black employees. This would appear to be the major distinction since both groups face difficult upward mobility paths, once employed. Further, Category I black employees are primarily relegated to the lower level salary grades while Category II black employees *enter* at higher salary grade levels.

Second, black employees experience less upward mobility overall than white employees. This is evident from the estimated measures of upward mobility and the MDC. The rates of upward mobility are higher for white employees than for black employees, and the MDC for black employees rises as salary grade levels rise.

Third, *length of service* is more strongly correlated with upward mobility than is *educational level*. The chosen interpretation is that the *quality* of length of service is the determining factor in rates of upward mobility. Educational level is determined outside the corporate organization and is not likely to influence upward mobility more directly than performance within the corporate organization—performance which can be qualitatively assessed and which is significantly a function of in-house training opportunities, constructive performance evaluations with appropriate feedback mechanisms, acceptance as a member of the team, and inclusion in the higher corporate communications networks. Under these circumstances, performance tends to improve and to be enhanced as length of service increases. While this is true for black and white employees alike, the analyses indicate that length of service for black employees has more of an impact on their upward mobility rates than does that factor on the upward mobility rate of white employees. However, the lower absolute values of upward mobility imply that black employees are not the beneficiaries of in-house performance supports, over time, to the same degree that white employees are.

Specifically, the length of service coefficients for males in Tables 8.9 and 10.1 reveal that the influence of that factor on the contrived measure of upward mobility is more positive for white male employees than for black male employees. That is, increases in length of service decrease the rates of upward mobility less for whites than for blacks. While this result is seen for both Category I and II employees, it is clear also that the *expected* rates of upward mobility decline generally with increases in length of service and entry points and tend to rise with increases in level of education.

Table 10.1 The Impact of Length of Service on Upward Mobility Rates—Male Employees

Employee Group	Salary Grade 1–2—7–8 Coefficients	
	Regression	Beta
White	−1.9803	−.878
Black	−2.1304	−.600

Source: See Table 8.9

Table 10.2 summarizes the length of service coefficients related to the Market Discrimination Coefficient for male employees. As length of service rises, the MDC falls as expected in the five salary grade groups. Moreover, the magnitudes of the black regression coefficients are consistently greater than those of the white regression coefficients, while the betas for white male employees are greater than the betas for black male employees in salary grades 1–2 and 3–4. This explains, in part, the uneven estimates of the MDC, given

Table 10.2 The Impact of Length of Service on the Market Discrimination
Coefficient

	Black Male Employees		White Male Employees	
Salary	Coefficients			
Grades	Regression	Beta	Regression	Beta
1–2	−.1052	−.764	−.0760	−.786
3–4	−.0894	−.847	−.0470	−.870
5–6	−.0767	−.929	−.0565	−.829
7–8	−.0871	−.972	−.0596	−.916
9–10	−.1163	−.997	−.0578	−.898

Source: See Table 9.4 for black employees. The MDC for white males was
computed, and regressions using education and length of service data were run. The
resulting length of service coefficients are shown here.

Table 10.3 Derived Market Discrimination Coefficients Assuming Selected
Levels of Education and Length of Service

Length of Service by Salary Grade Level	Black Males		White Males	
	High School	College	High School	College
Salary Grades 1–2				
Less than 2 yrs.	.0698	.0512	.0754	.0268
2–4 yrs.	−.0354	−.0540	−.0006	−.0492
5–9 yrs.	−.1406	−.1592	−.0766	−.1253
Salary Grades 3–4				
Less than 2 yrs.	.1347	.1212	.0912	.0873
2–4 yrs.	.0707	.0318	.0442	.0403
5–9 yrs.	−.0441	−.0576	−.0028	−.0067
Salary Grades 5–6				
Less than 2 yrs.	.2887	.2464	.1385	.1190
2–4 yrs.	.2120	.1697	.0820	.0625
5–9 yrs.	.1353	.0930	.0255	.0060
Salary Grades 7–8				
Less than 2 yrs.	.2928	.2499	.1921	.1942
2–4 yrs.	.2057	.1628	.1325	.1346
5–9 yrs.	.1186	.0757	.0729	.0750
Salary Grades 9–10				
Less than 2 yrs.	.2545	.3079	.2036	.2030
2–4 yrs.	.1382	.1916	.1458	.1452
5–9 yrs.	.0219	.0753	.0880	.0874

the assumptions of increasing length of service and changes in educational status. For example, from Table 10.3, the following observations are made:

1. Continuing the assumption that the "less than 2 yrs." category is equivalent to point of entry, note that for black male high school and college graduates, the MDCs are relatively close in the lower grades and, while increasing, diverge at the higher salary grade levels. Certainly, this would be a reasonable development until it is noted that for white male high school and college graduates, the significant divergence occurs in the salary grade group 1–2 and from thereon tends toward convergence at the point of entry for the higher salary grades. It seems clear, then, that the *quality* of the first two years of employment is probably different for Category II black male high school and college graduates but similar for Category II white male high school and college graduates. To the extent that the MDC reflects the quality of length of service, black males have opportunities for fewer and less of those experiences essential to a high quality length of service. Moreover, for salary grades 3–4—9–10, white male high school graduates have lower MDCs than black male college graduates in the first two years of employment.

2. Increases in length of service for each salary grade group are accompanied by declines in the MDCs for black and white males. While the rates of decline are greater for black male high school and college graduates than for their white counterparts through the ninth year of employment, the absolute values of the MDCs for blacks tend to remain above those for whites.

3. For Category I employees, the derived MDCs would seem to indicate that a college degree lowers the MDC for white males but has relatively little effect on the MDC for black males. As the salary grade level increases, however, college degrees lower the MDC more for blacks than for whites even though the absolute values for black employees tend to remain above those for whites irrespective of length of service.[8]

4. The values of the MDCs for Category II white males are strikingly close through the ninth year of employment, notwithstanding educational credentials. This is to say that Category II white male high school and college graduates face similar MDCs which imply that the quality of length of service is similar for both high school and college graduates. With respect to Category II black male employees, the values of the MDCs through the ninth year of employment tend to be higher for high school graduates than for college graduates.

---

[8]In salary grades 9–10, a statistical anomaly appears in Table 10.3. Here, the regression coefficient for education in the equation for black males takes a positive sign which causes the values of the MDC for black college graduates to exceed those derived for black high school graduates.

5. The race coefficients estimated in Chapter VIII were not statistically significant in terms of the contrived measures of upward mobility though they carried the expected sign. In Chapter IX, however, where race was a dummy variable used to explain variations in the MDC, it was statistically significant for each salary grade group for black males and females, and black males. As hypothesized, the importance of the race variable increases as black employees move to the higher salary grades within the corporation. Furthermore, a review of the beta coefficients in Tables 9.1 and 9.2 points to the dominance of race as an explanatory variable from salary grade group 5–6 through salary grade group 9–10.

This result, in our opinion, lends credibility to our earlier discussions and supports a theory of *employer expectations*, or a theory of *employment racism*. These significant race coefficients suggest that blacks generally are largely evaluated and judged for hiring, in-house training opportunities, promotions, and the like, on the basis of managers' preconceived notions of relatively low black productivity, and/or the practice of *discounting* the credentials and performance of black employees. At the point of hire, employer expectations, which are influenced not only by race but also employee portfolios, prevail and the role of race is increasingly dominant the higher the salary grade level applied for. Once inside the corporation, the dynamics of the internal labor market assume command on behalf of both black and white employees. Of major importance, however, is the fact that the dynamics reflect racism, and its perceived implications for lower productivity, in varying proportions when determining the flow of black employees.

GENERAL CONCLUSIONS

Though this book may raise more questions than it answers, its basic purpose is to add to the data base regarding racial discrimination in the corporate internal labor market and its impact on upward mobility for black employees. While the statistical analyses are limited to the available corporate data base, they and the discussions contained herein point to inadequacies in the neoclassical wage discrimination models and in the human capital theories for relevant explanations of upward mobility and support instead some theory of employment racism.

Discrimination in labor markets and in the employment process is generally described in terms of different wages paid to units of labor of equal ability and productivity. In view of empirical black-white wage differentials, economic wisdom either constructs a rationale for such wage differentials between black and white workers who are perfect substitutes in production; or it theorizes that in fact black and white workers are not perfect substitutes; or both. What we have been led to conclude in this study is that wage differentials are probably not the significant source of racial discrimination; rather, such differentials are a manifestation of an institutional racism which negatively impacts the quality of length of service for black employees. Thus, rates of promotion and upward mobility and, consequently, wage rates tend to be lower for black employees than for white employees. Moreover, the *patterns* of racially induced employment discrimination are sufficiently clear—in terms of the levels and types of jobs, their authorities and responsibilities, the decreasing rates of upward mobility relative to white employees, the increasing MDCs as black employees move to higher salary grades, and the apparently lower quality length of service experiences—to cast considerable doubt on the usefulness of a neoclassical theory with a "taste for discrimination" at its base. These patterns also undermine a human capital theory that propounds the view that black employees have not chosen to invest in their own human capital to the extent that white employees have as an explanation for black–white wage differentials. Such patterns could only be maintained, in all likelihood, if institutionalized, and it is this corporate institutionalization of the employment process which gives credence to the notion of *institutional racism* and its role in the corporate internal labor market.

More to the point, institutional racism is reflected in the values and customs embraced by organizations. Given that a major function of corporate internal labor markets is the allocation of career opportunities, it is clear that managers, who may be "independent" or "dependent," are themselves seeking upward mobility opportunities and, at the same time, determining rates of upward mobility for subordinates. Needless to say, adherence to organizational values and customs—which undergird the role and evaluation of "overall employee performance" and of communication networks—is key to the upward mobility process for managers and subordinates. Since managers have responsibilities for deciding promotions and assignments for all employees, it is likely that institutional racism, as well as personal values embraced by managers, negatively impacts the rate of upward mobility and the career aspirations of black corporate employees.

RECOMMENDATIONS

Many contemporary corporate leaders and managers vigorously resist, as individuals, the organizational and cultural forces which promote employment discrimination on the basis of race. Not only do these managers understand the economic importance of maximizing black and white labor resources in the production process, they also reflect a sensitivity to the concept of corporate social responsibility and its potential contributions to the viability of the social and economic environment. In addition, they see racial discrimination in the labor markets as an anachronism and as an assault upon human dignity. As a substantive basis for the recommendations which are to follow, a brief discussion of corporate social responsibility, the issue of equality versus efficiency, and the nature of corporate intervention is in order.

Corporate Social Responsibility

Specifically, corporate social responsibility is a concept that reflects the social concerns of corporations for the community and society in which they exist. It is not necessarily motivated by any particular altruism; rather, it is both a response to the demands of society for corporate involvement in its welfare and a recognition by corporations that their health, vitality, and viability are inextricably linked to that of the society. Thus, modern-day corporations have legitimate interests in many social issues and activities not *directly* related to those which generate profits.[9]

A 1973 Harris national poll revealed that the public's expectation of corporate leadership in a number of social areas has been increasing since 1966. Table 10.4 shows this change regarding selected areas of concern:

> What is clear is that it is generally recognized that many of the actions of business firms . . . affect the well-being of the society, and thus can be described as social actions. It is also clear that 'business is being asked to assume broader responsibilities to society than ever before and to serve a wider range of human values.'[10]

This role is consistent with Daniel Bell's notion of a changing corporate structure:

> A business corporation . . . with its hierarchy and status system . . . is now a lifetime experience for many of its members. Necessarily, therefore, it can no longer be an instrument satisfying

---

[9]Regarding this concept, see John J. Corson and George A. Steiner, *Measuring Business's Social Performance: The Corporate Social Audit* (New York: Committee for Economic Development, 1974).

[10]Ibid., p. 2.

Table 10.4 Nationwide Public Opinion Polls—Corporate Social
Responsibility
(Selected Issues)

	Corporations should give leadership		
Issues	1973	1971	1966
	(in percent)		
Controlling air and water pollution	92	89	69
Rebuilding our cities	85	84	74
Enabling people to use their creative talents fully	85	85	73
Eliminating racial discrimination	84	81	69
Wiping out poverty	83	81	69

Source: Summary of Lou Harris polls cited in Corson and Steiner, *Measuring Social Performance*, p. 15.

a single end—in the case of the business corporation, only turning out its goods and services—but it has to be a satisfactory way of life for its members.[11]

While corporate members are also members of the larger society which registers its social demands, black members make the assumption that they too are entitled to a "satisfactory way of life" within the corporate structure and, outside of that structure, that corporations have a social responsibility for contributing toward general improvements in the life of black communities. At least within the corporate internal labor market, it is fair to state that such an assumption is not broadly validated by experience or analysis.[12] What is validated is that the social and economic structures of the corporation, in Bell's terms, position blacks and define black/white relationships—even Category II blacks—in much the same manner as might be observed in the larger society. As a result, three rather obvious judgements may be formed:

1. The social structure of the internal labor market probably resembles societal class relationships. Michael J. Piore has noted that

[11]Daniel Bell, *The Coming of Post-Industrial Society* (New York: Basic Books, 1973), p. 288. Also see Peter B. Doeringer and Michael J. Piore, *Internal Labor Markets and Manpower Analysis* (Lexington: D.C. Heath, 1971), chap. 1.

[12]This statement simply means that in relative terms, corporate life for black employees is less rewarding and satisfying than for white employees.

"the characterization of the secondary sector and the upper and lower tiers of the primary sector suggest the distinctions made in the sociological literature between the lower-, working-, and middle-class subcultures."[13]

2. The workings of the internal labor market and the generated results cannot be analyzed solely in a strict economic/financial framework.

3. Corporate decisions and actions regarding the management of internal labor markets must be guided not entirely by reference to economic/financial factors but also by corporate social considerations, with an eye toward social responsibility and meeting the social, economic, and psychic needs of all its members.

These judgements notwithstanding, the fact is, with respect to internal labor markets, that questions abound regarding the classic tradeoff between socioeconomic equality and economic efficiency. Is "fair" consistent with that economic and financial success that ensures survival? What do "equality" and "fair" mean in an internal labor market context? Suffice it to state that while these and other questions deserve attention, their appropriate treatment is beyond the scope of this volume. Nonetheless, it is useful to describe some of the parameters governing the equality versus efficiency concept.

Equality versus Efficiency

With specific reference to internal labor markets, for example, Doeringer and Piore have taken the position that given the structure, rules, and customs regarding the pricing and the allocation of labor, and the reinforcing interests of employers and employees,

> it is not generally possible to change the distribution of jobs
> between the races without affecting the efficiency of recruitment,
> screening, and training. The elimination of racial discrimination
> is likely to raise the inefficiency of the labor force adjustment
> process, at least in the short run, thereby imposing costs upon
> both the employer and society.[14]

Bell offers a similar conclusion based on a somewhat different view— a disparaging one—of social attempts at equality. In the main, they

---

[13]As was pointed out earlier, "upper and lower tiers" are equivalent to Category II and Category I corporate employees. See Michael J. Piore, "Notes for a Theory of Labor Market Stratification," in *Labor Market Segmentation*, ed. Richard C. Edwards, Michael Reich, and David M. Gordon (Lexington: D.C. Heath, 1975), p. 127.

[14]Doeringer and Piore, *Internal Labor Markets*, p. 136.

are violative of the principles of a "meritocracy" which he maintains is essential in the postindustrial society. Of these attempts, he states that

> one sees this in the derogation of the IQ and the denunciation of theories espousing a genetic basis of intelligence . . . and the attack on "credentials" and even schooling itself as the determinant of a man's position in the society. A postindustrial society reshapes the class structure of society by creating new technical elites. The populist reaction, which has begun in the 1970s, raises the demand for greater "equality" as a defense against being excluded from that society. Thus the issue of meritocracy versus equality.[15]

The Doeringer and Piore contention ascribes to the internal labor markets a set of equilibria which account for employer and employee interests and a host of institutional customs and values, including racism. Intervention serves to disturb these equilibria and the results are market inefficiencies. Of course, this apologia for racism is neoclassicism at its best. Bell's "meritocracy," on the other hand, is an attack on those deprived of social and economic opportunities, the promotion of "technical skills and higher education" as a basis for status and earnings, and the presumption of the relative superiority of some groups (racial, class, or both).

One need not be an economist to suspect the obvious; namely, that the underemployment or underutilization of human resources, as a function of discrimination based on race, likely will result in misallocations which, in turn, create inefficiencies. Nor need one be a sociologist or political scientist to observe that interventions (e.g., government regulations, legal proscriptions) on behalf of society relative to profit-making goals are frequent and produce social policies that tend to outweigh private interests. From discrimination models developed by Shelly J. Lundberg and Richard Startz, a major conclusion was that

> the gain to society from discrimination, which reduces the small loss for the advantaged workers, is smaller than the loss to society from discrimination, which increases the large loss to the disadvantaged workers.[16]

And, consistent with a major theme of this volume, Arthur M. Okun writes:

---

[15] Bell, Post-Industrial Society, p. 410.

[16] Shelly J. Lundberg and Richard Startz, "Private Discrimination and Social Intervention in Competitive Labor Markets," American Economic Review, 73 (June 1983), 347.

Unequal opportunity at one point in time generates unequal opportunity over time. Once people are excluded from good jobs, they are deprived of the incentives and opportunities to develop the skills that would otherwise qualify them for good jobs. . . . If . . . [a black] . . . is blocked from his firm's ladder-climbing career program, he accumulates fewer skills on the job. Thus, inefficiency can grow at compound interest.[17]

If it is agreed, then, that employment discrimination is not in the social interest, and that social interventions produce inefficiencies through the disturbance of labor market equilibria, one is left with a market structure that tends not to respond to social desiderata. David H. Swinton convincingly argues that the automaticity of free market forces is not likely to correct the inequalities which characterize black/white relations.[18] As a matter of fact, such inequalities are likely to persist even in the face of economic equilibrium. Thus, government intervention may be necessary for the attainment of a "social equilibrium" where the absence of such "threaten[s] the social stability or the social welfare." Unlike Doeringer and Piore, and Bell, Swinton reminds us that

the phenomenon of discrimination is itself a social intervention into the determination of market equilibrium. There is nothing sacred about the market equilibrium which itself is just the outcome of a particular set of sociopolitical processes. Therefore, additional intervention can certainly be justified whenever the outcome is undesirable.[19]

In the final analysis, while markets governed by custom and institutional values may tend toward rigidity, there is, nonetheless, evidence that such interventions have brought about orderly and efficient changes in economic behavior. Okun observes that

when society opts for equal employment opportunity, it is overriding preferences for racial and sexual discrimination. . . . The record dramatizes the general point that political decisions about fair play can change economic behavior. It further illustrates the general possibility that what is good for equality may be good for efficiency.[20]

Thus, the equality versus efficiency issue is far from settled.

---

[17]Arthur M. Okun, *Equality and Efficiency*, p. 77.
[18]David H. Swinton, "Factors Affecting the Future Economic Prospects of Minorities," *American Economic Review*, Proceedings, 65 (May 1975), 53–58.
[19]Swinton, "Prospects of Minorities," p. 58.
[20]Okun, *Equality and Efficiency*, pp. 78–79.

From our viewpoint, however, the arguments in support of the mutual exclusivity of "equality" and "efficiency" are designed to perpetuate race and class distinctions on behalf of a privileged group. And *if* inefficiencies arise in the work place because racial barriers are lowered (intervention), they are more likely the result of racist responses than the inability of qualified black employees to perform efficiently.

Corporate Interventions

Even though equal employment opportunity and affirmative action legislation is on the books, and corporate policy statements of nondiscrimination are written, significant changes in the management of the corporate internal labor market requires, in particular, that senior management develop a commitment and determination to alter internal employment practices. Not so incidentally, a number of major corporations, and some smaller ones, led by visionaries and individuals committed to the principles of equal employment opportunity have had notable successes in their EEO efforts on behalf of blacks, other minorities, and women. Ultimately, such advances are built on internal interventions. Moreover, it is clear that the organizational leadership required for internal labor market change must originate with board chairmen and chief executive officers.[21]

John Diebold identifies four types of management tools found to be useful in implementing changes within the corporate structure.[22] First, there is the practice of "compliance management" based on a structure of incentives—managerial and financial—designed to induce desired performance. Second, "ethical standards management" anticipates the successful transfer of values, especially humanistic, to the organization from the chief executive. Third, by encouraging the positive embrace by employees of those values essential to organizational change, chief executives seek to promote the role of "value management." Last, the concept of "participative management" seeks to identify and uplift interests common to employees and managers through the involvement of these groups in the development and implementation of organizational goals.

With these four management tools in mind, we recommend consideration of four types of programs which can improve the utilization of black and other minority employees, heighten productivity, alter the pattern of black and minority representation in the

---

[21]Additional support for this point may be found in John Diebold, *The Role of Business in Society* (New York: Amacom, 1982), pp. 6–7; and Robert W. Ackerman, *The Social Challenge to Business* (Cambridge: Harvard University Press, 1975), p. 317.

[22]Diebold, *The Role of Business*, pp. 8–9.

corporation, and enhance the corporate equal employment opportunity image.

First, consider the design and implementation of a formal *mentor program*. The essential thrust of such an effort is to expose selected black employees (or other minorities and women) to the rigors of upper management and the wide range of day-to-day management concerns, including problem solving. This requires that various key members of the management team be willing to take on a black employee as a special assistant, or as an executive assistant, or as a special project manager, with an eye to providing developmental experiences geared to that employee's corporate interests and potential. The rotation of such employees among key managers is an added and useful dimension of a mentor program under many circumstances. The success of the program is highly correlated with chief executive officer commitment and that officer's involvement in the periodic monitoring and evaluation process. While it is likely that white males, in particular, will grumble and complain that black employees are receiving preferential treatment which damages their (white males) career prospects, it is sensible to address this perceived "wrong." Of several possible approaches, the one most consistent with principles of equal opportunity is to develop a company-wide mentor program which includes white males. A reasonable objective, of course, is to ensure a significant percentage of blacks, other minorities, and women in the program in any given time period.

Second, consider a corporate communications effort directed toward black employees. Several key programmatic pieces can form the basis for this activity: meetings called once or twice a year by the chief executive officer with selected black employees for the purpose of sharing corporate plans which may affect employees; a corporate mechanism for *upward communications*, i.e., from black employees to senior management, regarding black career development and corporate activities designed to support that development; and corporate promotion of special education and training programs for black employees.

Third, corporate leadership, with respect to needed changes in the management of internal labor markets, must be accompanied by value-oriented and prideful communications—oral or written—to the work force and to the larger community. Chief executive officers should consider: 1) writings in in-house organs and in the popular press; 2) addresses to community and civic groups; 3) the establishment of corporate workshops for various employee groups for the purposes of identifying and exploring barriers to internal mobility paths; 4) heightened involvement in black civic and educational organizations; and 5) other key forms of communication.

Fourth, the establishment of a system of social and organizational accountabilities ensures the participation of subordinate managers. This can be supported by the kind of incentives described by Diebold.

These and other efforts have been undertaken by many corporations with varying degrees of success. In addition to the corporate benefits mentioned above, the implementation of these recommendations contributes to: 1) the acceptance of blacks in nontraditional positions; 2) an improvement in the morale and outlook of black employees; 3) a reduction in discriminatory attitudes and behavior on the part of white managers and employees; 4) improved channels of communication between subordinates and superiors, and between black and white employees; and 5) a better understanding between racial groups.

Clearly, these recommendations address, in part, the problems associated with quality length of service and the issue of race. It is to be hoped that their design and implementation can improve the rates of upward mobility for black employees, encourage the removal of the artificial ceiling, and reduce the absolute values of the Market Discrimination Coefficient.

APPENDIX AND
BIBLIOGRAPHY

Appendix

THE DATA CONTAINED herein describe each of the 2,721 corporate employees in the 1978 data base by salary grades. In addition to the personnel data, the Market Discrimination Coefficient (MDC) was computed, as shown in the text, for each employee and is included in the data base.

Weekly salaries are in dollars and rounded to the nearest dollar; racial designations are: black = 1, white = 0; sex designations are: male = 1, female = 0; educational levels are: high school = 0, training or special education = 1, college—no degree = 2, college graduate = 3, beyond college = 4; length of service categories are: less than 2 years = 1, 2–4 years = 2, 5–9 years = 3, 10–14 years = 4, 15–19 years = 5, and more than 19 years = 6. These data are as of December 31, 1978.

	Salary Grades 1 & 2			Number of Employees: 244			
(1) Current Weekly Salary (black)	(2) Current Weekly Salary (white)	(3) MDC (black)	(4) MDC (white)	(5) Race	(6) Sex	(7) Educ Level	(8) Length of Service
0	138	0	.088	0	1	0	1
0	130	0	.155	0	1	0	1
0	140	0	.072	0	1	0	1

				Salary Grades 1 & 2 (continued)			
(1) Current Weekly Salary (black)	(2) Current Weekly Salary (white)	(3) MDC (black)	(4) MDC (white)	(5) Race	(6) Sex	(7) Educ Level	(8) Length of Service
0	146	0	.028	0	1	0	1
0	135	0	.112	0	1	0	1
0	142	0	.057	0	1	0	1
0	130	0	.155	0	1	0	1
0	146	0	.026	0	1	1	1
0	152	0	−.013	0	1	0	1
0	144	0	.042	0	1	0	1
0	135	0	.112	0	1	0	1
0	142	0	.057	0	1	0	1
0	140	0	.072	0	1	0	1
0	155	0	−.032	0	1	0	2
0	148	0	.014	0	1	0	2
0	156	0	−.038	0	1	2	2
0	145	0	.035	0	1	0	2
0	152	0	−.013	0	1	0	2
0	158	0	−.050	0	1	1	3
0	165	0	−.090	0	1	0	3
0	168	0	−.107	0	1	0	3
0	142	0	.057	0	0	0	1
0	135	0	.112	0	0	0	1
0	138	0	.088	0	0	0	1
0	130	0	.155	0	0	0	1
0	145	0	.035	0	0	0	1
0	132	0	.137	0	0	0	1
0	140	0	.072	0	0	0	1
0	148	0	.014	0	0	0	1
0	142	0	.057	0	0	0	1
0	135	0	.112	0	0	1	1
0	140	0	.072	0	0	0	1
0	134	0	.120	0	0	0	1
0	146	0	.026	0	0	0	1
0	142	0	.057	0	0	0	1
0	144	0	.042	0	0	0	1
0	138	0	.088	0	0	0	1
0	135	0	.112	0	0	0	1

Salary Grades 1 & 2 (continued)

(1) Current Weekly Salary (black)	(2) Current Weekly Salary (white)	(3) MDC (black)	(4) MDC (white)	(5) Race	(6) Sex	(7) Educ Level	(8) Length of Service
0	152	0	−.013	0	0	0	1
0	148	0	.014	0	0	1	1
0	132	0	.137	0	0	0	1
0	135	0	.112	0	0	0	1
0	140	0	.072	0	0	0	1
0	147	0	.021	0	0	0	1
0	142	0	.057	0	0	0	1
0	136	0	.104	0	0	0	1
0	152	0	−.013	0	0	0	1
0	130	0	.155	0	0	0	1
0	138	0	.088	0	0	1	1
0	135	0	.112	0	0	0	1
0	142	0	.057	0	0	0	1
0	140	0	.072	0	0	0	1
0	146	0	.026	0	0	1	1
0	138	0	.088	0	0	0	1
0	135	0	.112	0	0	0	1
0	142	0	.057	0	0	0	1
0	135	0	.112	0	0	0	1
0	142	0	.057	0	0	0	1
0	140	0	.072	0	0	0	1
0	138	0	.088	0	0	1	1
0	145	0	.035	0	0	0	1
0	144	0	.042	0	0	0	1
0	138	0	.088	0	0	0	1
0	132	0	.137	0	0	0	1
0	146	0	.028	0	0	0	1
0	142	0	.057	0	0	0	2
0	146	0	.028	0	0	1	2
0	158	0	−.050	0	0	0	2
0	152	0	−.013	0	0	0	2
0	145	0	.035	0	0	0	2
0	160	0	−.062	0	0	1	2
0	156	0	−.038	0	0	0	2
0	148	0	.014	0	0	0	2

Salary Grades 1 & 2 (continued)

(1) Current Weekly Salary (black)	(2) Current Weekly Salary (white)	(3) MDC (black)	(4) MDC (white)	(5) Race	(6) Sex	(7) Educ Level	(8) Length of Service
0	152	0	−.013	0	0	2	2
0	164	0	−.085	0	0	0	2
0	145	0	.035	0	0	0	2
0	156	0	−.038	0	0	0	2
0	150	0	.001	0	0	0	2
0	158	0	−.050	0	0	2	2
0	166	0	−.096	0	0	0	2
0	162	0	−.074	0	0	0	2
0	155	0	−.032	0	0	1	2
0	171	0	−.122	0	0	0	2
0	164	0	−.085	0	0	0	2
0	164	0	−.085	0	0	0	2
							3
0	178	0	−.157	0	0	0	3
0	172	0	−.127	0	0	2	3
0	165	0	−.090	0	0	0	3
0	174	0	−.138	0	0	0	3
0	158	0	−.050	0	0	1	3
0	166	0	−.096	0	0	0	3
0	172	0	−.127	0	0	0	3
0	165	0	−.090	0	0	0	3
0	168	0	−.107	0	0	0	3
0	174	0	−.138	0	0	1	3
0	166	0	−.096	0	0	0	3
0	160	0	−.062	0	0	2	3
0	178	0	−.157	0	0	0	3
0	170	0	−.117	0	0	0	3
0	166	0	−.096	0	0	0	4
0	180	0	−.166	0	0	1	4
0	172	0	−.127	0	0	0	4
0	176	0	−.147	0	0	0	4
0	168	0	−.107	0	0	1	5
0	165	0	−.090	0	0	2	5
0	178	0	−.157	0	0	0	6
140	0	.072	0	1	1	0	1

				Salary Grades 1 & 2 (continued)			
(1) Current Weekly Salary (black)	*(2)* Current Weekly Salary (white)	*(3)* MDC (black)	*(4)* MDC (white)	*(5)* Race	*(6)* Sex	*(7)* Educ Level	*(8)* Length of Service
135	0	.112	0	1	1	0	1
141	0	.064	0	1	1	0	1
144	0	.042	0	1	1	0	1
138	0	.088	0	1	1	1	1
132	0	.137	0	1	1	0	1
136	0	.104	0	1	1	0	1
140	0	.072	0	1	1	0	1
135	0	.112	0	1	1	0	1
130	0	.155	0	1	1	1	1
144	0	.042	0	1	1	0	1
140	0	.072	0	1	1	0	1
142	0	.057	0	1	1	0	1
138	0	.088	0	1	1	0	1
135	0	.112	0	1	1	0	1
146	0	.026	0	1	1	1	1
152	0	−.013	0	1	1	0	1
150	0	.001	0	1	1	0	1
144	0	.042	0	1	1	0	1
138	0	.088	0	1	1	0	1
142	0	.057	0	1	1	0	1
140	0	.072	0	1	1	0	1
152	0	−.013	0	1	1	1	1
145	0	.035	0	1	1	0	1
140	0	.072	0	1	1	0	1
138	0	.088	0	1	1	0	1
142	0	.057	0	1	1	0	1
136	0	.104	0	1	1	0	1
146	0	.026	0	1	1	0	2
154	0	−.026	0	1	1	2	2
150	0	.001	0	1	1	0	2
148	0	.014	0	1	1	1	2
162	0	−.074	0	1	1	0	2
154	0	−.026	0	1	1	0	2
168	0	−.107	0	1	1	0	2
175	0	−.142	0	1	1	1	2

Salary Grades 1 & 2 (continued)

(1) Current Weekly Salary (black)	(2) Current Weekly Salary (white)	(3) MDC (black)	(4) MDC (white)	(5) Race	(6) Sex	(7) Educ Level	(8) Length of Service
172	0	−.127	0	1	1	0	3
140	0	.072	0	1	0	0	1
136	0	.104	0	1	0	0	1
142	0	.057	0	1	0	0	1
130	0	.155	0	1	0	1	1
138	0	.088	0	1	0	0	1
148	0	.014	0	1	0	0	1
145	0	.035	0	1	0	0	1
138	0	.088	0	1	0	1	1
140	0	.072	0	1	0	0	1
135	0	.112	0	1	0	0	1
138	0	.088	0	1	0	0	1
136	0	.104	0	1	0	0	1
143	0	.050	0	1	0	0	1
138	0	.088	0	1	0	0	1
142	0	.057	0	1	0	1	1
140	0	.072	0	1	0	0	1
141	0	.064	0	1	0	0	1
135	0	.112	0	1	0	0	1
138	0	.088	0	1	0	1	1
132	0	.137	0	1	0	0	1
144	0	.042	0	1	0	0	1
137	0	.096	0	1	0	0	1
135	0	.112	0	1	0	0	1
144	0	.042	0	1	0	0	1
141	0	.064	0	1	0	2	1
143	0	.050	0	1	0	0	1
135	0	.112	0	1	0	0	1
138	0	.088	0	1	0	1	1
136	0	.104	0	1	0	0	1
141	0	.064	0	1	0	0	1
142	0	.057	0	1	0	2	1
138	0	.088	0	1	0	0	1
144	0	.042	0	1	0	0	1
139	0	.080	0	1	0	0	1

				Salary Grades 1 & 2 (continued)			
(1)	*(2)*	*(3)*	*(4)*	*(5)*	*(6)*	*(7)*	*(8)*
Current Weekly Salary (black)	*Current Weekly Salary (white)*	*MDC (black)*	*MDC (white)*	*Race*	*Sex*	*Educ Level*	*Length of Service*
143	0	.050	0	1	0	1	1
135	0	.112	0	1	0	0	1
137	0	.096	0	1	0	1	1
134	0	.120	0	1	0	0	1
142	0	.057	0	1	0	0	1
156	0	−.038	0	1	0	0	1
147	0	.021	0	1	0	1	1
142	0	.057	0	1	0	0	1
145	0	.035	0	1	0	0	1
138	0	.088	0	1	0	0	1
142	0	.057	0	1	0	1	1
151	0	−.006	0	1	0	0	1
140	0	.072	0	1	0	0	1
146	0	.026	0	1	0	0	1
135	0	.112	0	1	0	0	1
164	0	−.085	0	1	0	0	2
152	0	−.013	0	1	0	2	2
156	0	−.038	0	1	0	0	2
158	0	−.050	0	1	0	0	2
156	0	−.038	0	1	0	0	2
165	0	−.090	0	1	0	0	2
149	0	.007	0	1	0	1	2
157	0	−.044	0	1	0	2	2
162	0	−.074	0	1	0	0	2
174	0	−.138	0	1	0	0	2
164	0	−.085	0	1	0	0	2
158	0	−.050	0	1	0	0	2
152	0	−.013	0	1	0	1	2
164	0	−.085	0	1	0	0	2
160	0	−.062	0	1	0	1	2
155	0	−.032	0	1	0	0	2
176	0	−.147	0	1	0	0	2
172	0	−.127	0	1	0	0	2
180	0	−.166	0	1	0	0	2
175	0	−.142	0	1	0	0	2

Salary Grades 1 & 2 (continued)

(1) Current Weekly Salary (black)	(2) Current Weekly Salary (white)	(3) MDC (black)	(4) MDC (white)	(5) Race	(6) Sex	(7) Educ Level	(8) Length of Service
154	0	−.026	0	1	0	0	2
158	0	−.050	0	1	0	1	2
152	0	−.013	0	1	0	0	2
176	0	−.147	0	1	0	0	2
159	0	−.056	0	1	0	0	2
166	0	−.096	0	1	0	0	2
178	0	−.157	0	1	0	2	2
175	0	−.142	0	1	0	0	2
168	0	−.107	0	1	0	0	2
153	0	−.019	0	1	0	1	2
170	0	−.117	0	1	0	0	2
172	0	−.127	0	1	0	0	2
156	0	−.038	0	1	0	0	2
165	0	−.090	0	1	0	1	2
161	0	−.068	0	1	0	0	2
158	0	−.050	0	1	0	0	2
164	0	−.085	0	1	0	2	2
168	0	−.107	0	1	0	1	2
171	0	−.122	0	1	0	0	3
165	0	−.090	0	1	0	2	3
162	0	−.074	0	1	0	0	3
159	0	−.056	0	1	0	1	3
174	0	−.138	0	1	0	0	3
168	0	−.107	0	1	0	2	3
160	0	−.062	0	1	0	0	3
162	0	−.074	0	1	0	0	3
157	0	−.044	0	1	0	0	3
164	0	−.085	0	1	0	1	3
175	0	−.142	0	1	0	0	4
172	0	−.127	0	1	0	0	4
168	0	−.107	0	1	0	1	5
179	0	−.162	0	1	0	2	6

	Salary Grades 3 & 4			Number of Employees: 694			
(1) Current Weekly Salary (black)	(2) Current Weekly Salary (white)	(3) MDC (black)	(4) MDC (white)	(5) Race	(6) Sex	(7) Educ Level	(8) Length of Service
0	170	0	.144	0	1	0	1
0	166	0	.172	0	1	0	1
0	175	0	.112	0	1	1	1
0	172	0	.131	0	1	0	1
0	165	0	.179	0	1	0	1
0	184	0	.057	0	1	0	1
0	182	0	.069	0	1	0	1
0	177	0	.099	0	1	2	1
0	168	0	.158	0	1	0	1
0	170	0	.144	0	1	0	1
0	184	0	.057	0	1	0	1
0	178	0	.093	0	1	0	1
0	170	0	.144	0	1	0	1
0	165	0	.179	0	1	1	1
0	182	0	.069	0	1	0	1
0	175	0	.112	0	1	2	1
0	172	0	.131	0	1	0	1
0	184	0	.057	0	1	0	1
0	168	0	.158	0	1	0	1
0	176	0	.105	0	1	1	1
0	188	0	.035	0	1	0	1
0	170	0	.144	0	1	0	1
0	175	0	.112	0	1	1	1
0	174	0	.118	0	1	0	1
0	182	0	.069	0	1	0	2
0	194	0	.003	0	1	1	2
0	188	0	.035	0	1	0	2
0	180	0	.081	0	1	0	2
0	194	0	.003	0	1	0	2
0	185	0	.051	0	1	0	2
0	182	0	.069	0	1	1	2
0	187	0	.040	0	1	0	2
0	184	0	.057	0	1	2	2
0	178	0	.093	0	1	0	2
0	194	0	.003	0	1	0	2

Salary Grades 3 & 4 (continued)

(1) Current Weekly Salary (black)	(2) Current Weekly Salary (white)	(3) MDC (black)	(4) MDC (white)	(5) Race	(6) Sex	(7) Educ Level	(8) Length of Service
0	185	0	.051	0	1	1	2
0	188	0	.035	0	1	0	2
0	180	0	.081	0	1	1	2
0	192	0	.013	0	1	0	2
0	185	0	.051	0	1	0	2
0	196	0	−.008	0	1	2	2
0	190	0	.024	0	1	0	2
0	180	0	.081	0	1	0	2
0	176	0	.105	0	1	0	2
0	190	0	.024	0	1	0	2
0	182	0	.069	0	1	1	2
0	185	0	.051	0	1	0	2
0	175	0	.112	0	1	0	2
0	184	0	.057	0	1	2	2
0	195	0	−.003	0	1	0	2
0	190	0	.024	0	1	0	2
0	184	0	.057	0	1	0	2
0	189	0	.029	0	1	2	2
0	205	0	−.051	0	1	0	2
0	186	0	.046	0	1	0	2
0	195	0	−.003	0	1	0	2
0	198	0	−.018	0	1	2	2
0	184	0	.057	0	1	0	2
0	190	0	.024	0	1	0	2
0	185	0	.051	0	1	2	2
0	192	0	.013	0	1	0	2
0	195	0	−.003	0	1	1	2
0	184	0	.057	0	1	0	2
0	196	0	−.008	0	1	0	3
0	208	0	−.065	0	1	0	3
0	204	0	−.047	0	1	0	3
0	194	0	.003	0	1	2	3
0	220	0	−.116	0	1	0	3
0	214	0	−.091	0	1	1	3
0	196	0	−.008	0	1	0	3

			Salary Grades 3 & 4 (continued)				
(1)	*(2)*	*(3)*	*(4)*	*(5)*	*(6)*	*(7)*	*(8)*
Current Weekly Salary (black)	*Current Weekly Salary (white)*	*MDC (black)*	*MDC (white)*	*Race*	*Sex*	*Educ Level*	*Length of Service*
0	205	0	−.051	0	1	0	3
0	212	0	−.083	0	1	1	3
0	208	0	−.065	0	1	0	3
0	194	0	.003	0	1	1	4
0	202	0	−.037	0	1	0	4
0	214	0	−.091	0	1	0	4
0	220	0	−.116	0	1	0	4
0	228	0	−.147	0	1	0	4
0	218	0	−.108	0	1	2	4
0	225	0	−.136	0	1	0	4
0	212	0	−.083	0	1	0	4
0	222	0	−.124	0	1	1	4
0	217	0	−.104	0	1	0	4
0	206	0	−.056	0	1	0	5
0	210	0	−.074	0	1	0	5
0	200	0	−.028	0	1	2	5
0	224	0	−.132	0	1	0	5
0	195	0	−.003	0	1	0	5
0	230	0	−.154	0	1	0	5
0	228	0	−.147	0	1	2	5
0	223	0	−.128	0	1	1	5
0	218	0	−.108	0	1	0	6
0	209	0	−.069	0	1	0	6
0	216	0	−.100	0	1	1	6
0	211	0	−.078	0	1	0	6
0	224	0	−.132	0	1	0	6
0	221	0	−.120	0	1	2	6
0	228	0	−.147	0	1	0	6
0	220	0	−.116	0	1	0	6
0	217	0	−.104	0	1	0	6
0	225	0	−.136	0	1	1	6
0	214	0	−.091	0	1	0	6
0	220	0	−.116	0	1	2	6
0	224	0	−.132	0	1	0	6
0	227	0	−.143	0	1	0	6

	Salary Grades 3 & 4 (continued)						
(1)	*(2)*	*(3)*	*(4)*	*(5)*	*(6)*	*(7)*	*(8)*
Current Weekly Salary (black)	Current Weekly Salary (white)	MDC (black)	MDC (white)	Race	Sex	Educ Level	Length of Service
0	220	0	−.116	0	1	1	6
0	228	0	−.147	0	1	0	6
0	176	0	.105	0	0	0	1
0	164	0	.186	0	0	0	1
0	168	0	.158	0	0	0	1
0	165	0	.179	0	0	2	1
0	162	0	.201	0	0	0	1
0	174	0	.118	0	0	0	1
0	168	0	.158	0	0	0	1
0	175	0	.112	0	0	1	1
0	182	0	.069	0	0	0	1
0	160	0	.216	0	0	2	1
0	186	0	.046	0	0	0	1
0	175	0	.112	0	0	0	1
0	172	0	.131	0	0	0	1
0	170	0	.144	0	0	2	1
0	182	0	.069	0	0	0	1
0	176	0	.105	0	0	0	1
0	177	0	.099	0	0	1	1
0	185	0	.051	0	0	0	1
0	168	0	.158	0	0	0	1
0	188	0	.035	0	0	2	1
0	185	0	.051	0	0	0	1
0	174	0	.118	0	0	0	1
0	179	0	.087	0	0	0	1
0	172	0	.131	0	0	2	1
0	175	0	.112	0	0	1	1
0	180	0	.081	0	0	0	1
0	172	0	.131	0	0	0	1
0	168	0	.158	0	0	0	1
0	177	0	.099	0	0	0	1
0	181	0	.075	0	0	1	1
0	174	0	.118	0	0	0	1
0	179	0	.087	0	0	0	1
0	172	0	.131	0	0	0	1
0	170	0	.144	0	0	0	1

Salary Grades 3 & 4 (continued)

(1) Current Weekly Salary (black)	(2) Current Weekly Salary (white)	(3) MDC (black)	(4) MDC (white)	(5) Race	(6) Sex	(7) Educ Level	(8) Length of Service
0	165	0	.179	0	0	2	1
0	172	0	.131	0	0	0	1
0	186	0	.046	0	0	0	1
0	174	0	.118	0	0	0	1
0	168	0	.158	0	0	1	1
0	177	0	.099	0	0	2	1
0	172	0	.131	0	0	0	1
0	181	0	.075	0	0	1	1
0	184	0	.057	0	0	0	1
0	175	0	.112	0	0	0	1
0	182	0	.069	0	0	0	1
0	170	0	.144	0	0	0	1
0	184	0	.057	0	0	2	1
0	176	0	.105	0	0	0	1
0	175	0	.112	0	0	0	1
0	178	0	.093	0	0	2	1
0	182	0	.069	0	0	0	1
0	185	0	.051	0	0	0	1
0	178	0	.093	0	0	0	1
0	170	0	.144	0	0	0	1
0	182	0	.069	0	0	1	1
0	176	0	.105	0	0	0	1
0	182	0	.069	0	0	0	1
0	177	0	.099	0	0	1	1
0	180	0	.081	0	0	0	1
0	182	0	.069	0	0	2	1
0	177	0	.099	0	0	0	1
0	172	0	.131	0	0	0	1
0	176	0	.105	0	0	0	1
0	168	0	.158	0	0	0	1
0	164	0	.186	0	0	0	1
0	172	0	.131	0	0	2	1
0	166	0	.172	0	0	0	1
0	162	0	.201	0	0	0	1
0	180	0	.081	0	0	0	1

Salary Grades 3 & 4 (continued)							
(1) Current Weekly Salary (black)	(2) Current Weekly Salary (white)	(3) MDC (black)	(4) MDC (white)	(5) Race	(6) Sex	(7) Educ Level	(8) Length of Service
0	175	0	.112	0	0	0	2
0	190	0	.024	0	0	0	2
0	196	0	−.008	0	0	0	2
0	182	0	.069	0	0	2	2
0	185	0	.051	0	0	0	2
0	178	0	.093	0	0	0	2
0	184	0	.057	0	0	0	2
0	194	0	.003	0	0	0	2
0	198	0	−.018	0	0	0	2
0	190	0	.024	0	0	3	2
0	188	0	.035	0	0	0	2
0	194	0	.003	0	0	0	2
0	190	0	.024	0	0	0	2
0	185	0	.051	0	0	0	2
0	188	0	.035	0	0	1	2
0	194	0	.003	0	0	0	2
0	204	0	−.047	0	0	2	2
0	189	0	.029	0	0	0	2
0	194	0	.003	0	0	0	2
0	191	0	.018	0	0	0	2
0	186	0	.046	0	0	0	2
0	194	0	.003	0	0	0	2
0	190	0	.024	0	0	0	2
0	184	0	.057	0	0	2	2
0	192	0	.013	0	0	0	2
0	185	0	.051	0	0	0	2
0	196	0	−.008	0	0	1	2
0	204	0	−.047	0	0	0	2
0	195	0	−.003	0	0	2	2
0	190	0	.024	0	0	0	2
0	206	0	−.056	0	0	2	2
0	200	0	−.028	0	0	0	2
0	197	0	−.013	0	0	0	2
0	194	0	.003	0	0	0	2
0	206	0	−.056	0	0	1	2

Salary Grades 3 & 4 (continued)

(1) Current Weekly Salary (black)	(2) Current Weekly Salary (white)	(3) MDC (black)	(4) MDC (white)	(5) Race	(6) Sex	(7) Educ Level	(8) Length of Service
0	201	0	−.032	0	0	0	2
0	195	0	−.003	0	0	0	2
0	192	0	.013	0	0	0	2
0	198	0	−.018	0	0	0	2
0	185	0	.051	0	0	2	2
0	194	0	.003	0	0	0	2
0	206	0	−.056	0	0	2	2
0	195	0	−.003	0	0	0	2
0	188	0	.035	0	0	0	2
0	184	0	.057	0	0	0	2
0	193	0	.008	0	0	2	2
0	197	0	−.013	0	0	0	2
0	190	0	.024	0	0	2	2
0	178	0	.093	0	0	0	2
0	184	0	.057	0	0	0	2
0	202	0	−.037	0	0	0	2
0	190	0	.024	0	0	1	2
0	185	0	.051	0	0	0	2
0	182	0	.069	0	0	0	2
0	196	0	−.008	0	0	2	2
0	190	0	.024	0	0	0	2
0	194	0	.003	0	0	0	2
0	187	0	.040	0	0	0	2
0	191	0	.018	0	0	0	2
0	208	0	−.065	0	0	3	2
0	194	0	.003	0	0	0	2
0	186	0	.046	0	0	0	2
0	175	0	.112	0	0	0	2
0	185	0	.051	0	0	0	2
0	192	0	.013	0	0	2	2
0	190	0	.024	0	0	0	2
0	184	0	.057	0	0	1	2
0	188	0	.035	0	0	0	2
0	180	0	.081	0	0	2	2
0	196	0	−.008	0	0	0	2

			Salary Grades 3 & 4 (continued)				
(1) Current Weekly Salary (black)	(2) Current Weekly Salary (white)	(3) MDC (black)	(4) MDC (white)	(5) Race	(6) Sex	(7) Educ Level	(8) Length of Service
0	190	0	.024	0	0	0	2
0	194	0	.003	0	0	0	2
0	185	0	.051	0	0	0	2
0	203	0	−.042	0	0	2	2
0	187	0	.040	0	0	0	2
0	192	0	.013	0	0	0	2
0	187	0	.040	0	0	0	2
0	192	0	.013	0	0	1	2
0	184	0	.057	0	0	0	2
0	210	0	−.074	0	0	0	3
0	200	0	−.028	0	0	2	3
0	206	0	−.056	0	0	0	3
0	194	0	.003	0	0	1	3
0	204	0	−.047	0	0	0	3
0	216	0	−.100	0	0	0	3
0	205	0	−.051	0	0	0	3
0	198	0	−.018	0	0	1	3
0	195	0	−.003	0	0	0	3
0	202	0	−.037	0	0	0	3
0	198	0	−.018	0	0	0	3
0	206	0	−.056	0	0	2	3
0	188	0	.035	0	0	0	3
0	194	0	.003	0	0	3	3
0	190	0	.024	0	0	0	3
0	208	0	−.065	0	0	0	3
0	213	0	−.087	0	0	2	3
0	201	0	−.032	0	0	0	3
0	197	0	−.013	0	0	1	3
0	204	0	−.047	0	0	0	3
0	200	0	−.028	0	0	0	3
0	195	0	−.003	0	0	1	3
0	198	0	−.018	0	0	0	3
0	215	0	−.095	0	0	0	3
0	208	0	−.065	0	0	2	3
0	204	0	−.047	0	0	0	3

Salary Grades 3 & 4 (continued)

(1) Current Weekly Salary (black)	(2) Current Weekly Salary (white)	(3) MDC (black)	(4) MDC (white)	(5) Race	(6) Sex	(7) Educ Level	(8) Length of Service
0	215	0	−.095	0	0	0	3
0	194	0	.003	0	0	0	3
0	198	0	−.018	0	0	1	3
0	190	0	.024	0	0	0	3
0	204	0	−.047	0	0	0	3
0	196	0	−.008	0	0	2	3
0	209	0	−.069	0	0	1	3
0	206	0	−.056	0	0	0	3
0	190	0	.024	0	0	0	3
0	196	0	−.008	0	0	2	3
0	214	0	−.091	0	0	0	3
0	208	0	−.065	0	0	0	3
0	205	0	−.051	0	0	0	3
0	196	0	−.008	0	0	2	3
0	189	0	.029	0	0	1	3
0	195	0	−.003	0	0	0	3
0	200	0	−.028	0	0	0	3
0	198	0	−.018	0	0	1	3
0	206	0	−.056	0	0	0	3
0	210	0	−.074	0	0	0	3
0	200	0	−.028	0	0	3	3
0	206	0	−.056	0	0	0	3
0	194	0	.003	0	0	0	3
0	206	0	−.056	0	0	2	3
0	214	0	−.091	0	0	0	3
0	205	0	−.051	0	0	0	3
0	196	0	−.008	0	0	3	3
0	190	0	.024	0	0	0	3
0	203	0	−.042	0	0	1	3
0	196	0	−.008	0	0	0	3
0	194	0	.003	0	0	0	3
0	203	0	−.042	0	0	2	3
0	198	0	−.018	0	0	0	3
0	190	0	.024	0	0	0	3
0	195	0	−.003	0	0	2	3

			Salary Grades 3 & 4 (continued)				
(1) Current Weekly Salary (black)	*(2)* Current Weekly Salary (white)	*(3)* MDC (black)	*(4)* MDC (white)	*(5)* Race	*(6)* Sex	*(7)* Educ Level	*(8)* Length of Service
0	206	0	−.056	0	0	0	3
0	188	0	.035	0	0	0	3
0	197	0	−.013	0	0	0	3
0	206	0	−.056	0	0	2	3
0	202	0	−.037	0	0	0	3
0	194	0	.003	0	0	0	3
0	215	0	−.095	0	0	2	3
0	208	0	−.065	0	0	0	3
0	200	0	−.028	0	0	1	3
0	212	0	−.083	0	0	0	4
0	224	0	−.132	0	0	0	4
0	215	0	−.095	0	0	0	4
0	218	0	−.108	0	0	1	4
0	210	0	−.074	0	0	0	4
0	215	0	−.095	0	0	0	4
0	218	0	−.108	0	0	2	4
0	204	0	−.047	0	0	0	4
0	200	0	−.028	0	0	3	4
0	208	0	−.065	0	0	0	4
0	205	0	−.051	0	0	0	4
0	221	0	−.120	0	0	1	4
0	194	0	.003	0	0	0	4
0	206	0	−.056	0	0	1	4
0	202	0	−.037	0	0	0	4
0	218	0	−.108	0	0	0	4
0	215	0	−.095	0	0	2	4
0	209	0	−.069	0	0	0	4
0	222	0	−.124	0	0	1	5
0	217	0	−.104	0	0	0	5
0	208	0	−.065	0	0	0	5
0	205	0	−.051	0	0	2	5
0	212	0	−.083	0	0	0	5
0	206	0	−.056	0	0	0	5
0	225	0	−.136	0	0	0	5
0	219	0	−.112	0	0	3	5

Salary Grades 3 & 4 (continued)

(1) Current Weekly Salary (black)	(2) Current Weekly Salary (white)	(3) MDC (black)	(4) MDC (white)	(5) Race	(6) Sex	(7) Educ Level	(8) Length of Service
0	208	0	−.065	0	0	0	5
0	214	0	−.091	0	0	0	5
0	220	0	−.116	0	0	1	5
0	217	0	−.104	0	0	0	6
0	205	0	−.051	0	0	0	6
0	214	0	−.091	0	0	1	6
0	206	0	−.056	0	0	0	6
0	228	0	−.147	0	0	0	6
0	225	0	−.136	0	0	0	6
0	218	0	−.108	0	0	2	6
0	222	0	−.124	0	0	3	6
0	215	0	−.095	0	0	0	6
0	228	0	−.147	0	0	0	6
0	220	0	−.116	0	0	2	6
0	216	0	−.100	0	0	0	6
0	221	0	−.120	0	0	0	6
0	225	0	−.136	0	0	2	6
0	214	0	−.091	0	0	0	6
0	219	0	−.112	0	0	1	6
0	230	0	−.154	0	0	0	6
0	224	0	−.132	0	0	0	6
0	212	0	−.083	0	0	0	6
0	215	0	−.095	0	0	2	6
0	221	0	−.120	0	0	0	6
170	0	.144	0	1	1	0	1
165	0	.179	0	1	1	0	1
178	0	.093	0	1	1	0	1
172	0	.131	0	1	1	0	1
179	0	.087	0	1	1	0	1
171	0	.138	0	1	1	0	1
162	0	.201	0	1	1	0	1
178	0	.093	0	1	1	1	1
175	0	.112	0	1	1	0	1
165	0	.179	0	1	1	0	1
178	0	.093	0	1	1	1	1

	Salary Grades 3 & 4 (continued)						
(1) Current Weekly Salary (black)	(2) Current Weekly Salary (white)	(3) MDC (black)	(4) MDC (white)	(5) Race	(6) Sex	(7) Educ Level	(8) Length of Service
164	0	.186	0	1	1	0	1
176	0	.105	0	1	1	0	1
179	0	.087	0	1	1	0	1
178	0	.093	0	1	1	0	1
165	0	.179	0	1	1	0	1
174	0	.118	0	1	1	0	1
174	0	.118	0	1	1	0	2
168	0	.158	0	1	1	0	2
181	0	.075	0	1	1	0	2
175	0	.112	0	1	1	0	2
186	0	.046	0	1	1	1	2
177	0	.099	0	1	1	0	2
184	0	.057	0	1	1	2	2
199	0	−.023	0	1	1	0	2
182	0	.069	0	1	1	0	2
194	0	.003	0	1	1	0	2
188	0	.035	0	1	1	1	2
185	0	.051	0	1	1	0	2
186	0	.046	0	1	1	0	2
180	0	.081	0	1	1	1	2
194	0	.003	0	1	1	2	2
190	0	.024	0	1	1	0	2
185	0	.051	0	1	1	0	2
182	0	.069	0	1	1	2	2
193	0	.008	0	1	1	0	2
188	0	.035	0	1	1	0	2
180	0	.081	0	1	1	0	2
184	0	.057	0	1	1	2	2
178	0	.093	0	1	1	0	2
187	0	.040	0	1	1	0	2
190	0	.024	0	1	1	1	2
193	0	.008	0	1	1	0	2
186	0	.046	0	1	1	0	2
197	0	−.013	0	1	1	2	2

Salary Grades 3 & 4 (continued)

(1) Current Weekly Salary (black)	(2) Current Weekly Salary (white)	(3) MDC (black)	(4) MDC (white)	(5) Race	(6) Sex	(7) Educ Level	(8) Length of Service
192	0	.013	0	1	1	0	2
184	0	.057	0	1	1	1	2
178	0	.093	0	1	1	2	2
185	0	.051	0	1	1	0	2
198	0	−.018	0	1	1	0	2
182	0	.069	0	1	1	2	2
175	0	.112	0	1	1	1	2
190	0	.024	0	1	1	0	2
186	0	.046	0	1	1	2	2
182	0	.069	0	1	1	0	2
185	0	.051	0	1	1	0	2
191	0	.018	0	1	1	0	3
194	0	.003	0	1	1	2	3
202	0	−.037	0	1	1	0	3
196	0	−.008	0	1	1	0	3
207	0	−.060	0	1	1	0	3
202	0	−.037	0	1	1	3	3
212	0	−.083	0	1	1	0	3
196	0	−.008	0	1	1	1	3
203	0	−.042	0	1	1	0	3
197	0	−.013	0	1	1	0	3
201	0	−.032	0	1	1	0	3
215	0	−.095	0	1	1	1	3
224	0	−.132	0	1	1	0	3
215	0	−.095	0	1	1	2	3
209	0	−.069	0	1	1	0	3
217	0	−.104	0	1	1	2	3
212	0	−.083	0	1	1	0	3
205	0	−.051	0	1	1	0	3
214	0	−.091	0	1	1	1	3
224	0	−.132	0	1	1	0	3
215	0	−.095	0	1	1	2	3
206	0	−.056	0	1	1	0	3
219	0	−.112	0	1	1	0	3
227	0	−.143	0	1	1	2	3

				Salary Grades 3 & 4 (continued)			
(1) Current Weekly Salary (black)	(2) Current Weekly Salary (white)	(3) MDC (black)	(4) MDC (white)	(5) Race	(6) Sex	(7) Educ Level	(8) Length of Service
218	0	−.108	0	1	1	0	4
222	0	−.124	0	1	1	1	5
172	0	.131	0	1	0	0	1
164	0	.186	0	1	0	0	1
168	0	.158	0	1	0	0	1
175	0	.112	0	1	0	2	1
170	0	.144	0	1	0	0	1
168	0	.158	0	1	0	0	1
179	0	.087	0	1	0	0	1
165	0	.179	0	1	0	0	1
171	0	.138	0	1	0	0	1
174	0	.118	0	1	0	1	1
170	0	.144	0	1	0	0	1
163	0	.193	0	1	0	0	1
168	0	.158	0	1	0	2	1
179	0	.087	0	1	0	0	1
175	0	.112	0	1	0	1	1
182	0	.069	0	1	0	0	1
176	0	.105	0	1	0	0	1
172	0	.131	0	1	0	2	1
177	0	.099	0	1	0	1	1
170	0	.144	0	1	0	0	1
173	0	.124	0	1	0	0	1
175	0	.112	0	1	0	0	1
182	0	.069	0	1	0	0	1
168	0	.158	0	1	0	0	1
164	0	.186	0	1	0	0	1
173	0	.124	0	1	0	1	1
179	0	.087	0	1	0	0	1
175	0	.112	0	1	0	0	1
182	0	.069	0	1	0	0	1
188	0	.035	0	1	0	0	2
180	0	.081	0	1	0	2	2
176	0	.105	0	1	0	0	2
182	0	.069	0	1	0	0	2

Salary Grades 3 & 4 (continued)							
(1) Current Weekly Salary (black)	(2) Current Weekly Salary (white)	(3) MDC (black)	(4) MDC (white)	(5) Race	(6) Sex	(7) Educ Level	(8) Length of Service
189	0	.029	0	1	0	1	2
175	0	.112	0	1	0	0	2
184	0	.057	0	1	0	3	2
180	0	.081	0	1	0	0	2
186	0	.046	0	1	0	0	2
185	0	.051	0	1	0	1	2
178	0	.093	0	1	0	2	2
175	0	.112	0	1	0	0	2
170	0	.144	0	1	0	0	2
188	0	.035	0	1	0	0	2
184	0	.057	0	1	0	2	2
182	0	.069	0	1	0	0	2
191	0	.018	0	1	0	1	2
176	0	.105	0	1	0	0	2
180	0	.081	0	1	0	2	2
183	0	.063	0	1	0	0	2
172	0	.131	0	1	0	0	2
182	0	.069	0	1	0	0	2
175	0	.112	0	1	0	1	2
179	0	.087	0	1	0	0	2
171	0	.138	0	1	0	2	2
186	0	.046	0	1	0	0	2
182	0	.069	0	1	0	0	2
174	0	.118	0	1	0	1	2
180	0	.081	0	1	0	0	2
186	0	.046	0	1	0	1	2
190	0	.024	0	1	0	0	2
182	0	.069	0	1	0	0	2
174	0	.118	0	1	0	2	2
181	0	.075	0	1	0	0	2
179	0	.087	0	1	0	0	2
188	0	.035	0	1	0	1	2
185	0	.051	0	1	0	0	2
192	0	.013	0	1	0	0	2
184	0	.057	0	1	0	1	2

Salary Grades 3 & 4 (continued)

(1) Current Weekly Salary (black)	(2) Current Weekly Salary (white)	(3) MDC (black)	(4) MDC (white)	(5) Race	(6) Sex	(7) Educ Level	(8) Length of Service
178	0	.093	0	1	0	3	2
180	0	.081	0	1	0	0	2
176	0	.105	0	1	0	0	2
182	0	.069	0	1	0	2	2
180	0	.081	0	1	0	2	2
188	0	.035	0	1	0	0	2
185	0	.051	0	1	0	0	2
192	0	.013	0	1	0	0	2
183	0	.063	0	1	0	2	2
182	0	.069	0	1	0	0	2
179	0	.087	0	1	0	0	2
186	0	.046	0	1	0	2	2
174	0	.118	0	1	0	0	2
180	0	.081	0	1	0	1	2
182	0	.069	0	1	0	0	2
181	0	.075	0	1	0	0	2
188	0	.035	0	1	0	1	2
185	0	.051	0	1	0	3	2
192	0	.013	0	1	0	0	2
174	0	.118	0	1	0	0	2
181	0	.075	0	1	0	0	2
176	0	.105	0	1	0	2	2
168	0	.158	0	1	0	0	2
179	0	.087	0	1	0	2	2
182	0	.069	0	1	0	0	2
188	0	.035	0	1	0	1	2
172	0	.131	0	1	0	0	2
169	0	.151	0	1	0	0	2
183	0	.063	0	1	0	0	2
175	0	.112	0	1	0	2	2
192	0	.013	0	1	0	0	2
184	0	.057	0	1	0	0	2
178	0	.093	0	1	0	0	2
180	0	.081	0	1	0	0	2
186	0	.046	0	1	0	1	2

Salary Grades 3 & 4 (continued)

(1) Current Weekly Salary (black)	(2) Current Weekly Salary (white)	(3) MDC (black)	(4) MDC (white)	(5) Race	(6) Sex	(7) Educ Level	(8) Length of Service
177	0	.099	0	1	0	0	2
180	0	.081	0	1	0	0	2
178	0	.093	0	1	0	0	2
184	0	.057	0	1	0	0	2
168	0	.158	0	1	0	2	2
179	0	.087	0	1	0	0	2
185	0	.051	0	1	0	0	2
180	0	.081	0	1	0	1	2
174	0	.118	0	1	0	0	2
192	0	.013	0	1	0	0	2
183	0	.063	0	1	0	2	2
176	0	.105	0	1	0	0	2
188	0	.035	0	1	0	0	2
175	0	.112	0	1	0	0	2
172	0	.131	0	1	0	2	2
181	0	.075	0	1	0	1	2
186	0	.046	0	1	0	0	2
182	0	.069	0	1	0	2	2
193	0	.008	0	1	0	0	2
170	0	.144	0	1	0	0	2
175	0	.112	0	1	0	1	2
183	0	.063	0	1	0	0	2
187	0	.040	0	1	0	0	2
184	0	.057	0	1	0	0	3
175	0	.112	0	1	0	0	3
178	0	.093	0	1	0	0	3
192	0	.013	0	1	0	2	3
198	0	−.018	0	1	0	0	3
194	0	.003	0	1	0	0	3
190	0	.024	0	1	0	2	3
185	0	.051	0	1	0	0	3
193	0	.008	0	1	0	0	3
190	0	.024	0	1	0	3	3
189	0	.029	0	1	0	0	3
195	0	−.003	0	1	0	0	3

Salary Grades 3 & 4 (continued)

(1) Current Weekly Salary (black)	(2) Current Weekly Salary (white)	(3) MDC (black)	(4) MDC (white)	(5) Race	(6) Sex	(7) Educ Level	(8) Length of Service
206	0	−.056	0	1	0	0	3
202	0	−.037	0	1	0	0	3
194	0	.003	0	1	0	1	3
210	0	−.074	0	1	0	0	3
218	0	−.108	0	1	0	0	3
200	0	−.028	0	1	0	0	3
197	0	−.013	0	1	0	2	3
192	0	.013	0	1	0	0	3
204	0	−.047	0	1	0	1	3
211	0	−.078	0	1	0	0	3
198	0	−.018	0	1	0	0	3
195	0	−.003	0	1	0	0	3
206	0	−.056	0	1	0	2	3
197	0	−.013	0	1	0	0	3
190	0	.024	0	1	0	0	3
215	0	−.095	0	1	0	2	3
188	0	.035	0	1	0	0	3
207	0	−.060	0	1	0	0	3
198	0	−.018	0	1	0	0	3
204	0	−.047	0	1	0	2	3
210	0	−.074	0	1	0	1	3
197	0	−.013	0	1	0	0	3
206	0	−.056	0	1	0	0	3
205	0	−.051	0	1	0	2	3
196	0	−.008	0	1	0	0	3
192	0	.013	0	1	0	0	3
210	0	−.074	0	1	0	1	3
200	0	−.028	0	1	0	0	3
195	0	−.003	0	1	0	0	3
214	0	−.091	0	1	0	3	3
217	0	−.104	0	1	0	0	3
206	0	−.056	0	1	0	0	3
194	0	.003	0	1	0	2	3
198	0	−.018	0	1	0	0	3
185	0	.051	0	1	0	2	3

				Salary Grades 3 & 4 (continued)			
(1) Current Weekly Salary (black)	(2) Current Weekly Salary (white)	(3) MDC (black)	(4) MDC (white)	(5) Race	(6) Sex	(7) Educ Level	(8) Length of Service
197	0	−.013	0	1	0	0	3
202	0	−.037	0	1	0	0	3
180	0	.081	0	1	0	0	3
197	0	−.013	0	1	0	3	3
201	0	−.032	0	1	0	0	3
196	0	−.008	0	1	0	1	3
205	0	−.051	0	1	0	0	3
214	0	−.091	0	1	0	0	3
208	0	−.065	0	1	0	0	3
220	0	−.116	0	1	0	1	3
192	0	.013	0	1	0	0	3
198	0	−.018	0	1	0	2	3
212	0	−.083	0	1	0	0	3
200	0	−.028	0	1	0	0	3
207	0	−.060	0	1	0	2	3
195	0	−.003	0	1	0	0	3
188	0	.035	0	1	0	0	3
197	0	−.013	0	1	0	0	3
206	0	−.056	0	1	0	2	3
201	0	−.032	0	1	0	0	3
212	0	−.083	0	1	0	0	3
198	0	−.018	0	1	0	1	3
197	0	−.013	0	1	0	0	3
202	0	−.037	0	1	0	0	3
214	0	−.091	0	1	0	2	3
200	0	−.028	0	1	0	0	3
195	0	−.003	0	1	0	0	3
223	0	−.128	0	1	0	3	3
207	0	−.060	0	1	0	0	3
215	0	−.095	0	1	0	0	3
206	0	−.056	0	1	0	0	3
220	0	−.116	0	1	0	2	3
198	0	−.018	0	1	0	0	3
204	0	−.047	0	1	0	0	3
212	0	−.083	0	1	0	2	3

			Salary Grades 3 & 4 (continued)				
(1) Current Weekly Salary (black)	(2) Current Weekly Salary (white)	(3) MDC (black)	(4) MDC (white)	(5) Race	(6) Sex	(7) Educ Level	(8) Length of Service
195	0	−.003	0	1	0	0	3
198	0	−.018	0	1	0	0	3
200	0	−.028	0	1	0	0	3
218	0	−.108	0	1	0	2	3
207	0	−.060	0	1	0	0	3
215	0	−.095	0	1	0	0	3
196	0	−.008	0	1	0	1	3
214	0	−,091	0	1	0	0	3
205	0	−.051	0	1	0	1	3
208	0	−.065	0	1	0	0	3
203	0	−.042	0	1	0	2	3
218	0	−.108	0	1	0	2	3
195	0	−.003	0	1	0	0	3
204	0	−.047	0	1	0	2	3
198	0	−.018	0	1	0	0	3
218	0	−.108	0	1	0	0	3
207	0	−.060	0	1	0	0	3
194	0	.003	0	1	0	2	3
202	0	−.037	0	1	0	0	3
214	0	−.091	0	1	0	0	3
209	0	−.069	0	1	0	1	3
228	0	−.147	0	1	0	0	4
224	0	−.132	0	1	0	1	4
219	0	−.112	0	1	0	0	4
226	0	−.139	0	1	0	2	4
220	0	−.116	0	1	0	0	4
218	0	−.108	0	1	0	3	5
225	0	−.136	0	1	0	1	6
228	0	−.147	0	1	0	0	6

	Salary Grades 5 & 6			Number of Employees: 871			
(1) Current Weekly Salary (black)	(2) Current Weekly Salary (white)	(3) MDC (black)	(4) MDC (white)	(5) Race	(6) Sex	(7) Educ Level	(8) Length of Service
0	251	0	.207	0	1	3	1
0	236	0	.283	0	1	3	1
0	244	0	.241	0	1	3	1
0	235	0	.289	0	1	3	1
0	238	0	.273	0	1	0	1
0	243	0	.246	0	1	3	1
0	230	0	.317	0	1	3	1
0	262	0	.156	0	1	2	1
0	247	0	.226	0	1	1	1
0	238	0	.273	0	1	0	1
0	241	0	.257	0	1	3	1
0	230	0	.317	0	1	3	1
0	253	0	.197	0	1	3	1
0	250	0	.212	0	1	4	1
0	264	0	.147	0	1	1	1
0	252	0	.202	0	1	0	1
0	243	0	.246	0	1	0	1
0	248	0	.221	0	1	2	1
0	232	0	.306	0	1	3	1
0	257	0	.179	0	1	3	1
0	252	0	.202	0	1	3	1
0	263	0	.152	0	1	4	1
0	255	0	.188	0	1	0	1
0	244	0	.241	0	1	1	1
0	238	0	.273	0	1	1	1
0	247	0	.226	0	1	2	1
0	241	0	.257	0	1	2	1
0	258	0	.174	0	1	3	1
0	246	0	.231	0	1	3	1
0	253	0	.197	0	1	4	1
0	235	0	.289	0	1	3	1
0	274	0	.105	0	1	4	1
0	240	0	.262	0	1	1	1
0	236	0	.283	0	1	0	1
0	245	0	.236	0	1	2	1

			Salary Grades 5 & 6 (continued)				
(1) Current Weekly Salary (black)	(2) Current Weekly Salary (white)	(3) MDC (black)	(4) MDC (white)	(5) Race	(6) Sex	(7) Educ Level	(8) Length of Service
0	254	0	.192	0	1	3	1
0	258	0	.174	0	1	3	1
0	250	0	.212	0	1	3	1
0	261	0	.161	0	1	3	1
0	240	0	.262	0	1	4	1
0	252	0	.202	0	1	3	1
0	235	0	.289	0	1	0	1
0	278	0	.090	0	1	3	2
0	259	0	.169	0	1	3	2
0	264	0	.147	0	1	0	2
0	294	0	.030	0	1	2	2
0	265	0	.143	0	1	0	2
0	258	0	.174	0	1	0	2
0	293	0	.034	0	1	3	2
0	275	0	.101	0	1	3	2
0	264	0	.147	0	1	3	2
0	272	0	.114	0	1	1	2
0	283	0	.070	0	1	2	2
0	265	0	.143	0	1	0	2
0	274	0	.105	0	1	2	2
0	305	0	−.007	0	1	3	2
0	280	0	.082	0	1	3	2
0	274	0	.105	0	1	3	2
0	296	0	.023	0	1	4	2
0	268	0	.130	0	1	0	2
0	275	0	.101	0	1	2	2
0	279	0	.086	0	1	0	2
0	263	0	.152	0	1	1	2
0	281	0	.078	0	1	2	2
0	274	0	.105	0	1	1	2
0	285	0	.063	0	1	3	2
0	280	0	.082	0	1	3	2
0	276	0	.097	0	1	3	2
0	308	0	−.017	0	1	3	2
0	294	0	.030	0	1	4	2

			Salary Grades 5 & 6 (continued)				
(1)	*(2)*	*(3)*	*(4)*	*(5)*	*(6)*	*(7)*	*(8)*
Current Weekly Salary (black)	Current Weekly Salary (white)	MDC (black)	MDC (white)	Race	Sex	Educ Level	Length of Service
0	286	0	.059	0	1	0	2
0	270	0	.122	0	1	2	2
0	278	0	.090	0	1	2	2
0	294	0	.030	0	1	0	2
0	283	0	.070	0	1	3	2
0	285	0	.063	0	1	0	2
0	277	0	.093	0	1	0	2
0	294	0	.030	0	1	1	2
0	305	0	−.007	0	1	3	2
0	297	0	.020	0	1	3	2
0	274	0	.105	0	1	0	2
0	282	0	.074	0	1	0	2
0	278	0	.090	0	1	1	2
0	290	0	.044	0	1	0	2
0	285	0	.063	0	1	0	2
0	278	0	.090	0	1	1	2
0	283	0	.070	0	1	1	2
0	272	0	.114	0	1	0	2
0	307	0	−.013	0	1	2	2
0	294	0	.030	0	1	3	2
0	286	0	.059	0	1	3	2
0	280	0	.082	0	1	2	2
0	285	0	.063	0	1	3	2
0	276	0	.097	0	1	3	2
0	275	0	.101	0	1	3	2
0	300	0	.010	0	1	0	2
0	284	0	.067	0	1	2	2
0	280	0	.082	0	1	2	2
0	287	0	.055	0	1	1	2
0	278	0	.090	0	1	0	2
0	286	0	.059	0	1	0	2
0	275	0	.101	0	1	2	2
0	284	0	.067	0	1	3	2
0	296	0	.023	0	1	3	2
0	280	0	.082	0	1	2	2

Salary Grades 5 & 6 (continued)

(1) Current Weekly Salary (black)	(2) Current Weekly Salary (white)	(3) MDC (black)	(4) MDC (white)	(5) Race	(6) Sex	(7) Educ Level	(8) Length of Service
0	310	0	−.023	0	1	4	2
0	295	0	.027	0	1	3	2
0	288	0	.052	0	1	3	2
0	274	0	.105	0	1	0	2
0	280	0	.082	0	1	2	2
0	288	0	.052	0	1	0	2
0	294	0	.030	0	1	2	2
0	283	0	.070	0	1	3	2
0	280	0	.082	0	1	2	2
0	294	0	.030	0	1	3	2
0	290	0	.044	0	1	3	2
0	312	0	−.029	0	1	3	2
0	295	0	.027	0	1	0	2
0	306	0	−.010	0	1	2	2
0	284	0	.067	0	1	0	2
0	280	0	.082	0	1	0	2
0	292	0	.037	0	1	3	2
0	288	0	.052	0	1	2	2
0	278	0	.090	0	1	3	2
0	307	0	−.013	0	1	3	2
0	285	0	.063	0	1	1	2
0	278	0	.090	0	1	0	2
0	283	0	.070	0	1	0	2
0	298	0	.016	0	1	0	2
0	296	0	.023	0	1	3	3
0	314	0	−.035	0	1	2	3
0	295	0	.027	0	1	3	3
0	318	0	−.048	0	1	0	3
0	300	0	.010	0	1	1	3
0	302	0	.003	0	1	0	3
0	308	0	−.017	0	1	2	3
0	320	0	−.054	0	1	3	3
0	324	0	−.065	0	1	3	3
0	290	0	.044	0	1	0	3
0	311	0	−.026	0	1	3	3

<table>
<tr><td colspan="8" align="center">Salary Grades 5 & 6 (continued)</td></tr>
</table>

(1) Current Weekly Salary (black)	(2) Current Weekly Salary (white)	(3) MDC (black)	(4) MDC (white)	(5) Race	(6) Sex	(7) Educ Level	(8) Length of Service
0	315	0	−.039	0	1	2	3
0	294	0	.030	0	1	0	3
0	287	0	.055	0	1	0	3
0	320	0	−.054	0	1	1	3
0	308	0	−.017	0	1	2	3
0	316	0	−.042	0	1	3	3
0	295	0	.027	0	1	3	3
0	314	0	−.035	0	1	3	3
0	322	0	−.059	0	1	2	3
0	296	0	.023	0	1	3	3
0	302	0	.003	0	1	4	3
0	325	0	−.068	0	1	0	3
0	314	0	−.035	0	1	2	3
0	322	0	−.059	0	1	0	3
0	298	0	.016	0	1	0	3
0	334	0	−.093	0	1	3	3
0	321	0	−.057	0	1	3	3
0	328	0	−.077	0	1	3	3
0	300	0	.010	0	1	4	3
0	306	0	−.010	0	1	3	3
0	335	0	−.096	0	1	3	3
0	321	0	−.057	0	1	2	3
0	328	0	−.077	0	1	0	3
0	315	0	−.039	0	1	0	3
0	295	0	.027	0	1	1	3
0	330	0	−.082	0	1	0	3
0	318	0	−.048	0	1	3	3
0	315	0	−.039	0	1	2	3
0	335	0	−.096	0	1	3	3
0	322	0	−.059	0	1	3	3
0	328	0	−.077	0	1	1	3
0	331	0	−.085	0	1	3	3
0	319	0	−.051	0	1	3	3
0	324	0	−.065	0	1	0	3
0	306	0	−.010	0	1	2	3

Salary Grades 5 & 6 (continued)

(1) Current Weekly Salary (black)	(2) Current Weekly Salary (white)	(3) MDC (black)	(4) MDC (white)	(5) Race	(6) Sex	(7) Educ Level	(8) Length of Service
0	319	0	−.051	0	1	3	3
0	324	0	−.065	0	1	1	3
0	333	0	−.091	0	1	3	3
0	317	0	−.045	0	1	2	3
0	334	0	−.093	0	1	2	3
0	315	0	−.039	0	1	3	3
0	323	0	−.062	0	1	3	3
0	335	0	−.096	0	1	0	3
0	331	0	−.085	0	1	0	3
0	338	0	−.104	0	1	1	3
0	326	0	−.071	0	1	1	3
0	322	0	−.059	0	1	0	3
0	304	0	−.004	0	1	2	3
0	296	0	.023	0	1	0	3
0	320	0	−.054	0	1	2	3
0	334	0	−.093	0	1	2	3
0	336	0	−.099	0	1	3	3
0	325	0	−.068	0	1	3	3
0	328	0	−.077	0	1	4	3
0	321	0	−.057	0	1	3	3
0	326	0	−.071	0	1	3	3
0	315	0	−.039	0	1	2	3
0	324	0	−.065	0	1	2	3
0	320	0	−.054	0	1	0	3
0	333	0	−.091	0	1	1	3
0	328	0	−.077	0	1	2	3
0	334	0	−.093	0	1	3	3
0	317	0	−.045	0	1	3	3
0	324	0	−.065	0	1	3	3
0	302	0	.003	0	1	2	3
0	330	0	−.082	0	1	3	3
0	326	0	−.071	0	1	3	3
0	322	0	−.059	0	1	1	3
0	322	0	−.059	0	1	2	3
0	298	0	.016	0	1	0	3

				Salary Grades 5 & 6 (continued)			
(1) Current Weekly Salary (black)	(2) Current Weekly Salary (white)	(3) MDC (black)	(4) MDC (white)	(5) Race	(6) Sex	(7) Educ Level	(8) Length of Service
0	334	0	−.093	0	1	3	3
0	315	0	−.039	0	1	0	3
0	318	0	−.048	0	1	0	3
0	310	0	−.023	0	1	3	3
0	327	0	−.074	0	1	2	3
0	322	0	−.059	0	1	0	3
0	328	0	−.077	0	1	1	3
0	334	0	−.093	0	1	1	3
0	330	0	−.082	0	1	2	3
0	325	0	−.068	0	1	0	3
0	333	0	−.091	0	1	3	3
0	328	0	−.077	0	1	3	3
0	306	0	−.010	0	1	2	3
0	321	0	−.057	0	1	2	3
0	324	0	−.065	0	1	2	3
0	316	0	−.042	0	1	4	3
0	328	0	−.077	0	1	3	3
0	325	0	−.068	0	1	1	3
0	336	0	−.099	0	1	2	4
0	324	0	−.065	0	1	3	4
0	317	0	−.045	0	1	3	4
0	338	0	−.104	0	1	0	4
0	335	0	−.096	0	1	0	4
0	326	0	−.071	0	1	2	4
0	332	0	−.088	0	1	0	4
0	320	0	−.054	0	1	1	4
0	328	0	−.077	0	1	3	4
0	340	0	−.109	0	1	3	4
0	333	0	−.091	0	1	2	4
0	327	0	−.074	0	1	3	4
0	324	0	−.065	0	1	2	4
0	325	0	−.068	0	1	0	4
0	320	0	−.054	0	1	1	4
0	326	0	−.071	0	1	0	4
0	318	0	−.048	0	1	0	4

				Salary Grades 5 & 6 (continued)				

(1) Current Weekly Salary (black)	(2) Current Weekly Salary (white)	(3) MDC (black)	(4) MDC (white)	(5) Race	(6) Sex	(7) Educ Level	(8) Length of Service
0	327	0	−.074	0	1	2	4
0	338	0	−.104	0	1	3	4
0	321	0	−.057	0	1	0	4
0	335	0	−.096	0	1	3	4
0	332	0	−.088	0	1	3	4
0	337	0	−.101	0	1	2	4
0	324	0	−.065	0	1	2	4
0	336	0	−.099	0	1	2	4
0	321	0	−.057	0	1	0	4
0	328	0	−.077	0	1	0	4
0	332	0	−.088	0	1	1	4
0	330	0	−.082	0	1	0	4
0	334	0	−.093	0	1	2	4
0	326	0	−.071	0	1	3	4
0	332	0	−.088	0	1	3	4
0	321	0	−.057	0	1	3	4
0	325	0	−.068	0	1	2	4
0	314	0	−.035	0	1	3	4
0	335	0	−.096	0	1	1	4
0	332	0	−.088	0	1	1	4
0	324	0	−.065	0	1	0	4
0	340	0	−.109	0	1	0	4
0	332	0	−.088	0	1	2	4
0	328	0	−.077	0	1	3	4
0	336	0	−.099	0	1	3	4
0	335	0	−.096	0	1	2	4
0	322	0	−.059	0	1	2	4
0	330	0	−.082	0	1	2	4
0	328	0	−.077	0	1	0	4
0	335	0	−.096	0	1	2	4
0	320	0	−.054	0	1	0	5
0	338	0	−.104	0	1	2	5
0	333	0	−.091	0	1	3	5
0	341	0	−.112	0	1	2	5
0	334	0	−.093	0	1	3	5

			Salary Grades 5 & 6 (continued)				
(1)	*(2)*	*(3)*	*(4)*	*(5)*	*(6)*	*(7)*	*(8)*
Current Weekly Salary (black)	Current Weekly Salary (white)	MDC (black)	MDC (white)	Race	Sex	Educ Level	Length of Service
0	332	0	−.088	0	1	0	5
0	338	0	−.104	0	1	0	5
0	335	0	−.096	0	1	1	5
0	329	0	−.079	0	1	0	5
0	334	0	−.093	0	1	1	5
0	326	0	−.071	0	1	1	5
0	331	0	−.085	0	1	2	5
0	338	0	−.104	0	1	3	5
0	336	0	−.099	0	1	2	5
0	335	0	−.096	0	1	0	5
0	328	0	−.077	0	1	2	5
0	330	0	−.082	0	1	2	5
0	340	0	−.109	0	1	0	5
0	337	0	−.101	0	1	3	5
0	332	0	−.088	0	1	3	5
0	335	0	−.096	0	1	2	5
0	338	0	−.104	0	1	0	5
0	333	0	−.091	0	1	0	5
0	328	0	−.077	0	1	2	5
0	337	0	−.101	0	1	1	5
0	336	0	−.099	0	1	0	5
0	331	0	−.085	0	1	3	5
0	335	0	−.096	0	1	3	5
0	329	0	−.079	0	1	0	5
0	330	0	−.082	0	1	2	5
0	337	0	−.101	0	1	2	5
0	331	0	−.085	0	1	0	5
0	334	0	−.093	0	1	1	5
0	328	0	−.077	0	1	0	5
0	336	0	−.099	0	1	2	5
0	332	0	−.088	0	1	2	5
0	330	0	−.082	0	1	0	5
0	335	0	−.096	0	1	3	5
0	338	0	−.104	0	1	3	5
0	330	0	−.082	0	1	2	5

| | | | | *Salary Grades 5 & 6 (continued)* | | | | |

(1) Current Weekly Salary (black)	(2) Current Weekly Salary (white)	(3) MDC (black)	(4) MDC (white)	(5) Race	(6) Sex	(7) Educ Level	(8) Length of Service
0	334	0	−.093	0	1	2	5
0	335	0	−.096	0	1	0	5
0	332	0	−.088	0	1	1	5
0	340	0	−.109	0	1	2	5
0	325	0	−.068	0	1	0	5
0	332	0	−.088	0	1	0	6
0	337	0	−.101	0	1	0	6
0	334	0	−.093	0	1	2	6
0	335	0	−.096	0	1	2	6
0	328	0	−.077	0	1	0	6
0	340	0	−.109	0	1	0	6
0	333	0	−.091	0	1	0	6
0	336	0	−.099	0	1	2	6
0	341	0	−.112	0	1	3	6
0	330	0	−.082	0	1	2	6
0	328	0	−.077	0	1	2	6
0	342	0	−.114	0	1	3	6
0	337	0	−.101	0	1	3	6
0	335	0	−.096	0	1	2	6
0	332	0	−.088	0	1	2	6
0	333	0	−.091	0	1	0	6
0	330	0	−.082	0	1	0	6
0	328	0	−.077	0	1	0	6
0	335	0	−.096	0	1	0	6
0	341	0	−.112	0	1	2	6
0	338	0	−.104	0	1	2	6
0	337	0	−.101	0	1	2	6
0	338	0	−.104	0	1	1	6
0	330	0	−.082	0	1	2	6
0	332	0	−.088	0	1	2	6
0	337	0	−.101	0	1	2	6
0	335	0	−.096	0	1	1	6
0	328	0	−.077	0	1	2	6
0	334	0	−.093	0	1	0	6
0	336	0	−.099	0	1	0	6

		Salary Grades 5 & 6 (continued)					
(1) Current Weekly Salary (black)	(2) Current Weekly Salary (white)	(3) MDC (black)	(4) MDC (white)	(5) Race	(6) Sex	(7) Educ Level	(8) Length of Service
0	330	0	−.082	0	1	0	6
0	338	0	−.104	0	1	2	6
0	335	0	−.096	0	1	0	6
0	340	0	−.109	0	1	0	6
0	337	0	−.101	0	1	3	6
0	335	0	−.096	0	1	0	6
0	338	0	−.104	0	1	0	6
0	329	0	−.079	0	1	0	6
0	337	0	−.101	0	1	2	6
0	334	0	−.093	0	1	1	6
0	337	0	−.101	0	1	2	6
0	330	0	−.082	0	1	2	6
0	336	0	−.099	0	1	2	6
0	335	0	−.096	0	1	0	6
0	332	0	−.088	0	1	2	6
0	338	0	−.104	0	1	0	6
0	340	0	−.109	0	1	0	6
0	330	0	−.082	0	1	0	6
0	333	0	−.091	0	1	1	6
0	328	0	−.077	0	1	0	6
0	342	0	−.114	0	1	0	6
0	335	0	−.096	0	1	0	6
0	332	0	−.088	0	1	2	6
0	337	0	−.101	0	1	2	6
0	338	0	−.104	0	1	2	6
0	332	0	−.088	0	1	0	6
0	335	0	−.096	0	1	1	6
0	338	0	−.104	0	1	0	6
0	234	0	.294	0	0	3	1
0	243	0	.262	0	0	2	1
0	240	0	.246	0	0	2	1
0	231	0	.311	0	0	3	1
0	235	0	.289	0	0	3	1
0	232	0	.306	0	0	0	1
0	236	0	.283	0	0	0	1

				Salary Grades 5 & 6 (continued)			
(1) Current Weekly Salary (black)	(2) Current Weekly Salary (white)	(3) MDC (black)	(4) MDC (white)	(5) Race	(6) Sex	(7) Educ Level	(8) Length of Service
0	248	0	.221	0	0	1	1
0	242	0	.252	0	0	0	1
0	254	0	.192	0	0	3	1
0	241	0	.257	0	0	2	1
0	238	0	.273	0	0	3	1
0	232	0	.306	0	0	2	1
0	245	0	.236	0	0	2	1
0	246	0	.231	0	0	3	1
0	238	0	.273	0	0	3	1
0	241	0	.257	0	0	2	1
0	264	0	.147	0	0	2	1
0	253	0	.197	0	0	1	1
0	238	0	.273	0	0	0	1
0	232	0	.306	0	0	0	1
0	247	0	.226	0	0	2	1
0	240	0	.262	0	0	1	1
0	236	0	.283	0	0	3	1
0	245	0	.236	0	0	0	1
0	263	0	.152	0	0	3	1
0	252	0	.202	0	0	2	1
0	238	0	.273	0	0	1	1
0	230	0	.317	0	0	1	1
0	241	0	.257	0	0	3	1
0	246	0	.231	0	0	3	1
0	239	0	.267	0	0	2	1
0	242	0	.252	0	0	0	1
0	246	0	.231	0	0	0	1
0	254	0	.192	0	0	3	1
0	250	0	.212	0	0	3	1
0	253	0	.197	0	0	2	1
0	248	0	.221	0	0	3	2
0	265	0	.143	0	0	3	2
0	270	0	.122	0	0	2	2
0	242	0	.252	0	0	1	2
0	249	0	.216	0	0	2	2

Salary Grades 5 & 6 (continued)

(1) Current Weekly Salary (black)	(2) Current Weekly Salary (white)	(3) MDC (black)	(4) MDC (white)	(5) Race	(6) Sex	(7) Educ Level	(8) Length of Service
0	251	0	.207	0	0	3	2
0	245	0	.236	0	0	3	2
0	263	0	.152	0	0	1	2
0	258	0	.174	0	0	2	2
0	261	0	.161	0	0	0	2
0	266	0	.139	0	0	2	2
0	258	0	.174	0	0	0	2
0	255	0	.188	0	0	0	2
0	276	0	.097	0	0	3	2
0	265	0	.143	0	0	2	2
0	258	0	.174	0	0	0	2
0	270	0	.122	0	0	2	2
0	262	0	.156	0	0	2	2
0	268	0	.130	0	0	1	2
0	257	0	.179	0	0	0	2
0	274	0	.105	0	0	3	2
0	283	0	.070	0	0	3	2
0	264	0	.147	0	0	2	2
0	276	0	.097	0	0	2	2
0	258	0	.174	0	0	1	2
0	263	0	.152	0	0	2	2
0	275	0	.101	0	0	0	2
0	270	0	.122	0	0	3	2
0	274	0	.105	0	0	2	2
0	271	0	.118	0	0	3	2
0	268	0	.130	0	0	3	2
0	262	0	.156	0	0	2	2
0	276	0	.097	0	0	2	2
0	268	0	.130	0	0	3	2
0	274	0	.105	0	0	2	2
0	265	0	.143	0	0	2	2
0	258	0	.174	0	0	0	2
0	263	0	.152	0	0	1	2
0	280	0	.082	0	0	0	2
0	275	0	.101	0	0	2	2

Salary Grades 5 & 6 (continued)							
(1)	(2)	(3)	(4)	(5)	(6)	(7)	(8)
Current Weekly Salary (black)	Current Weekly Salary (white)	MDC (black)	MDC (white)	Race	Sex	Educ Level	Length of Service
0	277	0	.093	0	0	0	2
0	262	0	.156	0	0	2	2
0	274	0	.105	0	0	2	2
0	281	0	.078	0	0	3	2
0	263	0	.152	0	0	0	2
0	274	0	.105	0	0	2	2
0	279	0	.086	0	0	2	2
0	251	0	.207	0	0	1	3
0	278	0	.090	0	0	3	3
0	264	0	.147	0	0	2	3
0	272	0	.114	0	0	1	3
0	266	0	.139	0	0	0	3
0	271	0	.118	0	0	3	3
0	278	0	.090	0	0	3	3
0	263	0	.152	0	0	3	3
0	258	0	.174	0	0	2	3
0	263	0	.152	0	0	0	3
0	274	0	.105	0	0	0	3
0	270	0	.122	0	0	1	3
0	281	0	.078	0	0	3	3
0	272	0	.114	0	0	2	3
0	268	0	.130	0	0	2	3
0	273	0	.110	0	0	2	3
0	260	0	.165	0	0	2	3
0	264	0	.147	0	0	0	3
0	283	0	.070	0	0	1	3
0	275	0	.101	0	0	1	3
0	278	0	.090	0	0	0	3
0	262	0	.156	0	0	2	3
0	310	0	−.023	0	0	3	3
0	298	0	.016	0	0	3	3
0	317	0	−.045	0	0	3	3
0	284	0	.067	0	0	2	3
0	275	0	.101	0	0	2	3
0	278	0	.090	0	0	0	3

				Salary Grades 5 & 6 (continued)			
(1) Current Weekly Salary (black)	(2) Current Weekly Salary (white)	(3) MDC (black)	(4) MDC (white)	(5) Race	(6) Sex	(7) Educ Level	(8) Length of Service
0	286	0	.059	0	0	1	3
0	272	0	.114	0	0	0	3
0	288	0	.052	0	0	2	3
0	267	0	.134	0	0	0	3
0	274	0	.105	0	0	0	3
0	279	0	.086	0	0	2	3
0	295	0	.027	0	0	3	3
0	291	0	.041	0	0	2	3
0	306	0	−.010	0	0	3	3
0	312	0	−.029	0	0	3	3
0	284	0	.066	0	0	1	3
0	298	0	.016	0	0	3	3
0	281	0	.078	0	0	0	3
0	296	0	.023	0	0	2	3
0	272	0	.114	0	0	2	3
0	283	0	.070	0	0	2	3
0	280	0	.082	0	0	0	3
0	274	0	.105	0	0	0	3
0	296	0	.023	0	0	1	3
0	288	0	.052	0	0	0	3
0	285	0	.063	0	0	2	3
0	295	0	.027	0	0	3	3
0	292	0	.037	0	0	2	3
0	280	0	.082	0	0	2	3
0	284	0	.066	0	0	0	3
0	322	0	−.059	0	0	4	3
0	287	0	.055	0	0	2	3
0	293	0	.034	0	0	0	3
0	282	0	.074	0	0	0	3
0	320	0	−.054	0	0	3	3
0	309	0	−.020	0	0	3	3
0	284	0	.066	0	0	2	3
0	280	0	.082	0	0	2	3
0	286	0	.059	0	0	2	3
0	282	0	.074	0	0	0	3

	Salary Grades 5 & 6 (continued)						
(1)	(2)	(3)	(4)	(5)	(6)	(7)	(8)
Current Weekly Salary (black)	Current Weekly Salary (white)	MDC (black)	MDC (white)	Race	Sex	Educ Level	Length of Service
0	314	0	−.035	0	0	3	3
0	285	0	.063	0	0	0	3
0	291	0	.041	0	0	0	3
0	280	0	.082	0	0	0	3
0	288	0	.052	0	0	1	3
0	294	0	.030	0	0	2	3
0	297	0	.020	0	0	2	3
0	274	0	.105	0	0	2	3
0	302	0	.003	0	0	3	3
0	280	0	.082	0	0	0	3
0	283	0	.070	0	0	0	3
0	318	0	−.048	0	0	4	3
0	275	0	.101	0	0	2	3
0	282	0	.074	0	0	2	3
0	287	0	.055	0	0	0	3
0	323	0	−.062	0	0	3	3
0	312	0	−.029	0	0	3	3
0	280	0	.082	0	0	0	3
0	276	0	.097	0	0	0	4
0	294	0	.030	0	0	0	4
0	285	0	.063	0	0	1	4
0	281	0	.078	0	0	0	4
0	284	0	.066	0	0	2	4
0	297	0	.020	0	0	2	4
0	320	0	−.054	0	0	3	4
0	286	0	.059	0	0	2	4
0	300	0	.010	0	0	3	4
0	324	0	−.065	0	0	3	4
0	278	0	.090	0	0	0	4
0	294	0	.030	0	0	0	4
0	300	0	.010	0	0	1	4
0	306	0	−.010	0	0	3	4
0	294	0	.030	0	0	2	4
0	310	0	−.023	0	0	3	4
0	287	0	.055	0	0	2	4

Salary Grades 5 & 6 (continued)

(1) Current Weekly Salary (black)	(2) Current Weekly Salary (white)	(3) MDC (black)	(4) MDC (white)	(5) Race	(6) Sex	(7) Educ Level	(8) Length of Service
0	328	0	−.077	0	0	3	4
0	310	0	−.023	0	0	2	4
0	298	0	.016	0	0	2	4
0	304	0	−.004	0	0	0	4
0	307	0	−.013	0	0	1	4
0	318	0	−.048	0	0	0	4
0	310	0	−.023	0	0	1	4
0	313	0	−.032	0	0	1	4
0	320	0	−.054	0	0	0	4
0	315	0	−.039	0	0	2	4
0	306	0	−.010	0	0	0	4
0	300	0	.010	0	0	0	4
0	298	0	.016	0	0	2	4
0	308	0	−.017	0	0	2	4
0	319	0	−.051	0	0	2	4
0	340	0	−.109	0	0	3	4
0	322	0	−.059	0	0	0	4
0	317	0	−.045	0	0	0	4
0	336	0	−.099	0	0	3	4
0	320	0	−.054	0	0	2	4
0	304	0	−.004	0	0	2	4
0	306	0	−.010	0	0	0	4
0	314	0	−.035	0	0	0	4
0	327	0	−.074	0	0	1	4
0	321	0	−.057	0	0	0	4
0	309	0	−.020	0	0	2	4
0	327	0	−.074	0	0	3	4
0	318	0	−.048	0	0	2	4
0	315	0	−.039	0	0	0	5
0	321	0	−.057	0	0	0	5
0	314	0	−.035	0	0	2	5
0	328	0	−.077	0	0	0	5
0	335	0	−.096	0	0	0	5
0	308	0	−.017	0	0	1	5
0	311	0	−.026	0	0	2	5

			Salary Grades 5 & 6 (continued)				
(1)	*(2)*	*(3)*	*(4)*	*(5)*	*(6)*	*(7)*	*(8)*
Current Weekly Salary (black)	*Current Weekly Salary (white)*	*MDC (black)*	*MDC (white)*	*Race*	*Sex*	*Educ Level*	*Length of Service*
0	306	0	−.010	0	0	2	5
0	325	0	−.068	0	0	2	5
0	340	0	−.109	0	0	3	5
0	320	0	−.054	0	0	0	5
0	334	0	−.093	0	0	2	5
0	328	0	−.077	0	0	0	5
0	317	0	−.045	0	0	0	5
0	322	0	−.059	0	0	2	5
0	314	0	−.035	0	0	2	5
0	323	0	−.062	0	0	0	5
0	325	0	−.068	0	0	0	5
0	320	0	−.054	0	0	0	5
0	338	0	−.104	0	0	2	5
0	316	0	−.042	0	0	2	5
0	340	0	−.109	0	0	3	5
0	322	0	−.059	0	0	0	5
0	314	0	−.035	0	0	0	5
0	326	0	−.071	0	0	1	5
0	320	0	−.054	0	0	2	5
0	328	0	−.077	0	0	2	5
0	321	0	−.057	0	0	0	5
0	306	0	−.010	0	0	0	5
0	321	0	−.057	0	0	0	5
0	328	0	−.077	0	0	2	5
0	317	0	−.045	0	0	2	5
0	335	0	−.096	0	0	3	5
0	330	0	−.082	0	0	2	5
0	338	0	−.104	0	0	3	5
0	330	0	−.082	0	0	3	5
0	314	0	−.035	0	0	0	5
0	323	0	−.062	0	0	0	5
0	328	0	−.077	0	0	1	6
0	317	0	−.045	0	0	0	6
0	309	0	−.020	0	0	3	6
0	316	0	−.042	0	0	3	6

| | | | | Salary Grades 5 & 6 (continued) | | | | |

(1) Current Weekly Salary (black)	(2) Current Weekly Salary (white)	(3) MDC (black)	(4) MDC (white)	(5) Race	(6) Sex	(7) Educ Level	(8) Length of Service
0	324	0	−.065	0	0	2	6
0	327	0	−.074	0	0	1	6
0	320	0	−.054	0	0	0	6
0	331	0	−.085	0	0	0	6
0	329	0	−.079	0	0	3	6
0	322	0	−.059	0	0	2	6
0	334	0	−.093	0	0	3	6
0	315	0	−.039	0	0	2	6
0	335	0	−.096	0	0	2	6
0	332	0	−.088	0	0	0	6
0	336	0	−.099	0	0	0	6
0	330	0	−.082	0	0	1	6
0	334	0	−.093	0	0	2	6
0	340	0	−.109	0	0	2	6
0	322	0	−.059	0	0	0	6
0	325	0	−.068	0	0	0	6
0	318	0	−.048	0	0	1	6
0	334	0	−.093	0	0	2	6
0	330	0	−.082	0	0	1	6
0	321	0	−.057	0	0	2	6
0	324	0	−.065	0	0	0	6
0	332	0	−.088	0	0	0	6
0	341	0	−.112	0	0	3	6
0	324	0	−.065	0	0	2	6
0	318	0	−.048	0	0	2	6
0	320	0	−.054	0	0	2	6
0	324	0	−.065	0	0	0	6
0	336	0	−.099	0	0	2	6
0	315	0	−.039	0	0	2	6
0	311	0	−.026	0	0	0	6
0	322	0	−.059	0	0	0	6
0	325	0	−.068	0	0	0	6
0	328	0	−.077	0	0	0	6
0	324	0	−.065	0	0	2	6
0	332	0	−.088	0	0	0	6

			Salary Grades 5 & 6 (continued)				
(1) Current Weekly Salary (black)	(2) Current Weekly Salary (white)	(3) MDC (black)	(4) MDC (white)	(5) Race	(6) Sex	(7) Educ Level	(8) Length of Service
0	338	0	−.104	0	0	3	6
0	324	0	−.065	0	0	0	6
0	330	0	−.082	0	0	0	6
0	321	0	−.057	0	0	1	6
0	340	0	−.109	0	0	3	6
0	319	0	−.051	0	0	2	6
0	320	0	−.054	0	0	0	6
0	325	0	−.068	0	0	0	6
0	310	0	−.023	0	0	0	6
0	337	0	−.101	0	0	2	6
0	328	0	−.077	0	0	2	6
0	330	0	−.082	0	0	1	6
0	315	0	−.039	0	0	2	6
0	321	0	−.057	0	0	1	6
0	328	0	−.077	0	0	0	6
0	340	0	−.109	0	0	1	6
0	314	0	−.035	0	0	3	6
0	344	0	−.120	0	0	2	6
0	328	0	−.077	0	0	2	6
0	333	0	−.091	0	0	0	6
0	324	0	−.065	0	0	0	6
0	327	0	−.074	0	0	0	6
0	332	0	−.088	0	0	2	6
0	330	0	−.082	0	0	0	6
0	319	0	−.051	0	0	0	6
0	312	0	−.029	0	0	2	6
0	337	0	−.101	0	0	2	6
0	335	0	−.096	0	0	1	6
0	320	0	−.054	0	0	2	6
0	308	0	−.017	0	0	3	6
0	319	0	−.051	0	0	0	6
0	324	0	−.065	0	0	2	6
0	329	0	−.079	0	0	0	6
0	322	0	−.059	0	0	0	6
0	325	0	−.068	0	0	2	6

Salary Grades 5 & 6 (continued)

(1) Current Weekly Salary (black)	(2) Current Weekly Salary (white)	(3) MDC (black)	(4) MDC (white)	(5) Race	(6) Sex	(7) Educ Level	(8) Length of Service
0	320	0	−.054	0	0	0	6
0	314	0	−.035	0	0	0	6
0	335	0	−.096	0	0	0	6
0	328	0	−.077	0	0	2	6
0	311	0	−.026	0	0	0	6
0	324	0	−.065	0	0	0	6
0	331	0	−.085	0	0	1	6
0	327	0	−.074	0	0	0	6
0	320	0	−.054	0	0	2	6
0	332	0	−.088	0	0	2	6
0	341	0	−.112	0	0	3	6
0	318	0	−.048	0	0	0	6
0	332	0	−.088	0	0	3	6
0	324	0	−.065	0	0	2	6
0	328	0	−.077	0	0	2	6
0	321	0	−.057	0	0	0	6
0	336	0	−.099	0	0	0	6
0	340	0	−.109	0	0	2	6
0	332	0	−.088	0	0	0	6
0	324	0	−.065	0	0	0	6
0	329	0	−.079	0	0	0	6
0	333	0	−.091	0	0	2	6
0	337	0	−.101	0	0	2	6
0	330	0	−.082	0	0	1	6
0	318	0	−.048	0	0	0	6
0	342	0	−.114	0	0	1	6
0	338	0	−.104	0	0	2	6
0	331	0	−.085	0	0	0	6
0	335	0	−.096	0	0	0	6
0	332	0	−.088	0	0	2	6
232	0	.306	0	1	1	2	1
240	0	.262	0	1	1	3	1
248	0	.221	0	1	1	3	1
235	0	.289	0	1	1	2	1
230	0	.317	0	1	1	0	1

Salary Grades 5 & 6 (continued)

(1) Current Weekly Salary (black)	(2) Current Weekly Salary (white)	(3) MDC (black)	(4) MDC (white)	(5) Race	(6) Sex	(7) Educ Level	(8) Length of Service
238	0	.273	0	1	1	1	1
240	0	.262	0	1	1	0	1
232	0	.306	0	1	1	2	1
236	0	.283	0	1	1	2	1
252	0	.202	0	1	1	3	1
258	0	.174	0	1	1	3	1
237	0	.278	0	1	1	2	1
255	0	.188	0	1	1	3	1
231	0	.311	0	1	1	0	1
232	0	.306	0	1	1	2	1
249	0	.216	0	1	1	3	1
247	0	.226	0	1	1	2	2
263	0	.152	0	1	1	3	2
260	0	.165	0	1	1	3	2
252	0	.202	0	1	1	0	2
263	0	.152	0	1	1	1	2
254	0	.192	0	1	1	0	2
258	0	.174	0	1	1	2	2
270	0	.122	0	1	1	3	2
256	0	.183	0	1	1	3	2
263	0	.152	0	1	1	2	2
238	0	.273	0	1	1	0	2
244	0	.241	0	1	1	2	2
253	0	.197	0	1	1	1	2
248	0	.221	0	1	1	2	2
240	0	.262	0	1	1	0	2
265	0	.143	0	1	1	3	2
245	0	.236	0	1	1	2	2
259	0	.169	0	1	1	3	2
273	0	.110	0	1	1	3	2
254	0	.192	0	1	1	0	2
248	0	.221	0	1	1	3	2
260	0	.165	0	1	1	2	3
253	0	.197	0	1	1	2	3
247	0	.226	0	1	1	0	3

Salary Grades 5 & 6 (continued)

(1) Current Weekly Salary (black)	(2) Current Weekly Salary (white)	(3) MDC (black)	(4) MDC (white)	(5) Race	(6) Sex	(7) Educ Level	(8) Length of Service
259	0	.169	0	1	1	0	3
271	0	.118	0	1	1	1	3
268	0	.130	0	1	1	0	3
270	0	.122	0	1	1	0	3
273	0	.110	0	1	1	2	3
264	0	.147	0	1	1	2	3
283	0	.070	0	1	1	3	3
255	0	.188	0	1	1	0	3
276	0	.097	0	1	1	3	3
281	0	.078	0	1	1	2	3
270	0	.122	0	1	1	0	3
263	0	.152	0	1	1	0	3
254	0	.192	0	1	1	0	3
273	0	.110	0	1	1	2	3
261	0	.161	0	1	1	0	3
258	0	.174	0	1	1	3	3
280	0	.082	0	1	1	0	3
275	0	.101	0	1	1	2	3
283	0	.070	0	1	1	1	3
278	0	.090	0	1	1	0	3
274	0	.105	0	1	1	0	3
285	0	.063	0	1	1	2	3
282	0	.074	0	1	1	2	3
274	0	.105	0	1	1	3	3
288	0	.052	0	1	1	2	3
263	0	.152	0	1	1	2	3
277	0	.093	0	1	1	0	3
268	0	.130	0	1	1	3	3
279	0	.086	0	1	1	3	3
275	0	.101	0	1	1	0	3
282	0	.074	0	1	1	2	3
293	0	.034	0	1	1	0	4
298	0	.016	0	1	1	0	4
286	0	.059	0	1	1	2	4
314	0	−.035	0	1	1	2	4

Salary Grades 5 & 6 (continued)

(1) Current Weekly Salary (black)	(2) Current Weekly Salary (white)	(3) MDC (black)	(4) MDC (white)	(5) Race	(6) Sex	(7) Educ Level	(8) Length of Service
322	0	−.059	0	1	1	1	4
308	0	−.017	0	1	1	2	4
312	0	−.029	0	1	1	1	4
296	0	.023	0	1	1	0	4
305	0	−.007	0	1	1	3	5
337	0	−.101	0	1	1	2	5
328	0	−.077	0	1	1	2	6
330	0	−.082	0	1	1	0	6
322	0	−.059	0	1	1	2	6
324	0	−.065	0	1	1	0	6
244	0	.241	0	1	0	3	1
236	0	.283	0	1	0	0	1
253	0	.197	0	1	0	3	1
251	0	.207	0	1	0	2	1
258	0	.174	0	1	0	3	1
235	0	.289	0	1	0	1	1
238	0	.273	0	1	0	0	1
244	0	.241	0	1	0	2	1
253	0	.197	0	1	0	0	2
261	0	.161	0	1	0	2	2
255	0	.188	0	1	0	0	2
270	0	.122	0	1	0	3	2
276	0	.097	0	1	0	3	2
258	0	.174	0	1	0	0	2
251	0	.207	0	1	0	2	2
248	0	.221	0	1	0	2	2
259	0	.169	0	1	0	1	2
253	0	.197	0	1	0	2	3
277	0	.093	0	1	0	3	3
260	0	.165	0	1	0	2	3
255	0	.188	0	1	0	0	3
278	0	.090	0	1	0	1	3
284	0	.067	0	1	0	0	3
275	0	.101	0	1	0	0	3
287	0	.055	0	1	0	2	3

			Salary Grades 5 & 6 (continued)				
(1) Current Weekly Salary (black)	(2) Current Weekly Salary (white)	(3) MDC (black)	(4) MDC (white)	(5) Race	(6) Sex	(7) Educ Level	(8) Length of Service
266	0	.139	0	1	0	0	3
275	0	.101	0	1	0	2	3
268	0	.130	0	1	0	0	3
280	0	.082	0	1	0	0	3
272	0	.114	0	1	0	2	3
283	0	.070	0	1	0	2	3
276	0	.097	0	1	0	3	3
282	0	.074	0	1	0	2	3
274	0	.105	0	1	0	2	3
290	0	.044	0	1	0	3	3
297	0	.020	0	1	0	3	3
261	0	.161	0	1	0	1	3
308	0	−.017	0	1	0	4	3
263	0	.152	0	1	0	2	3
273	0	.110	0	1	0	0	3
264	0	.147	0	1	0	0	3
281	0	.078	0	1	0	0	3
287	0	.055	0	1	0	2	3
275	0	.101	0	1	0	2	3
294	0	.030	0	1	0	0	3
263	0	.152	0	1	0	2	3
296	0	.023	0	1	0	3	3
275	0	.101	0	1	0	2	3
278	0	.090	0	1	0	0	3
302	0	.003	0	1	0	3	3
281	0	.078	0	1	0	0	4
269	0	.126	0	1	0	0	4
297	0	.020	0	1	0	2	4
296	0	.023	0	1	0	0	4
308	0	−.017	0	1	0	2	5
297	0	.020	0	1	0	0	6

	Salary Grades 7 & 8			Number of Employees: 569			
(1) Current Weekly Salary (black)	(2) Current Weekly Salary (white)	(3) MDC (black)	(4) MDC (white)	(5) Race	(6) Sex	(7) Educ Level	(8) Length of Service
0	352	0	.252	0	1	3	1
0	334	0	.320	0	1	3	1
0	336	0	.312	0	1	3	1
0	344	0	.281	0	1	2	1
0	368	0	.198	0	1	3	1
0	350	0	.259	0	1	2	1
0	354	0	.245	0	1	2	1
0	362	0	.218	0	1	3	1
0	358	0	.231	0	1	3	1
0	335	0	.316	0	1	4	1
0	374	0	.179	0	1	3	1
0	365	0	.208	0	1	4	1
0	371	0	.188	0	1	4	1
0	360	0	.224	0	1	3	1
0	345	0	.278	0	1	4	1
0	341	0	.293	0	1	4	1
0	352	0	.252	0	1	3	1
0	338	0	.304	0	1	4	1
0	343	0	.285	0	1	4	1
0	372	0	.185	0	1	4	1
0	362	0	.218	0	1	3	1
0	340	0	.296	0	1	3	1
0	348	0	.267	0	1	4	1
0	360	0	.224	0	1	4	1
0	374	0	.179	0	1	3	2
0	348	0	.267	0	1	3	2
0	356	0	.238	0	1	3	2
0	351	0	.256	0	1	4	2
0	376	0	.172	0	1	3	2
0	384	0	.148	0	1	3	2
0	365	0	.208	0	1	4	2
0	374	0	.179	0	1	3	2
0	391	0	.127	0	1	4	2
0	383	0	.151	0	1	4	2
0	375	0	.175	0	1	2	2

Salary Grades 7 & 8 (continued)

(1) Current Weekly Salary (black)	(2) Current Weekly Salary (white)	(3) MDC (black)	(4) MDC (white)	(5) Race	(6) Sex	(7) Educ Level	(8) Length of Service
0	378	0	.166	0	1	3	2
0	364	0	.211	0	1	3	2
0	387	0	.139	0	1	2	2
0	410	0	.075	0	1	2	2
0	405	0	.088	0	1	3	2
0	394	0	.119	0	1	4	2
0	376	0	.172	0	1	3	2
0	385	0	.145	0	1	3	2
0	392	0	.124	0	1	3	2
0	377	0	.169	0	1	2	2
0	388	0	.136	0	1	0	2
0	392	0	.124	0	1	3	2
0	380	0	.160	0	1	3	2
0	406	0	.086	0	1	1	2
0	391	0	.127	0	1	3	2
0	370	0	.191	0	1	4	2
0	384	0	.148	0	1	3	2
0	397	0	.110	0	1	3	2
0	382	0	.154	0	1	3	2
0	408	0	.080	0	1	2	2
0	400	0	.102	0	1	3	2
0	385	0	.145	0	1	3	2
0	396	0	.113	0	1	4	2
0	378	0	.166	0	1	3	2
0	384	0	.148	0	1	3	2
0	410	0	.075	0	1	2	2
0	394	0	.119	0	1	3	2
0	395	0	.116	0	1	3	2
0	404	0	.091	0	1	3	2
0	380	0	.160	0	1	0	2
0	386	0	.142	0	1	3	2
0	377	0	.169	0	1	1	2
0	410	0	.075	0	1	4	2
0	395	0	.116	0	1	3	3
0	422	0	.044	0	1	3	3

Salary Grades 7 & 8 (continued)

(1) Current Weekly Salary (black)	(2) Current Weekly Salary (white)	(3) MDC (black)	(4) MDC (white)	(5) Race	(6) Sex	(7) Educ Level	(8) Length of Service
0	396	0	.113	0	1	2	3
0	412	0	.070	0	1	3	3
0	418	0	.054	0	1	2	3
0	400	0	.102	0	1	1	3
0	412	0	.070	0	1	3	3
0	390	0	.130	0	1	3	3
0	406	0	.086	0	1	1	3
0	388	0	.136	0	1	0	3
0	395	0	.116	0	1	3	3
0	382	0	.154	0	1	2	3
0	420	0	.049	0	1	3	3
0	412	0	.070	0	1	3	3
0	424	0	.040	0	1	3	3
0	385	0	.145	0	1	4	3
0	395	0	.116	0	1	2	3
0	408	0	.080	0	1	3	3
0	400	0	.102	0	1	0	3
0	426	0	.035	0	1	3	3
0	414	0	.065	0	1	3	3
0	398	0	.107	0	1	2	3
0	402	0	.096	0	1	3	3
0	432	0	.020	0	1	2	3
0	418	0	.054	0	1	0	3
0	385	0	.145	0	1	3	3
0	416	0	.060	0	1	1	3
0	400	0	.102	0	1	4	3
0	428	0	.030	0	1	3	3
0	420	0	.049	0	1	3	3
0	394	0	.119	0	1	2	3
0	405	0	.088	0	1	3	3
0	390	0	.130	0	1	3	3
0	400	0	.102	0	1	0	3
0	427	0	.032	0	1	3	3
0	420	0	.049	0	1	1	3
0	398	0	.107	0	1	3	3

				Salary Grades 7 & 8 (continued)			
(1) Current Weekly Salary (black)	(2) Current Weekly Salary (white)	(3) MDC (black)	(4) MDC (white)	(5) Race	(6) Sex	(7) Educ Level	(8) Length of Service
0	414	0	.065	0	1	0	3
0	396	0	.113	0	1	3	3
0	422	0	.044	0	1	3	3
0	417	0	.057	0	1	2	3
0	439	0	.004	0	1	4	3
0	422	0	.044	0	1	3	3
0	415	0	.062	0	1	4	3
0	390	0	.130	0	1	3	3
0	416	0	.060	0	1	2	3
0	424	0	.040	0	1	2	3
0	397	0	.110	0	1	3	3
0	409	0	.078	0	1	0	3
0	436	0	.011	0	1	3	3
0	421	0	.047	0	1	3	3
0	428	0	.030	0	1	2	3
0	388	0	.136	0	1	3	3
0	444	0	−.007	0	1	4	3
0	432	0	.020	0	1	3	3
0	435	0	.013	0	1	1	3
0	402	0	.096	0	1	3	3
0	416	0	.060	0	1	1	3
0	400	0	.102	0	1	2	3
0	456	0	−.033	0	1	4	3
0	438	0	.006	0	1	3	3
0	405	0	.088	0	1	3	3
0	422	0	.044	0	1	3	3
0	431	0	.023	0	1	2	3
0	414	0	.065	0	1	1	3
0	420	0	.049	0	1	3	3
0	433	0	.018	0	1	4	3
0	425	0	.037	0	1	3	3
0	438	0	.006	0	1	3	3
0	429	0	.027	0	1	0	3
0	444	0	−.007	0	1	2	3
0	431	0	.023	0	1	3	3

			Salary Grades 7 & 8 (continued)				
(1)	(2)	(3)	(4)	(5)	(6)	(7)	(8)
Current Weekly Salary (black)	Current Weekly Salary (white)	MDC (black)	MDC (white)	Race	Sex	Educ Level	Length of Service
0	398	0	.107	0	1	0	3
0	425	0	.037	0	1	1	3
0	418	0	.054	0	1	3	3
0	436	0	.011	0	1	3	3
0	422	0	.044	0	1	3	3
0	440	0	.002	0	1	3	4
0	436	0	.011	0	1	2	4
0	442	0	−.003	0	1	3	4
0	448	0	−.016	0	1	2	4
0	440	0	.002	0	1	2	4
0	432	0	.020	0	1	3	4
0	466	0	−.054	0	1	3	4
0	455	0	−.031	0	1	4	4
0	442	0	−.003	0	1	3	4
0	458	0	−.038	0	1	2	4
0	432	0	.020	0	1	3	4
0	462	0	−.046	0	1	3	4
0	450	0	−.021	0	1	0	4
0	441	0	−.001	0	1	3	4
0	447	0	−.014	0	1	0	4
0	435	0	.013	0	1	0	4
0	452	0	−.025	0	1	2	4
0	439	0	.004	0	1	3	4
0	444	0	−.007	0	1	0	4
0	453	0	−.027	0	1	2	4
0	440	0	.002	0	1	3	4
0	456	0	−.033	0	1	2	4
0	447	0	−.014	0	1	0	4
0	430	0	.025	0	1	2	4
0	468	0	−.058	0	1	3	4
0	455	0	−.031	0	1	3	4
0	462	0	−.046	0	1	0	4
0	470	0	−.062	0	1	4	4
0	461	0	−.044	0	1	3	4
0	465	0	−.052	0	1	3	4

Salary Grades 7 & 8 (continued)

(1) Current Weekly Salary (black)	(2) Current Weekly Salary (white)	(3) MDC (black)	(4) MDC (white)	(5) Race	(6) Sex	(7) Educ Level	(8) Length of Service
0	450	0	−.021	0	1	3	4
0	462	0	−.046	0	1	2	4
0	468	0	−.058	0	1	2	4
0	445	0	−.010	0	1	3	4
0	453	0	−.027	0	1	1	4
0	450	0	−.021	0	1	3	4
0	462	0	−.046	0	1	1	4
0	470	0	−.062	0	1	2	4
0	443	0	−.005	0	1	0	4
0	452	0	−.025	0	1	3	4
0	445	0	−.010	0	1	0	4
0	461	0	−.044	0	1	0	4
0	453	0	−.027	0	1	3	4
0	438	0	.006	0	1	1	4
0	455	0	−.031	0	1	0	4
0	447	0	−.014	0	1	2	4
0	440	0	.002	0	1	3	4
0	453	0	−.027	0	1	2	4
0	450	0	−.021	0	1	3	4
0	468	0	−.058	0	1	4	4
0	460	0	−.042	0	1	0	4
0	462	0	−.046	0	1	3	4
0	445	0	−.010	0	1	2	4
0	470	0	−.062	0	1	2	4
0	452	0	−.025	0	1	3	4
0	448	0	−.016	0	1	0	4
0	440	0	.002	0	1	1	4
0	453	0	−.027	0	1	3	4
0	450	0	−.021	0	1	0	4
0	463	0	−.048	0	1	2	4
0	460	0	−.042	0	1	4	4
0	452	0	−.025	0	1	3	4
0	470	0	−.062	0	1	2	4
0	468	0	−.058	0	1	2	4
0	462	0	−.046	0	1	1	4

	Salary Grades 7 & 8 (continued)						
(1)	(2)	(3)	(4)	(5)	(6)	(7)	(8)
Current Weekly Salary (black)	Current Weekly Salary (white)	MDC (black)	MDC (white)	Race	Sex	Educ Level	Length of Service
0	467	0	−.056	0	1	0	4
0	451	0	−.023	0	1	3	4
0	458	0	−.038	0	1	1	4
0	446	0	−.012	0	1	4	4
0	453	0	−.027	0	1	1	4
0	460	0	−.042	0	1	3	4
0	455	0	−.031	0	1	3	4
0	462	0	−.046	0	1	3	4
0	452	0	−.025	0	1	2	4
0	447	0	−.014	0	1	3	4
0	451	0	−.023	0	1	3	4
0	463	0	−.048	0	1	4	4
0	472	0	−.066	0	1	0	4
0	449	0	−.018	0	1	2	4
0	465	0	−.052	0	1	0	5
0	483	0	−.088	0	1	0	5
0	472	0	−.066	0	1	3	5
0	460	0	−.042	0	1	2	5
0	468	0	−.058	0	1	3	5
0	462	0	−.046	0	1	3	5
0	473	0	−.068	0	1	4	5
0	484	0	−.089	0	1	1	5
0	452	0	−.025	0	1	3	5
0	473	0	−.068	0	1	0	5
0	468	0	−.058	0	1	3	5
0	474	0	−.070	0	1	2	5
0	483	0	−.088	0	1	0	5
0	475	0	−.072	0	1	1	5
0	468	0	−.058	0	1	0	5
0	480	0	−.082	0	1	1	5
0	472	0	−.066	0	1	3	5
0	478	0	−.078	0	1	3	5
0	486	0	−.093	0	1	2	5
0	480	0	−.082	0	1	3	5
0	462	0	−.046	0	1	4	5

Salary Grades 7 & 8 (continued)

(1) Current Weekly Salary (black)	(2) Current Weekly Salary (white)	(3) MDC (black)	(4) MDC (white)	(5) Race	(6) Sex	(7) Educ Level	(8) Length of Service
0	475	0	−.072	0	1	3	5
0	471	0	−.064	0	1	4	5
0	483	0	−.088	0	1	3	5
0	462	0	−.046	0	1	3	5
0	473	0	−.068	0	1	3	5
0	464	0	−.050	0	1	3	5
0	478	0	−.078	0	1	1	5
0	458	0	−.038	0	1	3	5
0	469	0	−.060	0	1	3	5
0	463	0	−.048	0	1	2	5
0	454	0	−.029	0	1	4	5
0	475	0	−.072	0	1	3	5
0	462	0	−.046	0	1	0	5
0	474	0	−.070	0	1	3	5
0	460	0	−.042	0	1	3	5
0	466	0	−.054	0	1	0	5
0	472	0	−.066	0	1	3	5
0	481	0	−.084	0	1	3	5
0	460	0	−.042	0	1	0	5
0	473	0	−.068	0	1	1	5
0	476	0	−.074	0	1	0	5
0	468	0	−.058	0	1	0	5
0	465	0	−.052	0	1	2	5
0	479	0	−.080	0	1	0	5
0	453	0	−.027	0	1	3	5
0	462	0	−.046	0	1	3	5
0	470	0	−.062	0	1	0	5
0	461	0	−.044	0	1	3	5
0	478	0	−.078	0	1	3	5
0	472	0	−.066	0	1	4	5
0	465	0	−.052	0	1	3	5
0	454	0	−.029	0	1	2	5
0	463	0	−.048	0	1	0	5
0	475	0	−.072	0	1	2	5
0	468	0	−.058	0	1	1	5

Salary Grades 7 & 8 (continued)

(1) Current Weekly Salary (black)	(2) Current Weekly Salary (white)	(3) MDC (black)	(4) MDC (white)	(5) Race	(6) Sex	(7) Educ Level	(8) Length of Service
0	462	0	−.046	0	1	3	5
0	475	0	−.072	0	1	3	5
0	483	0	−.088	0	1	2	5
0	460	0	−.042	0	1	3	5
0	454	0	−.029	0	1	0	5
0	473	0	−.068	0	1	3	5
0	462	0	−.046	0	1	3	5
0	469	0	−.060	0	1	1	5
0	451	0	−.023	0	1	3	5
0	463	0	−.048	0	1	0	5
0	475	0	−.072	0	1	0	5
0	468	0	−.058	0	1	3	5
0	483	0	−.088	0	1	2	6
0	476	0	−.074	0	1	3	6
0	485	0	−.091	0	1	2	6
0	482	0	−.086	0	1	3	6
0	474	0	−.070	0	1	0	6
0	488	0	−.097	0	1	0	6
0	480	0	−.082	0	1	0	6
0	493	0	−.106	0	1	3	6
0	482	0	−.086	0	1	3	6
0	473	0	−.068	0	1	2	6
0	484	0	−.089	0	1	1	6
0	481	0	−.084	0	1	0	6
0	476	0	−.074	0	1	1	6
0	492	0	−.104	0	1	3	6
0	487	0	−.095	0	1	0	6
0	475	0	−.072	0	1	2	6
0	480	0	−.082	0	1	3	6
0	483	0	−.085	0	1	3	6
0	491	0	−.102	0	1	2	6
0	478	0	−.078	0	1	2	6
0	472	0	−.066	0	1	3	6
0	483	0	−.088	0	1	0	6
0	475	0	−.072	0	1	3	6

Salary Grades 7 & 8 (continued)

(1) Current Weekly Salary (black)	(2) Current Weekly Salary (white)	(3) MDC (black)	(4) MDC (white)	(5) Race	(6) Sex	(7) Educ Level	(8) Length of Service
0	486	0	−.093	0	1	0	6
0	480	0	−.082	0	1	2	6
0	482	0	−.086	0	1	1	6
0	472	0	−.066	0	1	0	6
0	493	0	−.106	0	1	1	6
0	476	0	−.074	0	1	0	6
0	483	0	−.088	0	1	0	6
0	487	0	−.095	0	1	3	6
0	480	0	−.082	0	1	3	6
0	489	0	−.099	0	1	2	6
0	467	0	−.056	0	1	0	6
0	472	0	−.066	0	1	3	6
0	478	0	−.078	0	1	0	6
0	465	0	−.052	0	1	2	6
0	488	0	−.097	0	1	2	6
0	482	0	−.086	0	1	3	6
0	485	0	−.091	0	1	0	6
0	476	0	−.074	0	1	1	6
0	470	0	−.062	0	1	0	6
0	482	0	−.086	0	1	3	6
0	475	0	−.072	0	1	3	6
0	478	0	−.078	0	1	3	6
0	470	0	−.062	0	1	3	6
0	488	0	.097	0	1	0	6
0	481	0	−.084	0	1	1	6
0	465	0	−.052	0	1	0	6
0	478	0	−.078	0	1	1	6
0	475	0	−.072	0	1	2	6
0	483	0	−.088	0	1	2	6
0	497	0	−.113	0	1	3	6
0	488	0	−.097	0	1	3	6
0	478	0	−.078	0	1	4	6
0	486	0	−.093	0	1	3	6
0	475	0	−.072	0	1	2	6
0	470	0	−.062	0	1	3	6

			Salary Grades 7 & 8 (continued)				
(1)	(2)	(3)	(4)	(5)	(6)	(7)	(8)
Current Weekly Salary (black)	Current Weekly Salary (white)	MDC (black)	MDC (white)	Race	Sex	Educ Level	Length of Service
0	483	0	−.088	0	1	0	6
0	472	0	−.066	0	1	0	6
0	488	0	−.097	0	1	3	6
0	480	0	−.082	0	1	2	6
0	478	0	−.078	0	1	2	6
0	481	0	−.084	0	1	0	6
0	470	0	−.062	0	1	3	6
0	482	0	−.086	0	1	0	6
0	489	0	−.099	0	1	0	6
0	472	0	−.066	0	1	1	6
0	465	0	−.052	0	1	0	6
0	478	0	−.078	0	1	1	6
0	484	0	−.089	0	1	3	6
0	480	0	−.082	0	1	3	6
0	473	0	−.068	0	1	3	6
0	488	0	−.097	0	1	2	6
0	480	0	−.082	0	1	1	6
0	465	0	−.052	0	1	2	6
0	470	0	−.062	0	1	0	6
0	462	0	−.046	0	1	3	6
0	485	0	−.091	0	1	3	6
0	493	0	−.106	0	1	0	6
0	482	0	−.086	0	1	1	6
0	496	0	−.111	0	1	4	6
0	478	0	−.078	0	1	0	6
0	483	0	−.088	0	1	0	6
0	480	0	−.082	0	1	2	6
0	489	0	−.099	0	1	0	6
0	475	0	−.072	0	1	3	6
0	482	0	−.086	0	1	3	6
0	493	0	−.106	0	1	0	6
0	480	0	−.082	0	1	1	6
0	472	0	−.066	0	1	2	6
0	490	0	−.101	0	1	2	6
0	483	0	−.088	0	1	3	6

			Salary Grades 7 & 8 (continued)				
_(1)_	_(2)_	_(3)_	_(4)_	_(5)_	_(6)_	_(7)_	_(8)_
Current Weekly Salary (black)	Current Weekly Salary (white)	MDC (black)	MDC (white)	Race	Sex	Educ Level	Length of Service
0	476	0	−.074	0	1	3	6
0	470	0	−.062	0	1	2	6
0	483	0	−.088	0	1	0	6
0	482	0	−.086	0	1	0	6
0	494	0	−.108	0	1	1	6
0	485	0	−.091	0	1	0	6
0	480	0	−.082	0	1	0	6
0	483	0	−.088	0	1	2	6
0	475	0	−.072	0	1	2	6
0	472	0	−.066	0	1	1	6
0	488	0	−.097	0	1	0	6
0	480	0	−.082	0	1	3	6
0	486	0	−.093	0	1	0	6
0	474	0	−.070	0	1	3	6
0	493	0	−.106	0	1	3	6
0	466	0	−.054	0	1	2	6
0	478	0	−.078	0	1	3	6
0	470	0	−.062	0	1	1	6
0	482	0	−.086	0	1	0	6
0	476	0	−.074	0	1	0	6
0	494	0	−.108	0	1	4	6
0	485	0	−.091	0	1	3	6
0	497	0	−.113	0	1	3	6
0	483	0	−.088	0	1	3	6
0	471	0	−.064	0	1	3	6
0	482	0	−.086	0	1	2	6
0	480	0	−.082	0	1	3	6
0	486	0	−.093	0	1	1	6
0	473	0	−.068	0	1	3	6
0	462	0	−.046	0	1	0	6
0	488	0	−.097	0	1	3	6
0	485	0	−.091	0	1	0	6
0	476	0	−.074	0	1	0	6
0	495	0	−.110	0	1	3	6
0	480	0	−.082	0	1	2	6

Salary Grades 7 & 8 (continued)

(1) Current Weekly Salary (black)	(2) Current Weekly Salary (white)	(3) MDC (black)	(4) MDC (white)	(5) Race	(6) Sex	(7) Educ Level	(8) Length of Service
0	344	0	.281	0	0	3	1
0	335	0	.316	0	0	3	1
0	340	0	.296	0	0	4	1
0	347	0	.270	0	0	4	1
0	342	0	.289	0	0	3	1
0	338	0	.304	0	0	3	1
0	351	0	.256	0	0	3	1
0	370	0	.191	0	0	3	1
0	368	0	.198	0	0	1	1
0	352	0	.252	0	0	3	1
0	335	0	.316	0	0	4	1
0	347	0	.270	0	0	4	1
0	352	0	.252	0	0	3	1
0	360	0	.224	0	0	4	1
0	358	0	.231	0	0	4	1
0	345	0	.278	0	0	3	2
0	364	0	.211	0	0	3	2
0	370	0	.191	0	0	3	2
0	353	0	.249	0	0	3	2
0	375	0	.175	0	0	4	2
0	383	0	.151	0	0	3	2
0	370	0	.191	0	0	4	2
0	376	0	.172	0	0	4	2
0	384	0	.148	0	0	3	2
0	392	0	.124	0	0	3	2
0	360	0	.224	0	0	2	2
0	378	0	.166	0	0	3	2
0	375	0	.175	0	0	2	2
0	392	0	.124	0	0	3	3
0	386	0	.142	0	0	3	3
0	405	0	.088	0	0	4	3
0	396	0	.113	0	0	3	3
0	388	0	.136	0	0	2	3
0	410	0	.075	0	0	2	3
0	400	0	.102	0	0	3	3

Salary Grades 7 & 8 (continued)

(1) Current Weekly Salary (black)	(2) Current Weekly Salary (white)	(3) MDC (black)	(4) MDC (white)	(5) Race	(6) Sex	(7) Educ Level	(8) Length of Service
0	392	0	.124	0	0	2	3
0	387	0	.139	0	0	0	3
0	395	0	.116	0	0	1	3
0	415	0	.062	0	0	3	3
0	408	0	.080	0	0	3	3
0	411	0	.072	0	0	1	3
0	396	0	.113	0	0	2	3
0	405	0	.088	0	0	1	3
0	387	0	.139	0	0	3	3
0	394	0	.119	0	0	3	3
0	421	0	.047	0	0	0	3
0	414	0	.065	0	0	1	3
0	409	0	.078	0	0	1	3
0	392	0	.124	0	0	2	3
0	385	0	.145	0	0	0	3
0	397	0	.110	0	0	3	3
0	410	0	.075	0	0	3	3
0	402	0	.096	0	0	2	4
0	396	0	.113	0	0	3	4
0	456	0	−.033	0	0	0	4
0	464	0	−.050	0	0	2	4
0	452	0	−.025	0	0	3	4
0	468	0	−.058	0	0	3	4
0	464	0	−.050	0	0	2	4
0	455	0	−.031	0	0	3	4
0	470	0	−.062	0	0	4	4
0	462	0	−.046	0	0	3	4
0	460	0	−.042	0	0	3	4
0	469	0	−.060	0	0	1	4
0	448	0	−.016	0	0	0	4
0	456	0	−.033	0	0	1	4
0	465	0	−.052	0	0	2	5
0	474	0	−.070	0	0	3	5
0	483	0	−.088	0	0	2	5
0	470	0	−.062	0	0	0	5

Salary Grades 7 & 8 (continued)

(1) Current Weekly Salary (black)	(2) Current Weekly Salary (white)	(3) MDC (black)	(4) MDC (white)	(5) Race	(6) Sex	(7) Educ Level	(8) Length of Service
0	463	0	−.048	0	0	1	5
0	470	0	−.062	0	0	1	5
0	460	0	−.042	0	0	0	5
0	481	0	−.084	0	0	2	5
0	475	0	−.072	0	0	2	5
0	478	0	−.078	0	0	2	5
0	469	0	−.060	0	0	3	5
0	473	0	−.068	0	0	3	5
0	483	0	−.088	0	0	2	6
0	478	0	−.078	0	0	0	6
0	492	0	−.104	0	0	1	6
0	468	0	−.058	0	0	0	6
0	473	0	−.068	0	0	3	6
0	479	0	−.080	0	0	3	6
0	470	0	−.062	0	0	2	6
0	486	0	−.093	0	0	0	6
0	482	0	−.086	0	0	1	6
0	491	0	−.102	0	0	1	6
0	476	0	−.074	0	0	0	6
0	477	0	−.076	0	0	0	6
0	484	0	−.089	0	0	0	6
0	475	0	−.072	0	0	3	6
0	484	0	−.089	0	0	2	6
0	493	0	−.106	0	0	2	6
0	490	0	−.101	0	0	2	6
0	478	0	−.078	0	0	3	6
0	486	0	−.093	0	0	0	6
0	480	0	−.082	0	0	0	6
0	483	0	−.088	0	0	2	6
0	475	0	−.072	0	0	1	6
0	481	0	−.084	0	0	0	6
0	493	0	−.106	0	0	3	6
0	472	0	−.066	0	0	3	6
0	477	0	−.076	0	0	1	6
0	486	0	−.093	0	0	0	6

Salary Grades 7 & 8 (continued)

(1) Current Weekly Salary (black)	(2) Current Weekly Salary (white)	(3) MDC (black)	(4) MDC (white)	(5) Race	(6) Sex	(7) Educ Level	(8) Length of Service
0	483	0	−.088	0	0	0	6
0	495	0	−.110	0	0	1	6
0	482	0	−.086	0	0	2	6
0	477	0	−.076	0	0	2	6
0	470	0	−.062	0	0	3	6
0	483	0	−.088	0	0	2	6
0	480	0	−.082	0	0	3	6
0	476	0	−.074	0	0	3	6
344	0	.281	0	1	1	4	1
352	0	.252	0	1	1	4	1
341	0	.293	0	1	1	4	1
365	0	.208	0	1	1	3	1
358	0	.231	0	1	1	3	1
350	0	.259	0	1	1	3	1
380	0	.160	0	1	1	3	2
376	0	.172	0	1	1	4	2
402	0	.096	0	1	1	3	2
395	0	.116	0	1	1	3	2
415	0	.062	0	1	1	4	3
403	0	.094	0	1	1	2	3
410	0	.075	0	1	1	3	3
396	0	.113	0	1	1	3	3
390	0	.130	0	1	1	0	3
400	0	.102	0	1	1	1	3
405	0	.088	0	1	1	2	3
388	0	.136	0	1	1	2	3
424	0	.040	0	1	1	3	3
456	0	−.033	0	1	1	3	4
472	0	−.066	0	1	1	4	4
465	0	−.052	0	1	1	4	4
476	0	−.074	0	1	1	3	5
470	0	−.062	0	1	1	3	5
340	0	.296	0	1	0	3	1
345	0	.278	0	1	0	4	1
356	0	.238	0	1	0	3	2

		Salary Grades 7 & 8 (continued)					
(1) Current Weekly Salary (black)	*(2)* Current Weekly Salary (white)	*(3)* MDC (black)	*(4)* MDC (white)	*(5)* Race	*(6)* Sex	*(7)* Educ Level	*(8)* Length of Service
371	0	.188	0	1	0	3	2
376	0	.172	0	1	0	3	3
380	0	.160	0	1	0	3	3
375	0	.175	0	1	0	4	3
392	0	.124	0	1	0	3	3
421	0	.047	0	1	0	4	4
464	0	−.050	0	1	0	3	5
488	0	−.097	0	1	0	3	6
482	0	−.086	0	1	0	2	6

	Salary Grades 9 & 10			Number of Employees: 343			
(1) Current Weekly Salary (black)	(2) Current Weekly Salary (white)	(3) MDC (black)	(4) MDC (white)	(5) Race	(6) Sex	(7) Educ Level	(8) Length of Service
0	536	0	.306	0	1	3	1
0	560	0	.250	0	1	3	1
0	554	0	.264	0	1	3	1
0	535	0	.309	0	1	3	1
0	520	0	.346	0	1	3	1
0	554	0	.264	0	1	4	1
0	560	0	.250	0	1	3	1
0	572	0	.224	0	1	4	1
0	543	0	.289	0	1	3	1
0	515	0	.360	0	1	3	1
0	530	0	.321	0	1	3	1
0	522	0	.341	0	1	3	1
0	547	0	.280	0	1	3	1
0	572	0	.224	0	1	1	1
0	563	0	.244	0	1	3	1
0	535	0	.309	0	1	3	1
0	548	0	.278	0	1	4	1
0	524	0	.336	0	1	3	1
0	540	0	.297	0	1	3	1
0	558	0	.255	0	1	3	2
0	523	0	.339	0	1	3	2
0	552	0	.268	0	1	3	2
0	587	0	.193	0	1	4	2
0	575	0	.218	0	1	3	2
0	620	0	.129	0	1	1	2
0	594	0	.179	0	1	3	2
0	587	0	.193	0	1	3	2
0	608	0	.152	0	1	3	2
0	587	0	.193	0	1	3	2
0	621	0	.127	0	1	3	2
0	594	0	.179	0	1	0	2
0	603	0	.161	0	1	3	2
0	614	0	.140	0	1	4	2
0	590	0	.187	0	1	3	2
0	625	0	.120	0	1	3	2

Salary Grades 9 & 10 (continued)

(1) Current Weekly Salary (black)	(2) Current Weekly Salary (white)	(3) MDC (black)	(4) MDC (white)	(5) Race	(6) Sex	(7) Educ Level	(8) Length of Service
0	605	0	.157	0	1	1	2
0	594	0	.179	0	1	3	2
0	615	0	.138	0	1	3	2
0	575	0	.218	0	1	0	2
0	564	0	.241	0	1	3	2
0	610	0	.148	0	1	3	3
0	643	0	.089	0	1	3	3
0	622	0	.126	0	1	4	3
0	615	0	.138	0	1	3	3
0	638	0	.097	0	1	4	3
0	658	0	.064	0	1	3	3
0	684	0	.024	0	1	3	3
0	670	0	.045	0	1	3	3
0	678	0	.033	0	1	3	3
0	662	0	.058	0	1	3	3
0	655	0	.069	0	1	4	3
0	669	0	.047	0	1	4	3
0	675	0	.037	0	1	3	3
0	660	0	.061	0	1	3	3
0	654	0	.071	0	1	1	3
0	680	0	.030	0	1	3	3
0	670	0	.045	0	1	3	3
0	666	0	.051	0	1	3	3
0	685	0	.022	0	1	3	3
0	682	0	.027	0	1	3	3
0	669	0	.047	0	1	3	3
0	660	0	.061	0	1	4	3
0	694	0	.009	0	1	3	3
0	685	0	.022	0	1	3	3
0	678	0	.033	0	1	4	3
0	680	0	.030	0	1	0	3
0	665	0	.053	0	1	3	3
0	687	0	.019	0	1	3	3
0	682	0	.027	0	1	3	3
0	675	0	.037	0	1	3	3

Salary Grades 9 & 10 (continued)

(1) Current Weekly Salary (black)	(2) Current Weekly Salary (white)	(3) MDC (black)	(4) MDC (white)	(5) Race	(6) Sex	(7) Educ Level	(8) Length of Service
0	688	0	.018	0	1	4	3
0	669	0	.047	0	1	3	3
0	688	0	.018	0	1	3	3
0	700	0	.001	0	1	0	3
0	695	0	.007	0	1	3	3
0	682	0	.027	0	1	0	3
0	674	0	.039	0	1	3	3
0	685	0	.022	0	1	4	3
0	694	0	.009	0	1	3	3
0	672	0	.042	0	1	3	3
0	682	0	.027	0	1	4	3
0	670	0	.045	0	1	1	3
0	675	0	.037	0	1	3	3
0	684	0	.024	0	1	0	3
0	673	0	.040	0	1	3	3
0	684	0	.024	0	1	3	3
0	689	0	.016	0	1	3	3
0	670	0	.045	0	1	3	3
0	704	0	−.006	0	1	3	3
0	685	0	.022	0	1	3	3
0	676	0	.036	0	1	3	3
0	688	0	.018	0	1	3	3
0	694	0	.009	0	1	1	3
0	690	0	.015	0	1	3	3
0	682	0	.027	0	1	4	3
0	685	0	.022	0	1	3	3
0	670	0	.045	0	1	0	3
0	720	0	−.028	0	1	3	4
0	698	0	.003	0	1	3	4
0	705	0	−.007	0	1	1	4
0	690	0	.015	0	1	3	4
0	687	0	.019	0	1	2	4
0	694	0	.009	0	1	3	4
0	706	0	−.008	0	1	3	4
0	717	0	−.024	0	1	1	4

			Salary Grades 9 & 10 (continued)				
(1)	(2)	(3)	(4)	(5)	(6)	(7)	(8)
Current Weekly Salary (black)	Current Weekly Salary (white)	MDC (black)	MDC (white)	Race	Sex	Educ Level	Length of Service
0	703	0	−.004	0	1	3	4
0	698	0	.003	0	1	3	4
0	725	0	−.034	0	1	0	4
0	710	0	−.014	0	1	3	4
0	698	0	.003	0	1	3	4
0	732	0	−.044	0	1	3	4
0	718	0	−.025	0	1	3	4
0	724	0	−.033	0	1	3	4
0	690	0	.015	0	1	3	4
0	735	0	−.047	0	1	3	4
0	718	0	−.025	0	1	4	4
0	726	0	−.036	0	1	3	4
0	715	0	−.021	0	1	3	4
0	706	0	−.088	0	1	4	4
0	722	0	−.030	0	1	3	4
0	711	0	−.015	0	1	3	4
0	730	0	−.041	0	1	4	4
0	704	0	−.006	0	1	3	4
0	712	0	−.017	0	1	0	4
0	709	0	−.013	0	1	3	4
0	725	0	−.034	0	1	3	4
0	718	0	−.025	0	1	3	4
0	727	0	−.037	0	1	3	4
0	704	0	−.006	0	1	4	4
0	718	0	−.025	0	1	3	4
0	710	0	−.014	0	1	3	4
0	695	0	.007	0	1	1	4
0	722	0	−.030	0	1	3	4
0	735	0	−.047	0	1	3	5
0	728	0	−.038	0	1	3	5
0	706	0	−.008	0	1	3	5
0	714	0	−.019	0	1	3	5
0	721	0	−.029	0	1	4	5
0	715	0	−.021	0	1	3	5
0	725	0	−.034	0	1	3	5

		Salary Grades 9 & 10 (continued)					
(1)	(2)	(3)	(4)	(5)	(6)	(7)	(8)
Current Weekly Salary (black)	Current Weekly Salary (white)	MDC (black)	MDC (white)	Race	Sex	Educ Level	Length of Service
0	705	0	−.007	0	1	3	5
0	732	0	−.044	0	1	3	5
0	721	0	−.029	0	1	0	5
0	726	0	−.036	0	1	3	5
0	708	0	−.011	0	1	3	5
0	720	0	−.028	0	1	3	5
0	736	0	−.049	0	1	1	5
0	742	0	−.056	0	1	3	5
0	722	0	−.030	0	1	3	5
0	717	0	−.024	0	1	3	5
0	704	0	−.006	0	1	4	5
0	732	0	−.044	0	1	3	5
0	725	0	−.034	0	1	3	5
0	718	0	−.025	0	1	1	5
0	727	0	−.037	0	1	3	5
0	702	0	−.003	0	1	3	5
0	716	0	−.022	0	1	2	5
0	724	0	−.033	0	1	3	5
0	715	0	−.021	0	1	3	5
0	736	0	−.049	0	1	0	5
0	717	0	−.024	0	1	3	5
0	745	0	−.060	0	1	3	5
0	722	0	−.030	0	1	3	5
0	734	0	−.046	0	1	4	5
0	715	0	−.021	0	1	3	5
0	723	0	−.032	0	1	0	5
0	732	0	−.044	0	1	3	5
0	718	0	−.025	0	1	3	5
0	752	0	−.069	0	1	3	5
0	728	0	−.038	0	1	3	5
0	721	0	−.029	0	1	3	5
0	734	0	−.046	0	1	3	5
0	718	0	−.025	0	1	2	5
0	722	0	−.030	0	1	3	5
0	731	0	−.042	0	1	1	5

Salary Grades 9 & 10 (continued)

(1) Current Weekly Salary (black)	(2) Current Weekly Salary (white)	(3) MDC (black)	(4) MDC (white)	(5) Race	(6) Sex	(7) Educ Level	(8) Length of Service
0	725	0	−.034	0	1	3	5
0	717	0	−.024	0	1	3	5
0	728	0	−.038	0	1	2	5
0	735	0	−.047	0	1	4	5
0	730	0	−.041	0	1	3	5
0	718	0	−.025	0	1	4	5
0	744	0	−.059	0	1	3	5
0	735	0	−.047	0	1	1	5
0	712	0	−.017	0	1	3	5
0	726	0	−.036	0	1	3	5
0	720	0	−.028	0	1	0	5
0	732	0	−.044	0	1	3	5
0	728	0	−.038	0	1	3	5
0	733	0	−.045	0	1	0	5
0	725	0	−.034	0	1	3	5
0	748	0	−.064	0	1	2	5
0	734	0	−.046	0	1	3	5
0	723	0	−.032	0	1	3	5
0	736	0	−.049	0	1	4	5
0	727	0	−.037	0	1	3	5
0	738	0	−.051	0	1	0	5
0	748	0	−.064	0	1	3	6
0	765	0	−.085	0	1	3	6
0	732	0	−.044	0	1	0	6
0	740	0	−.054	0	1	3	6
0	748	0	−.064	0	1	1	6
0	732	0	−.044	0	1	3	6
0	750	0	−.067	0	1	3	6
0	747	0	−.063	0	1	1	6
0	735	0	−.047	0	1	3	6
0	741	0	−.055	0	1	2	6
0	730	0	−.041	0	1	3	6
0	758	0	−.076	0	1	3	6
0	750	0	−.067	0	1	2	6
0	744	0	−.059	0	1	3	6

Salary Grades 9 & 10 (continued)

(1) Current Weekly Salary (black)	(2) Current Weekly Salary (white)	(3) MDC (black)	(4) MDC (white)	(5) Race	(6) Sex	(7) Educ Level	(8) Length of Service
0	755	0	−.073	0	1	0	6
0	738	0	−.051	0	1	3	6
0	740	0	−.054	0	1	3	6
0	743	0	−.058	0	1	0	6
0	760	0	−.079	0	1	4	6
0	752	0	−.069	0	1	3	6
0	758	0	−.076	0	1	3	6
0	744	0	−.059	0	1	0	6
0	747	0	−.063	0	1	3	6
0	753	0	−.070	0	1	1	6
0	748	0	−.064	0	1	3	6
0	742	0	−.056	0	1	3	6
0	765	0	−.085	0	1	3	6
0	738	0	−.051	0	1	3	6
0	740	0	−.054	0	1	3	6
0	752	0	−.069	0	1	2	6
0	738	0	−.051	0	1	3	6
0	750	0	−.067	0	1	3	6
0	756	0	−.074	0	1	2	6
0	748	0	−.064	0	1	3	6
0	740	0	−.054	0	1	3	6
0	756	0	−.074	0	1	3	6
0	750	0	−.067	0	1	3	6
0	753	0	−.070	0	1	1	6
0	741	0	−.055	0	1	0	6
0	765	0	−.085	0	1	3	6
0	753	0	−.070	0	1	3	6
0	758	0	−.076	0	1	4	6
0	752	0	−.069	0	1	3	6
0	760	0	−.079	0	1	2	6
0	745	0	−.060	0	1	3	6
0	738	0	−.051	0	1	0	6
0	742	0	−.056	0	1	1	6
0	759	0	−.078	0	1	3	6
0	755	0	−.073	0	1	3	6

			Salary Grades 9 & 10 (continued)				

(1) Current Weekly Salary (black)	(2) Current Weekly Salary (white)	(3) MDC (black)	(4) MDC (white)	(5) Race	(6) Sex	(7) Educ Level	(8) Length of Service
0	757	0	−.075	0	1	0	6
0	749	0	−.065	0	1	3	6
0	762	0	−.081	0	1	0	6
0	750	0	−.067	0	1	3	6
0	744	0	−.059	0	1	3	6
0	750	0	−.067	0	1	2	6
0	756	0	−.074	0	1	3	6
0	757	0	−.075	0	1	3	6
0	738	0	−.051	0	1	3	6
0	742	0	−.056	0	1	3	6
0	750	0	−.067	0	1	3	6
0	754	0	−.071	0	1	3	6
0	737	0	−.050	0	1	0	6
0	749	0	−.065	0	1	3	6
0	745	0	−.060	0	1	3	6
0	758	0	−.076	0	1	2	6
0	752	0	−.069	0	1	3	6
0	747	0	−.063	0	1	3	6
0	765	0	−.085	0	1	4	6
0	752	0	−.069	0	1	3	6
0	740	0	−.054	0	1	3	6
0	756	0	−.074	0	1	0	6
0	752	0	−.069	0	1	3	6
0	763	0	−.082	0	1	3	6
0	742	0	−.056	0	1	3	6
0	750	0	−.067	0	1	1	6
0	746	0	−.062	0	1	3	6
0	748	0	−.064	0	1	1	6
0	761	0	−.080	0	1	3	6
0	750	0	−.067	0	1	3	6
0	735	0	−.047	0	1	3	6
0	758	0	−.076	0	1	4	6
0	752	0	−.069	0	1	3	6
0	744	0	−.059	0	1	3	6
0	747	0	−.063	0	1	3	6

			Salary Grades 9 & 10 (continued)				
(1)	(2)	(3)	(4)	(5)	(6)	(7)	(8)
Current Weekly Salary (black)	Current Weekly Salary (white)	MDC (black)	MDC (white)	Race	Sex	Educ Level	Length of Service
0	758	0	−.076	0	1	3	6
0	732	0	−.044	0	1	3	6
0	746	0	−.062	0	1	3	6
0	740	0	−.054	0	1	0	6
0	756	0	−.074	0	1	3	6
0	753	0	−.070	0	1	2	6
0	745	0	−.060	0	1	2	6
0	740	0	−.054	0	1	3	6
0	747	0	−.063	0	1	3	6
0	744	0	−.059	0	1	1	6
0	758	0	−.076	0	1	3	6
0	765	0	−.085	0	1	1	6
0	757	0	−.075	0	1	0	6
0	743	0	−.058	0	1	3	6
0	749	0	−.065	0	1	3	6
0	740	0	−.054	0	1	0	6
0	754	0	−.071	0	1	3	6
0	760	0	−.079	0	1	3	6
0	752	0	−.069	0	1	4	6
0	741	0	−.055	0	1	3	6
0	759	0	−.078	0	1	3	6
0	755	0	−.073	0	1	2	6
0	758	0	−.076	0	1	0	6
0	740	0	−.054	0	1	3	6
0	753	0	−.070	0	1	3	6
0	538	0	.301	0	0	3	1
0	527	0	.329	0	0	4	1
0	540	0	.297	0	0	4	1
0	532	0	.316	0	0	3	1
0	563	0	.244	0	0	3	2
0	581	0	.205	0	0	3	2
0	622	0	.126	0	0	3	3
0	640	0	.094	0	0	4	3
0	635	0	.103	0	0	3	3
0	656	0	.067	0	0	0	3

			Salary Grades 9 & 10 (continued)				
(1) Current Weekly Salary (black)	(2) Current Weekly Salary (white)	(3) MDC (black)	(4) MDC (white)	(5) Race	(6) Sex	(7) Educ Level	(8) Length of Service
0	628	0	.115	0	0	3	3
0	715	0	−.021	0	0	3	4
0	708	0	−.011	0	0	1	4
0	735	0	−.047	0	0	3	4
0	720	0	−.028	0	0	3	4
0	732	0	−.044	0	0	2	5
0	728	0	−.038	0	0	3	5
0	738	0	−.051	0	0	3	5
0	732	0	−.044	0	0	4	5
0	753	0	−.070	0	0	3	6
0	748	0	−.064	0	0	3	6
0	756	0	−.074	0	0	3	6
0	754	0	−.071	0	0	0	6
0	738	0	−.051	0	0	3	6
0	742	0	−.056	0	0	2	6
0	746	0	−.062	0	0	3	6
0	739	0	−.053	0	0	1	6
0	754	0	−.071	0	0	3	6
0	750	0	−.067	0	0	3	6
535	0	.309	0	1	1	4	1
572	0	.224	0	1	1	4	2
577	0	.213	0	1	1	3	2
664	0	.054	0	1	1	3	3
710	0	−.014	0	1	1	4	4
722	0	−.030	0	1	1	4	4
528	0	.326	0	1	0	4	1
552	0	.268	0	1	0	4	2
620	0	.129	0	1	0	3	3

Bibliography

Ackerman, Robert W. *The Social Challenge to Business.* Cambridge: Harvard University Press, 1975.

Aigner, Dennis J., and Cain, Glen G. "Statistical Theories of Discrimination in Labor Markets." *Industrial and Labor Relations Review*, 30 (Jan. 1977), 175–87.

Alexis, Marcus. "A Theory of Labor Market Discrimination with Interdependent Utilities." *American Economic Review*, 63 (May 1973), 296–302.

America, Richard F., and Anderson, Bernard E. "Black Managers: How They Manage Their Emotions." *Across the Board*, April 1979, pp. 80–87.

————. *Moving Ahead: Black Managers in American Business.* New York: McGraw-Hill, 1978.

Anderson, Bernard E., and Wallace, Phyllis A. "Public Policy and Black Economic Progress: A Review of the Evidence." *American Economic Review*, 65 (May 1975), 47–52.

Arrow, Kenneth J. *Some Models of Racial Discrimination in the Labor Market.* Santa Monica: The Rand Corporation, 1971.

Ashenfelter, Orley, and Rees, Albert, eds. *Discrimination in Labor Markets.* Princeton: Princeton University Press, 1973.

Auletta, Ken. *The Underclass.* New York: Vintage Books, 1982.

Baron, Harold M. "The Web of Urban Racism." In *Institutional Racism in America*, edited by Louis L. Knowles and Kenneth Prewitt, pp. 154–76. Englewood Cliffs: Prentice-Hall, 1969.

Baron, Harold M., and Hymer, Bennett. "Racial Dualism in an Urban Labor Market." In *Problems in Political Economy: An Urban*

Perspective. 2nd ed., edited by David M. Gordon. Lexington: D.C. Heath, 1977.

Batchelder, Alan B. "Decline in the Relative Income of Negro Men." *Quarterly Journal of Economics*, 77 (Nov. 1964), 525–48.

Becker, Gary S. *Human Capital.* New York: National Bureau of Economic Research, 1964.

———. *Human Capital and the Personal Distribution of Income.* Ann Arbor: University of Michigan Press, 1967.

———. *The Economics of Discrimination.* 2nd ed. Chicago: University of Chicago Press, 1971.

Bell, Daniel. *The Coming of Post-Industrial Society.* New York: Basic Books, 1973.

Bell, Duran. "Occupational Discrimination as a Source of Income Differences: Lessons of the 1960's." *American Economic Review*, 62 (May 1972), 363–72.

Ben-Porath, Yoram. "The Production of Human Capital and the Life Cycle of Earnings." *Journal of Political Economy*, 75 (Aug. 1967), 352–65.

Bennett, Lerone, Jr. *Before the Mayflower: A History of the Negro in America, 1619–1964.* Rev. ed. Baltimore: Penguin Books, 1966.

Bergmann, Barbara R. "The Effect on White Incomes of Discrimination in Employment." *Journal of Political Economy* (Jan.–Feb. 1971), pp. 294–313.

Brown, Henry Phelps. *The Inequality of Pay.* Berkeley: University of California Press, 1977.

Brown, Martha A. "Values—A Necessary but Neglected Ingredient of Motivation on the Job." *Academy of Management Review* (Oct. 1976), pp. 15–23.

Bureau of the Census. *The Social and Economic Status of the Black Population in the United States, 1790–1978.* Washington, D.C.: Government Printing Office, Special Studies, Series p–23, No. 80.

Cairnes, J. E. *Political Economy.* New York: Harper, 1874.

Carmichael, Stokely, and Hamilton, Charles V. *Black Power: The Politics of Liberation in America.* New York: Vintage Books, 1967.

Clark, Kenneth B. *Dark Ghetto: Dilemmas of Social Power.* New York: Harper and Row, 1965.

Comanor, William S. "Racial Discrimination in American Industry." *Economica*, 40 (Nov. 1973), 363–78.

Corson, John J., and Steiner, George A. *Measuring Business's Social Performance: The Corporate Social Audit.* New York: Committee for Economic Development, 1974.

Davis, David Brion. *The Problem of Slavery in the Age of Revolution 1770–1823.* Ithaca: Cornell University Press, 1975.

Davis, George, and Watson, Glegg. *Black Life in Corporate America.* Garden City: Anchor/Doubleday, 1982.

Dickens, Floyd, Jr., and Dickens, Jacqueline B. *The Black Manager: Making It in the Corporate World.* New York: Amacom, 1982.

Diebold, John. *The Role of Business in Society.* New York: Amacom, 1982.

Doeringer, Peter B., and Piore, Michael J. *Internal Labor Markets and Manpower Analysis.* Lexington: D.C. Heath, 1971.

Draper, N. R., and Smith, H. *Applied Regression Analysis.* New York: John Wiley, 1966.

DuBois, W.E.B. *Black Reconstruction in America.* New York: Harcourt, Brace, 1935.

———. *Dusk of Dawn.* 1940 Reprint. New York: Schocken Books, 1968.

Elbaum, Bernard. "The Internalization of Labor Markets: Causes and Consequences." *American Economic Review,* 73 (May 1983), 260–65.

Ezeani, Eboh C. "Economic Conditions of Freed Black Slaves in the United States, 1870–1920." *Review of Black Political Economy,* 8 (Fall 1977), 104–18.

Ezekiel, Mordecai, and Fox, Karl A. *Methods of Correlation and Regression Analysis.* 3rd ed. New York: John Wiley, 1959.

Fernandez, John P. *Black Managers in White Corporations.* New York: John Wiley, 1975.

Flanagan, Robert J. "Discrimination Theory, Labor Turnover, and Racial Unemployment Differentials." *Journal of Human Resources,* 13 (Spring 1978), 187–207.

Fogel, Robert William, and Engerman, Stanley L. *Time on the Cross: The Economics of American Negro Slavery.* Boston: Little, Brown, 1974.

Foner, Philip S., and Lewis, Ronald L., eds. *The Black Worker: A Documentary History from Colonial Times to the Present.* 3 vols. Philadelphia: Temple University Press, 1978.

Franklin, John Hope. *From Slavery to Freedom.* New York: Alfred A. Knopf, 1947.

———. *Reconstruction: After the Civil War.* Chicago: University of Chicago Press, 1961.

Frazier, E. Franklin. *The Negro in the United States.* New York: Macmillan, 1949.

Freeman, Richard B. "Decline of Labor Market Discrimination and Economic Analysis." *American Economic Review,* 63 (May 1973), 280–86.

Friedman, Milton. *Capitalism and Freedom.* Chicago: University of Chicago Press, 1982.

Gagala, Ken. "The Dual Urban Labor Market." *Journal of Black Studies,* 3 (Mar. 1973), 350–70.

Gallaway, Lowell E. *Manpower Economics.* Homewood: Richard D. Irwin, 1971.

Gatewood, Lucian B. "The Black Artisan in the U.S., 1890–1930." *Review of Black Political Economy*, 5 (Fall 1974), 19–33.

Genovese, Eugene D. *Roll, Jordan, Roll: The World the Slaves Made.* New York: Vintage Books, 1974.

———. *The Political Economy of Slavery.* New York: Random House, 1965.

Ginzberg, Eli, ed. *The Negro Challenge to the Business Community.* New York: McGraw-Hill, 1964.

Glazer, Nathan. *Affirmative Discrimination: Ethnic Inequality and Public Policy.* New York: Basic Books, 1975.

Goodman, Leo A. "Multiplicative Models for the Analysis of Occupational Mobility Tables and Other Kinds of Cross-Classification Tables." *American Journal of Sociology*, 84 (Jan. 1979), 804–19.

Gordon, David M. *Theories of Poverty and Underemployment.* Lexington: D.C. Heath, 1972.

Gossett, Thomas F. *Race: The History of an Idea in America.* New York: Schocken Books, 1963.

Green, Philip. *The Pursuit of Inequality.* New York: Pantheon, 1981.

Greenbaum, Howard H., and Falcione, Raymond L. *Organizational Communication: Abstracts, Analysis, and Overview.* Vol. 6. Beverly Hills: Sage Publications, 1981.

Gwartney, James. "Changes in the Nonwhite/White Income Ratio—1939–67." *American Economic Review*, 55 (Dec. 1970), 872–83.

———. "Discrimination and Income Differentials." *American Economic Review*, 55 (June 1970), 396–408.

——— and Long, James E. "The Relative Earnings of Blacks and Other Minorities." *Industrial and Labor Relations Review*, 31 (April 1978), 336–46.

Haber, Sheldon E. "The Mobility of Professional Workers and Fair Hiring." *Industrial and Labor Relations Review*, 34 (Jan. 1981), 257–64.

Harris, Abram L., and Spero, Sterling D. *The Black Worker.* New York: Kennikat, 1966.

Harrison, Bennett. *Education, Training and the Urban Ghetto.* Baltimore: Johns Hopkins University Press, 1972.

———. "Education and Underemployment in the Urban Ghetto." *American Economic Review*, 62 (Dec. 1972), 796–811.

Haworth, Joan Gustafson; Gwartney, James; and Haworth, Charles. "Earnings, Productivity, and Changes in Employment Discrimination During the 1960's." *American Economic Review*, 65 (Mar. 1975), 158–68.

Heilbroner, Robert L., ed. *Economic Means and Social Ends: Essays in Political Economics.* Englewood Cliffs: Prentice-Hall, 1969.

Hernton, Calvin C. *Sex and Racism in America*. New York: Grove, 1965.

Hiestand, Dale L. *Economic Growth and Employment Opportunities for Minorities*. New York: Columbia University Press, 1964.

Hill, Robert B. *The Widening Economic Gap*. Washington, D.C.: National Urban League, 1979.

Hirsch, Barry T. "Earnings Inequality Across Labor Markets: A Test of the Human Capital Model." *Southern Economic Journal* (July 1978), pp. 32–45.

Hodson, Randy. *Workers' Earnings and Corporate Economic Structure*. New York: Academic Press, 1983.

Hogan, Lloyd L. *Principles of Black Political Economy*. Unpublished manuscript, 1982.

————, and Harris, Harry. "The Occupational-Industrial Structure of Black Employment in the United States." *Review of Black Political Economy*, 6 (Fall 1975), 14–26.

Huggins, Nathan I.; Kilson, Martin; and Fox, Daniel M., eds. *Key Issues in the Afro-American Experience*. Vol. 2. New York: Harcourt Brace Jovanovich, 1971.

Hurd, Michael D. "Changes in Wage Rates Between 1959–1967." *Review of Economics and Statistics*, 53 (May 1971), 189–99.

Jencks, Christopher. *Who Gets Ahead?: The Determinants of Economic Success in America*. New York: Basic Books, 1979.

Johnson, George E., and Welch, Finis. "The Labor Market Implications of an Economywide Affirmative Action Program." *Industrial and Labor Relations Review*, 29 (July 1976), 508–22.

Johnson, William R. "Racial Wage Discrimination and Industrial Structure." *Bell Journal of Economics* (Spring 1978), 70–81.

Jordan, Winthrop D. *White Over Black: American Attitudes Toward the Negro, 1550–1812*. Chapel Hill: University of North Carolina Press, 1968.

Kain, John F., ed. *Race and Poverty: The Economics of Discrimination*. Englewood Cliffs: Prentice-Hall, 1969.

Kanter, Rosabeth Moss. *Men and Women of the Corporation*. New York: Basic Books, 1977.

Kartz, Irwin, and Gurin, Patricia. *Race and the Social Sciences*. New York: Basic Books, 1969.

Kerr, Clark. *Labor Markets and Wage Determination: The Balkanization of Labor Markets and Other Essays*. Berkeley: University of California Press, 1977.

King, Allan G., and Knapp, Charles B. "Race and the Determinants of Lifetime Earnings." *Industrial and Labor Relations Review*, 31 (April 1978), 347–55.

Kluegel, James R. "The Causes and Cost of Racial Exclusion from Job Authority." *American Sociological Review*, 43 (June 1978), 285–301.

Knowles, Louis L., and Prewitt, Kenneth, eds. *Institutional Racism in America*. Englewood Cliffs: Prentice-Hall, 1969.

Krueger, Anne O. "The Economics of Discrimination." *Journal of Political Economy*, 71 (Oct. 1963), 481–86.

Lacy, Dan. *The White Use of Blacks in America*. New York: McGraw-Hill, 1972.

Lazear, Edward. "The Narrowing of Black-White Wage Differentials is Illusory." *American Economic Review*, 69 (Sept. 1979), 553–64.

Leigh, Duane E. *An Analysis of the Determinants of Occupational Upgrading*. New York: Academic Press, 1978.

Litwack, Leon F. *Been in the Storm So Long: The Aftermath of Slavery*. New York: Alfred A. Knopf, 1979.

Lundberg, Shelly J., and Startz, Richard. "Private Discrimination and Social Intervention in Competitive Labor Markets." *American Economic Review*, 73 (June 1983), 340–47.

Lyon, Larry, and Abell, Troy. "Social Mobility Among Young Black and White Men." *Pacific Sociological Review*, 22 (April 1979), 201–22.

Marshall, Ray. *The Negro Worker*. New York: Random House, 1967.

Mashayekhi, G. H. "Economic Situation of Non-Whites After 1964: An Empirical Analysis." *Review of Black Political Economy*, 8 (Summer 1978), 336–45.

Meier, August, and Rudwick, Elliott. *From Plantation to Ghetto*. 3rd ed. New York: Hill and Wang, 1976.

Mills, C. Wright. *White Collar: The American Middle Classes*. New York: Oxford University Press, 1951.

Mincer, Jacob. "The Distribution of Labor Incomes: A Survey." *Journal of Economic Literature*, 8 (1970), 1–26.

———. *Schooling, Experience, and Earnings*. New York: National Bureau of Economic Research, 1974.

Munnell, Alicia H. "The Economic Experience of Blacks, 1964–1974." *New England Economic Review* (Jan.–Feb. 1978), 5–18.

Myrdal, Gunnar, with the assistance of Richard Sterner and Arnold Rose. *An American Dilemma: The Negro Problem and Modern Democracy*. 2 vols. New York: Harper, 1944.

Niemi, Albert W. "Occupational/Educational Discrimination Against Black Males." *Journal of Black Studies*, 9 (1978), 87–92.

Norgren, Paul H., and Hill, Samuel E. *Toward Fair Employment*. New York: Columbia University Press, 1964.

Okun, Arthur M. *Equality and Efficiency: The Big Tradeoff*. Washington, D.C.: The Brookings Institution, 1975.

Orleans, Peter, and Ellis, William Russell, Jr., eds. *Race, Change, and Urban Society*. Beverly Hills: Sage Publications, 1971.

Osterman, Paul. "An Empirical Study of Labor Market Segmentation." *Industrial and Labor Relations Review*, 28 (July 1975), 508–21.

Parcel, Toby L., and Mueller, Charles W. *Ascription and Labor Markets: Race and Sex Differences in Earnings.* New York: Academic Press, 1983.

Parnes, H.S.; Fleisher, B.M.; Miljus, R.C.; and Spitz, R.S. *The Pre-Retirement Years: A Longitudinal Study of the Labor Market Experience of Men.* Vol. I. Washington, D.C.: Department of Labor, 1970.

Parsons, Talcott, and Clark, Kenneth B., eds. *The American Negro.* Boston: Beacon Press, 1967.

Pascal, Anthony H., ed. *Racial Discrimination in Economic Life.* Lexington: D.C. Heath, 1972.

Perlman, Richard. *The Economics of Poverty.* New York: McGraw-Hill, 1976.

Perlo, Victor. *Economics of Racism U.S.A.* 2nd. ed. New York: International Publishers, 1976.

Phelps, Edmund S. "The Statistical Theory of Racism and Sexism." *American Economic Review*, 62 (Sept. 1972), 659–61.

Piore, Michael J. "Labor Market Segmentation: To What Paradigm Does It Belong?" *American Economic Review*, 73 (May 1983), 249–53.

———. "Notes for a Theory of Labor Market Stratification." In *Labor Market Segmentation*, edited by R.C. Edwards; M. Reich; and D.M. Gordon. Lexington: D.C. Heath, 1975.

———. "The Dual Labor Market: Theory and Implications." In *Problems in Political Economy: An Urban Perspective.* 2nd ed., edited by David M. Gordon. Lexington: D.C. Heath, 1977.

Quarles, Benjamin. *The Negro in the Making of America.* Rev. ed. New York: Collier, 1969.

Reich, Michael. *Racial Inequality: A Political-Economic Analysis.* Princeton: Princeton University Press, 1981.

———. "The Economics of Racism." *Problems in Political Economy: An Urban Perspective.* 2nd. ed., edited by David M. Gordon. Lexington: D.C. Heath, 1977.

———. "The Persistence of Racial Inequality in Urban Areas and Industries, 1950–1970." *American Economic Review*, 70 (May 1980), 128–31.

———; Gordon, David M.; and Edwards, Richard C. "A Theory of Labor Market Segmentation." *American Economic Review*, Proceedings, 63 (May 1973), 359–65.

Report of the National Advisory Commission on Civil Disorders. New York: Bantam Books, 1968.

Rose, Arnold M. *The Negro in America.* Boston: Beacon Press, 1956.

Rosen, Sherwin. "A Theory of Life Earnings." *Journal of Political Economy,* 84 (1976), S45–S67.

———. "Learning and Experience in the Labor Market." *Journal of Human Resources,* 7 (Summer 1972), 326–42.

———, ed. *Studies in Labor Markets.* Chicago: University of Chicago Press, 1981.

Rosow, Jerome M. "Quality of Working Life and Productivity." *Vital Speeches of the Day,* 43 (June 1977), 496.

Ross, Arthur M. "The Negro in the American Economy." In *Employment, Race and Poverty,* edited by Arthur M. Ross and Herbert Hill. New York: Harcourt, Brace and World, 1967.

Russell, G. Hugh, and Black, Kenneth, Jr. *Human Behavior in Business.* New York: Meredith Corporation, 1972.

Sackrey, Charles. *The Political Economy of Urban Poverty.* New York: Norton, 1973.

Samuelson, Paul. *Economics.* 11th ed. New York: McGraw-Hill, 1980.

Saracheck, Bernard. "Career Concerns of Black Managers." *Management Review* (October 1974).

Schelling, Thomas C. "A Process of Residential Segregation: Neighborhood Tipping." In *Racial Discrimination in Economic Life,* edited by Anthony H. Pascal. Lexington: D.C. Heath, 1972.

Schiller, Bradley R. "Class Discrimination vs. Racial Discrimination." *Review of Economics and Statistics,* 53 (Aug. 1971), 263–69.

Shepherd, William G., and Levin, Sharon G. "Managerial Discrimination in Large Firms." *Review of Economics and Statistics,* 55 (1973), 412–22.

Smith, James, and Welch, Finis. "Black-White Male Wage Rates: 1960–70." *American Economic Review,* 67 (June 1977), 323–38.

———. *Race Differences in Earnings: New Evidence.* Santa Monica: The Rand Corporation, R–2295–NSF, 1978.

Smith, Marvin M. "Towards a General Equilibrium Theory of Wage Discrimination." *Southern Economic Journal* (Oct. 1978), 458–68.

Sowell, Thomas. "Economics and Black People." *Review of Black Political Economy,* 1 (Winter/Spring 1971), 3–34.

———. *Race and Economics.* New York: David McKay, 1975.

Spiller, G., with Introduction by Herbert Aptheker. *Inter-Racial Problems: Papers from the First Universal Races Congress Held in London in 1911.* New York: Citadel, 1970.

Stampp, Kenneth M. *The Peculiar Institution: Slavery in the Ante-Bellum South.* New York: Vintage Books, 1956.

Stiglitz, Joseph E. "Approaches to the Economics of Discrimination." *American Economic Review,* 63 (May 1973), 287–95.

Streifford, David M. "Racial Economic Dualism in St. Louis." *Review of Black Political Economy*, 4 (Spring 1974), 63–81.

Swanson, Gordon I., and Michaelson, Jon, eds. *Manpower Research and Labor Economics*. Beverly Hills: Sage Publications, 1979.

Swinton, David H. "A Labor Force Competition Model of Racial Discrimination in the Labor Market." *Review of Black Political Economy*, 9 (Fall 1978), 5–42.

———. "Factors Affecting the Future Economic Prospects of Minorities." *American Economic Review*, 65 (May 1975), 53–58.

Tabb, William K. *The Political Economy of the Black Ghetto*. New York: Norton, 1970.

Terry, Robert W. *For Whites Only*. Detroit: Detroit Industrial Mission, 1970.

Thieblot, Armand J., Jr., and Fletcher, Linda Pickthorne. *Negro Employment in Finance*. Philadelphia: University of Pennsylvania Press, 1970.

Thurow, Lester C. *Generating Inequality*. New York: Basic Books, 1975.

———. *Investment in Human Capital*. Los Angeles: Wadsworth, 1970.

———. *Poverty and Discrimination*. Washington, D.C.: The Brookings Institution, 1969.

U.S. Department of Labor, Manpower Administration. *A Study of Black Male Professionals in Industry*. Manpower Research Monograph No. 26, 1973. Based on a larger study by Evelyn S. Freeman and Charles L. Fields.

Vroman, Wayne. "Worker Upgrading and the Business Cycle." *Brookings Papers on Economic Activity*, 1 (1977), 229–50.

Wachtel, Howard M., and Betsey, Charles. "Employment at Low Wages." *The Review of Economics and Statistics*, 54 (1972), 121–29.

———. "Low Wage Workers and the Dual Labor Market: An Empirical Investigation." *Review of Black Political Economy*, 5 (1975), 288–301.

Welch, Finis. "Human Capital Theory: Education, Discrimination, and Life Cycles." *American Economic Review*, 65 (May 1975), 63–73.

———. "Labor Market Discrimination: An Interpretation of Income Differences in the Rural South." *Journal of Political Economy*, 75 (June 1967), 225–40.

Wesley, Charles H. *Negro Labor in the United States, 1850–1925*. 1927. Reprint New York: Russell and Russell, 1967.

Wilkinson, Frank, ed. *The Dynamics of Labour Market Segmentation*. New York: Academic Press, 1981.

Williams, Chancellor. *The Destruction of Black Civilization: Great Issues of a Race from 4500 B.C. to 2000 A.D.* Chicago: Third World Press, 1976.

Wilson, Kenneth L. "Toward an Improved Explanation of Income
    Attainment: Recalibrating Education and Occupation." Amer-
    ican Journal of Sociology, 84 (Nov. 1978), 684–97.
Wilson, William Julius. The Declining Significance of Race. 2nd ed.
    Chicago: University of Chicago Press, 1980.
Woodward, C. Vann. The Strange Career of Jim Crow. 2nd rev. ed.
    New York: Oxford University Press, 1966.
Work, John W. "Management Blacks and the Internal Labor Market:
    Responses to a Questionnaire." Human Resource Management
    (Fall 1980), pp. 27–31.
Wright, Erik Olin. "Race, Class, and Income Inequality." American
    Journal of Sociology, 83 (May 1978), 1368–97.
Younger, Mary Sue. Handbook for Linear Regression. North Scituate:
    Duxbury Press, 1979.

INDEX

Index